ANTARCTICA
Music, sounds and cultural connections

ANTARCTICA
Music, sounds and cultural connections

Edited by Bernadette Hince, Rupert Summerson
and Arnan Wiesel

Published by ANU Press
The Australian National University
Acton ACT 2601, Australia
Email: anupress@anu.edu.au
This title is also available online at http://press.anu.edu.au

---

National Library of Australia Cataloguing-in-Publication entry

Title: Antarctica - music, sounds and cultural connections / edited by Bernadette Hince, Rupert Summerson, Arnan Wiesel.

ISBN: 9781925022285 (paperback) 9781925022292 (ebook)

Subjects: Australasian Antarctic Expedition (1911-1914)--Centennial celebrations, etc.
Music festivals--Australian Capital Territory--Canberra.
Antarctica--Discovery and exploration--Australian--Congresses.
Antarctica--Songs and music--Congresses.

Other Creators/Contributors:
Hince, B. (Bernadette), editor.
Summerson, Rupert, editor.
Wiesel, Arnan, editor.
Australian National University School of Music.
Antarctica - music, sounds and cultural connections (2011 : Australian National University).

Dewey Number: 780.789471

All rights reserved. No part of this publication may be reproduced, stored in a retrieval system or transmitted in any form or by any means, electronic, mechanical, photocopying or otherwise, without the prior permission of the publisher.

Cover design and layout by ANU Press

Cover photo: Moonrise over Fram Bank, Antarctica. Photographer: Steve Nicol ©

This edition © 2015 ANU Press

Contents

Preface: Music and Antarctica ix
   Arnan Wiesel

Introduction: Listening to Antarctica 1
   Tom Griffiths

Mawson's musings and Morse code: Antarctic silence at the end of the 'Heroic Era', and how it was lost 15
   Mark Pharaoh

Thulia: a Tale of the Antarctic (1843): The earliest Antarctic poem and its musical setting. 23
   Elizabeth Truswell

Nankyoku no kyoku: The cultural life of the Shirase Antarctic Expedition 1910–12 37
   Rupert Summerson

The first published music from Antarctica? Captain Doorly's piano and its roots in older traditions of polar exploration and an imperial guilty conscience. 51
   Jeff Brownrigg

Eating the audience. 73
   Bernadette Hince

Musical adventures in Antarctica. 83
   Alice Giles

Mentions of music in the Antarctic diaries of Cecil T Madigan . . 89
   Arnan Wiesel

Body of ice: The movement of Antarctic ice through dance . . . 101
   Christina Evans

The poetry of Antarctic sound and the sound of Antarctic poetry 107
   Elizabeth Leane

Playing Antarctica: Making music with natural objects and sounds from the Antarctic Peninsula 121
   Cheryl E Leonard

And I may be some time 133
   Craig Cormick

The nature of sound and the sound of Nature 139
   Philip Samartzis

Kiwis on ice: Defining the ways in which the New Zealand
   identity is reflected in the Antarctic-inspired works of four
   New Zealand composers 151
   Patrick Shepherd

Antarctica: 'Surround Sound' 161
   Stephen Nicol

Frozen voices: Women, silence and Antarctica 169
   Jesse Blackadder

Frames of silence: Some descriptions of the sounds of
   Antarctica. 179
   Stephen Martin

Made and played in Antarctica: People's music in a far-flung
   place 189
   Bruce Watson

'A Vast Scale: Evocations of Antarctica' 205
   Rupert Summerson and Claire Beynon

Index 223

The idea for the 'Antarctica and Music' conference and music festival in Canberra at ANU School of Music was devised by Arnan Wiesel to commemorate the centenary of the Australasian Antarctic Expedition of 1911–14.

Preface: Music and Antarctica

Arnan Wiesel[1]

Music and Antarctica

Sound and nature are inseparable. Silence and nature are inseparable. These parameters of our world are often neglected. 'Sonically, an extraordinary silence embraces much of Antarctica. In this regard, my most profound listening was inward. Sitting on a scree slope in the Taylor Valley, on a windless afternoon, the only sound I heard was that of my pulse, a dull thud and swish against the hood of my parka.'[2]

The Antarctica Music Festival and Conference at The Australian National University's School of Music on 25–29 June 2011 generated a great sense of excitement. Concerts at the festival included the dawn performance of John Luther Adams' 'Inuksuit' at the James Turrell Skyspace in the Australian National Gallery, the inspired playing of harpist Alice Giles, the movement of dancer, animator and choreographer Lisa Roberts, and the cold magic of Norwegian percussionist Terje Isungset with his monolithic ice instruments in front of a capacity outdoor audience at the School of Music in Canberra, in 0°C on a winter's night. The conference 'Antarctica — Music, Sounds and Cultural Connections' on 27–29 June 2011 was unique in celebrating the theme of music in Antarctica. This volume presents papers from the conference.

Humans have been attracted to the polar regions for centuries. Consciousness of sounds — in particular, musical ones — has not been at the forefront of our aims in polar endeavours, although listening to and appreciating sounds (including the sounds of silence) *has* been a source of support and comfort, and a basis for social rituals, there as elsewhere. The Antarctic environment, with its extremes of climate and environment, offers great potential for creative achievements, including those in the world of music and sound.

Douglas Mawson's Australasian Antarctic Expedition of 1911–14 was the first Australian-led expedition to Antarctica. It crystallised Australia's interest in the southern continent. Our involvement has brought cultural and emotional challenges, as well as political and scientific ones, as Tom Griffiths writes in

---

1   Mr Arnan Wiesel, pianist and former Head of Keyboard, ANU School of Music, Arnan.Wiesel@me.com.
2   Quin, Douglas, 'Antarctica: Austral Soundscapes 1997–1998', dqmedia, http://www.dqmedia.com/articles/austral.pdf.

this volume. 'Antarctica does not only prompt logistical, political or intellectual questions; it implicates and challenges our humanity,' he says. In the years 2011–14, the centenary of the Australasian Antarctic Expedition stimulated many intellectual and creative celebrations. This volume is the result of one such celebration.

The diaries of meteorologist Cecil Madigan show the importance of music and sound for members of the expedition. In a small society isolated from external contacts, even the sound of morse code, far removed from the more obvious musical elements of English, could be regarded as part of the men's vital rituals of communications.

Crossing boundaries between performing arts disciplines and other mediums is not new, but the 21st century offers us the possibility of new approaches through a new suite of technological tools. In the concerts of the 'Antarctica and Music' Festival and Conference, dance, harp playing, natural instruments and sound recordings used various applications of modern technology.

Silence is an important element of any sonic environment. In Antarctica the almost constant sounds of extreme winds and blizzards affect the human spirit and behaviour. On the rare occasions when the noise of the wind dropped completely at Commonwealth Bay, men paused, initially at a loss to say what had changed.

In this volume, Mark Pharaoh discusses the loss of silence from Antarctica with the arrival of the radio and morse code, as well as other technological sounds of the era (especially the indoor ones), while in her project *Antarctica: Music From the Ice*, artist Cheryl Leonard uses the natural found objects and sounds of the Antarctic Peninsula.

In *Thulia: a Tale of the Antarctic,* artist and scientist Elizabeth Truswell examines the earliest Antarctic poem and its musical setting. Shakuhachi player, polar explorer and scholar Rupert Summerson writes in *Nankyoku no kyoku* of the cultural life of the Shirase Antarctic Expedition of 1910–12 — almost contemporaneous with Mawson's expedition but far less well known, despite its intersections with Australian history. With New Zealand artist Claire Beynon in *A Vast Scale*, Summerson also canvasses responses to imagery and music chosen to evoke Antarctic.

Music historian Jeff Brownrigg discusses the roots of the first music known to have been composed in Antarctica, on the relief expedition by Captain Gerard Doorly on the *Morning*. Dictionary-maker and historian Bernadette Hince discusses an occasion on which Gilbert Kerr of the 1902–04 Scottish National Antarctic Expedition played his bagpipes to a seemingly curious emperor penguin, a moment captured in photographs and often discussed since.

Harpist Alice Giles has a personal account of giving a concert in Antarctica, an extraordinary experience given greater depth by her connection through her grandfather Cecil Madigan with the Australasian Antarctic Expedition, whose centenary prompted the festival and conference. In the concert she used words from Madigan's diaries, songs, hymns, music mentioned in the diaries, and music written by contemporary Australian composers for the occasion. Another Antarctic Arts Fellow, dance artist Tina (Christina) Evans, writes of capturing the movement of Antarctic ice through dance.

Literary scholar Elizabeth Leane canvasses the relationship between sound, music and literature in an Antarctic context. She deals particularly with poetry because, as she says, 'poets tend to be interested in sound'. Writer Craig Cormick's short story *And I may be some time...* takes us to the world of Lawrence ('Titus') Oates, 'alone on the ice tonight' with the shrill song of the wind.

Composer and teacher Patrick Shepherd discusses his Antarctic-inspired work and that of three other New Zealand composers — Chris Cree Brown, Phil Dadson and Gareth Farr. Sound artist Philip Samartzis looks at the work of sound artists in extreme locations. Works such as Douglas Quin's *Antarctica* (1998) and Peter Cusack's *Baikal Ice* (2003), he says, provide 'insight into remote and inhospitable environments that are usually inaccessible to the rest of us'. In *Antarctica: 'Surround Sound'*, glaciologist and writer Stephen Nicol provides a counterview to the belief that Antarctica is 'a colourless, sterile environment where the only sound is the howling of the wind'. And writer Jesse Blackadder seeks to explore 'a different kind of Antarctic silence ... the silence of the earliest female travellers to Antarctica'.

'As you travel south you experience a moving away from the density and complexity of human culture', says writer Stephen Martin. 'Into this sense of change and sensory confusion tumble the sights and smells and sounds of one of the world's most extraordinary places'.

Folk musician and historian Bruce Watson writes of the music made at Australia's Antarctic bases, little of which has been published or systematically studied.

The number of artists looking to Antarctica as a source of inspiration is growing. Some presenters at this festival and conference had received Antarctic Arts Fellowships from the Australian Antarctic Division, which each year supports creative endeavours based around Antarctic subjects through these fellowships.

This is the first volume dedicated to the subject of Antarctica and music. One of the responsibilities of musicians is to bring individual creative elements to our society. I hope that the work represented here will encourage other Antarctic-inspired music and sound.

Acknowledgement

Sincere thanks from the editors and contributors for the excellent work of the ANU Press editors David Gardiner and Emily Tinker, designer Nausica Pinar and indexer Beth Battrick, to the ANU Publication Subsidy Committee for funding an index, and to the School of Music for funding author copies of this work.

Introduction: Listening to Antarctica

Tom Griffiths[1]

In 2011, we commemorated a series of Antarctic anniversaries: the centenary of Douglas Mawson's Australasian Antarctic Expedition, 100 years since the attainment of the South Pole, 75 years since the coming into force of the Australian Antarctic Territory and 50 years since the ratification of the Antarctic Treaty. On planet Earth today, it could be said that we inhabit the Antarctic moment. Each year now, tens of thousands of tourists visit a realm that, just a few generations ago, was virtually unknown. Over the past century we have learned just how different is the Antarctic from the Arctic, and Antarctica has moved from the geographical periphery of our consciousness to the centre of our scientific and intellectual concerns. The physics and politics of global warming have turned our eyes towards the great southern ice cap, which has 90 per cent of the world's land ice and 70 per cent of the globe's fresh water. The same industrial capitalism that has unleashed carbon has given us a planetary consciousness that reveals a calving berg as not just a random, local act of nature, but instead as the frightening frontier of a possibly irreversible global, historical event. Understanding ice — its history and its future — has turned out to be a key to understanding climate change and to securing a human future. The great white continent has never before gripped our imagination or dictated our destiny with such power.

It is a great pleasure to contribute to this volume, which follows a wonderful Antarctic Music Festival in Canberra in 2011 involving so many talented thinkers and performers. This event stimulated us to consider what it is that constitutes the culture of the ice. It also reminded us that Antarctica presents a cultural challenge to us, as well as a scientific and political one. How are we to make sense of such a remarkable, otherworldly part of the planet? How are we to imagine and experience it; how are we to respond ethically and emotionally to it; how are we to depict or distil it; what social and cultural experiments does it demand; what stimulus to human hope and creativity might it offer; what sensations, insights and ideas might it foster? Antarctica does not only prompt logistical, political or intellectual questions; it implicates and challenges our humanity.

The recent Antarctic anniversaries sketch out not just an evolving human engagement with the South Pole, but also a peculiarly Australian story. Voyagers,

---

[1] Professor Tom Griffiths, William Keith Hancock Professor of History, Centre for Environmental History, The Australian University, Canberra ACT 0200, tom.griffiths@anu.edu.au.

sealers and whalers headed south from colonial ports and, from the 1880s, Australian colonists themselves began to turn an imperial gaze towards the ice. Exploring Antarctica became a proud initiative of the newly federated nation in the early 20th century. Douglas Mawson's Australasian Antarctic Expedition of 1911–14 was part of that assertion of national interest; it was also the most earnestly scientific expedition of the heroic era, and one that put geographical exploration ahead of the race to the pole. That early, unambiguous Australian commitment to the priority of science offers us a proud inheritance, and one that has strengthened in the last 50 years of the Antarctic Treaty era.

After the Great War, Australia exerted strong pressure on Britain to secure sovereignty over the vast region of Antarctica south of Australia. This region was as close to Australia as Hobart was to Fremantle, and Australians felt a growing affinity with, and responsibility for, what was sometimes referred to as our 'Great Frozen Neighbour'.[2] Throughout the 1920s and 1930s, energetic Australian diplomacy was instrumental in expanding the frontiers of the British Empire into the Antarctic. Australia was no 'passive witness' to imperial events but, instead, acted on a clear conception of its distinctive outlook and material self-interest in Antarctic affairs.[3] Historian Marie Kawaja at ANU has been doing pioneering research in the diplomatic cables and official memoranda of the National Archives of Australia, and unearthing a new, vital story about the tenacity and expertise that underpinned Australia's political interest in Antarctica from the beginning.[4] This version of Australian history has been largely overlooked by historians of Australian diplomacy and foreign policy. It reminds us what stirring insights can be dug out of official archives, and also how coming to terms with Antarctica tends to make one see one's country — and the world — differently.

Of course, part of the Australian Antarctic story was Douglas Mawson's return to Antarctica in the summers of 1929–31, when he led the British, Australian and New Zealand Antarctic Research Expedition (known as the BANZARE voyages) in Scott's old ship, the *Discovery*. Mawson's secret instructions from the Australian Prime Minister were to 'plant the British flag wherever you find it practicable to do so'.[5] The passing of the *Australian Antarctic Territory Acceptance Act 1933* by the Commonwealth parliament formalised

---

2 'Our great frozen neighbour'. *Adelaide Advertiser*, 26 February 1929, NAA: Series A 461/8, Item H413/2, quoted in Marie Kawaja and Tom Griffiths (2011) "Our great frozen neighbour": Australia and Antarctica before the Treaty, 1880–1945'. In Marcus Haward and Tom Griffiths, eds, *Australia and the Antarctic Treaty system: 50 years of influence*. UNSW Press, Sydney, pp. 9–47.
3 Marie Kawaja (2010) Politics and diplomacy of the Australian Antarctic, 1901–1945. PhD thesis, The Australian National University, Canberra.
4 See Kawaja (2010) 'Politics and diplomacy', and Kawaja and Griffiths (2011) 'Our great frozen neighbour'.
5 WM Bush, ed. (1982) *Antarctica and international law: a collection of inter-state and national documents*, vol. II, London, Doc. AU12091929, pp. 117–18. See also Phillip Ayres (1999) *Mawson: a life*. Melbourne University Press, Carlton, p. 173.

the constitutional arrangements that allowed the Australian government to be the controlling authority over the Australian Antarctic Territory, a sovereignty claim for more than 42 per cent of Antarctica.

In the post-war period, a remarkable resolution of Antarctic territorial claims and rivalries emerged in the form of the Antarctic Treaty, which was signed by 12 nations (including Australia) in Washington in 1959, and which came into force in 1961. Just over 50 years ago, the first Antarctic Treaty Consultative Meeting — the annual assembly for Antarctic governance — was held in Canberra in (Old) Parliament House. It is unusual for an international treaty document to mention a city, but the text of the Antarctic Treaty does mention just one, and it is Canberra. Article IX names the City of Canberra as the first place that contracting parties shall meet 'within two months after the date of entry into force of the Treaty'. The choice of Canberra was, in part, recognition of the crucial role played in the treaty negotiations by Australia's Richard Casey.

And so it was that, on a typical Canberra winter morning on 10 July 1961, Prime Minister Robert Menzies welcomed delegates to Parliament House, saying 'As a matter of fact, I thought this morning, as I peered through the fog, that we had gone to some trouble to give you a proper Antarctic welcome.' Senator John Gorton was elected as chairman of the gathering, and Lady Mawson, the widow of Douglas Mawson, was present. Mr Menzies explained to the assembled delegates that Australians 'have a deep sense of neighbourhood about the Antarctic'. The leader of the Norwegian delegation declared: 'We feel that this might be a great stepping stone towards world peace, that examples from this treaty might be embodied elsewhere, and that the spirit of this treaty might prevail in other spheres.'[6] The construction of the Berlin Wall commenced just after the gathering in Canberra in July 1961 and, a year later, the world held its breath during the Cuban missile crisis. People were desperate for a different model of international relations.[7]

The Antarctic Treaty has provided that, and with remarkable success. It arose, like a kind of miracle, out of the tensions of the Cold War, in some senses was created *by* them. So, in 2011, we commemorated 50 years of the Treaty as well as the Mawson expedition centenary. Mawson died just one year before the Treaty was signed and he didn't foresee it, or even particularly want it. Today we recognise, with hindsight, that the Antarctic Treaty was not only a significant achievement in its own right, but that it was also a precursor, a model for the rest of the world and for the future. It was the first arms control

---

6   Commonwealth of Australia (1961) *Antarctic Treaty. Report of the First Consultative Meeting*, p. 30.
7   For further details on the negotiation of the Treaty, see Tom Griffiths (2010) 'The Antarctic Treaty in 1959'. In *Australia and the Antarctic Treaty – then and now*. IMAS, University of Tasmania, pp. 9–15.

treaty of the Cold War.⁸ It became an inspiration for the governance of other places — for management of the sea and outer space. As we today confront the global management of climate change and the lingering disappointment of the Copenhagen summit, the Antarctic Treaty offers an inspiring example of how respect for science can constructively inform world politics.⁹

Australia has been a major and positive player in the Antarctic Treaty System, and was, for example, a leader in the political revolution of 1989–91 when Treaty nations abandoned a mining convention and negotiated instead the Madrid Protocol on Environmental Protection. Over the last few years, the political scientist Marcus Haward and I have been working with a range of scholars and practitioners on a book about Australia's influence in the Antarctic Treaty System over 50 years. It was available when Australia hosted the Antarctic Treaty Consultative Meeting in 2012 in Hobart.¹⁰ The story of Australia's creative engagement in this international political regime deserves to be better known in our own country.

...

These, then, are some of the political and strategic foundations of Australia's relationship with Antarctica. But what of our cultural relationship to our southern neighbour? The culture of the ice remains one of the least studied aspects of the place, yet understanding of it is vital. Culture, of course, suffuses everything we do and say. It is ineffable and all-pervasive. How should you behave when arriving at an Antarctic station at the end of the polar winter? What is 'the changeover'? Whose ghostly footfalls do you hear when you enter the heroic-era huts? What did it mean to 'pont'?¹¹ How close should you get to an Adélie penguin? Where is 'the Daintree of Antarctica'? What is a true wilderness? What could the gift of a pebble imply? How exactly might one claim a tract of ice for one's country? Is it dangerous to be alone? What is a ventifact? Is it wise to disagree openly in a small community? How do you feel when you see green? When should you — and when shouldn't you — use the word 'sovereignty'? These are some of the countless delicate questions whose answers demand immersion in Antarctic culture.

---

8   Rob Hall and Marie Kawaja (2011) 'Australia and the negotiation of the Antarctic Treaty'. In Haward and Griffiths, eds, *Australia and the Antarctic Treaty system*, p. 91.
9   The 'official narrative' of the Treaty suggests that scientific idealism has largely trumped political rivalry, and equates science with international cooperation. However, this view has been challenged by careful accounts of how the mentality of settler colonialism underpins Antarctic history and continues to operate in subtle and effective ways under the Treaty. See the scholarship of Klaus Dodds, Christy Collis, Adrian Howkins, Peder Roberts, Alan Hemmings and Alessandro Antonello.
10   Marcus Haward and Tom Griffiths, eds (2011) *Australia and the Antarctic Treaty system: 50 years of influence*. UNSW Press, Sydney.
11   The verb 'to pont' means to pose, in polar discomfort, for a photograph, and is drawn from the name of Herbert George Ponting, photographer on Scott's last expedition. See Bernadette Hince (2000) *The Antarctic dictionary: a complete guide to Antarctic English*. CSIRO Publishing and Museum of Victoria, Melbourne.

Those who participated in this conference are pursuing this mission — to create and appreciate art, words, music, poetry, sculpture, dance, prose, objects, images, performances that make us think and feel with more perception, understanding and discrimination about a place that seems almost to defy human affiliation and scrutiny. The disciplinary boundaries between art and science melt in the quest for holistic understanding. At the 2011 Antarctica and Music conference, we were lucky to have Tim Bowden capturing Antarctic stories, Bernadette Hince investigating polar words, Rupert Summerson analysing wilderness, Elle Leane reading Antarctic literature, Steve Martin, Heather Rossiter and Mark Pharaoh sifting the legacy of the Australian Antarctic Expedition, Arnan Wiesel and Alice Giles stimulating us to think about Antarctic music. We need this work. The historian Stephen Murray-Smith asserted its importance during a heated debate in the ship's bar on his return voyage from Antarctica in 1986. He challenged his companions: 'Don't you think ideas and ideals are important? I tell you this, if this country has a future in Antarctica it will be because people have *ideas* about it.'[12]

One view of Antarctic culture is that it has all been about coming to terms with the immensity and meaning of the continent's vast icy outback. Antarctic voyagers of the 19th century had originally wanted rock. They wanted rock and soil they could plant a flag in and claim for their country. The ice was in the way: it was a nuisance, an obstacle. Later, the ice became a testing ground for physical endeavour, a source of beauty and fear, but still essentially an obstruction stopping them from reaching, studying and claiming the land beneath. But by the mid-20th century, the ice itself had become a primary scientific focus and was no longer regarded just as an obscuring and frustrating 'barrier' between visitors and the much-desired land. Scientists began to see ice as a mineral of interest in itself; they began to see glaciers as geological and Antarctica as a vestigial landscape, a giant white fossil.

In the early 1950s, it was discovered that the ice sheets were not just a few hundred metres thick but actually kilometres deep, and so the driest of all continents was actually a vast elevated plateau of frozen water. This startling discovery revealed that world sea level is principally controlled by the state of the Antarctic ice sheet. Questions about the ice changed from how frustrating, to how vast, how continental, how deep, how old, and then to how stable? Recent observable changes in the ice cap became anxiously assessed. The confirmation of global warming due to human influence came not only from the behaviour of the ice sheet, but also from the air bubbles trapped within it. Before Antarctica was even seen by humans, it was recording our impact.

---

12   Stephen Murray-Smith (1988) *Sitting on penguins: people and politics in Australian Antarctica*. Hutchinson Australia, Sydney, p. 125.

If 100 years ago the defining Antarctic journey was the sledging expedition across the surface of the ice, and 50 years ago it was the tractor traverse that, with seismic soundings, measured the volume of the ice sheet, then the defining Antarctic journey of our own era goes straight down, with the help of a drill, from the top of the ice dome to the continental bedrock, a vertical journey back through time. And the ice core thus extracted enables us to see our civilisation in the humbling context of hundreds of thousands of years of climate history. Right now in Antarctica, the international race is on again — not for the South Pole, not for the first trans-Antarctic traverse, but for the first million-year ice core.[13]

The dominant historical narratives of this international continent are nationalist. Nationalism is not contrary to the spirit of the Antarctic Treaty, for national endeavour is the means of contributing to the treaty system and there is national pride in becoming an influential party. But, as well as being a site of international cooperation, Antarctica has generated patriotism and competition, and sectors of the ice sheet have been integrated in distinctive and exclusive ways into dozens of national histories. Argentine and Chilean Antarctic territories appear on those nations' domestic maps; Richard Byrd established a 'colony' at what he called 'Little America'; Amundsen's triumph consolidated early 20th-century Norwegian nationhood; and in Australia, Mawson's huts have been seen to be 'as much a part of the national psyche as the Hills Hoist, Uluru, [and] the Eureka Stockade'.[14] Antarctic scholars have been wary of embracing postcolonial perspectives of Antarctic history and geography because of the continent's lack of indigenous people and its extreme environment, but as Klaus Dodds, Sanjay Chaturvedi and Christy Collis have argued, these factors make Antarctic colonialism a fascinating special case.[15]

For adventurous and scientific Australians of the 20th century, two frontiers beckoned: the white desert and the red heart, the far south and the outback. Adelaide, where Mawson gained a lecturing post in his twenties, was sandwiched between these frontiers; it was a city exposed to the winds of both deserts. Mawson, Cecil Madigan, Charles Laseron, Edgeworth David, Griffith Taylor and Syd Kirkby ventured in both directions, and Baldwin Spencer and JW Gregory went inland after almost going south. A contemporary expeditioner of this kind is Peter Campbell, the Casey plant inspector and diesel mechanic on my voyage south in late 2002. Peter, who has a big red beard and hence is known

---

13 For an elaboration of these paragraphs and for the meaning of ice in the climate crisis, see Tom Griffiths (2010) 'A humanist on thin ice: science and the humanities, people and climate change'. *Griffith Review* 29, August: http://griffithreview.com/edition-29-prosper-or-perish/a-humanist-on-thin-ice.
14 *Sydney Morning Herald* article (1997) quoted on p. 22 of Christy Collis (2000) 'Mawson's hut: emptying post-colonial Antarctica'. *Journal of Australian Studies* 63: 22–29.
15 Klaus J Dodds (2006) 'Post-colonial Antarctica: an emerging engagement'. *Polar Record* 42, 220: 59–70; Sanjay Chaturvedi (1996) *The polar regions; a political geography*. John Wiley, Chichester; Collis (2000) 'Mawson's hut'; and Christy Collis and Quentin Stevens (2007) 'Cold colonies: Antarctic spatialities at Mawson and McMurdo Stations', *Cultural Geographies* 14: 234–54.

as 'Bloo', came from Humpty Doo in the Northern Territory. So he continued the Australian tradition of comparing blizzards to dust storms, and wrote for *BushMag: Journal of the Outback* about the similarities of his two frontiers, 'the white and red deserts'.[16] Bloo marked his mid-winter at Casey by adding the name of his tiny town to the tall pole outside the station indicating the direction and distances of settlements. It now reads: London 15,966; Bucharest 14,211; Hobart 3,424; Vostok 1,383; Humpty Doo 6,141 ...

Although inhabitants of an arid land may seem strange colonisers of the ice, Australians *do* know something about deserts. Christy Collis has argued that, in the 20th century, the Australian desert of the imagination — the place of imperial opportunity and continental conquest — effectively moved to Antarctica.[17] Certainly there is a fascinating parallel cultural history of the two deserts to be teased out. Part of the sustained power for Australians of Douglas Stewart's radio play *The Fire on the Snow* (about Captain Scott's tragic polar expedition) must lie in this correspondence. Literary scholars have suggested that Australian writers like Stewart and Thomas Keneally (who wrote two novels inspired by heroic-era expeditions) use Antarctica as 'a surrogate land for Australia', as an alternative template for imagining a continental colonisation.[18] Sidney Nolan, one of Australia's great artists of the mythic outback, relished the opportunity he gained in 1964 to paint the white desert. In the same year that he was working on his paintings of the lost inland explorers Burke and Wills, Nolan visited Antarctica and found it provided 'an intensification' of what he had experienced in the heart of his own country.[19] It is not just a matter of Australians learning to look south and to secure their national interest there; it is also a story of Gondwanan cousins — one claimed by fire and the other by ice — providing vital, formative experiences of the frontier in a settler nation.

Mawson thought Antarctica might become an 'Alaska' to Australia's United States, a new frontier for a 'young' nation.[20] Brigid Hains, in *The ice and the inland*, studied the lives of Douglas Mawson and John Flynn (of the Inland) to explore the myth of the frontier in a rapidly modernising Australian nation. She argued that for settler Australians of the early 20th century, anxious to assert a national identity and worried about the mental and physical effects of an urbanising population, the Antarctic frontier, like the outback, was a place

---

16 Bloo Campbell, 'Notes from the Antarctic desert', *BushMag: Journal of the Outback*, 2003 http://www.bushmag.com.au, viewed 1 November 2006.
17 Collis (2000) 'Mawson's hut', p. 24.
18 Elizabeth Leane (2007) 'A place of ideals in conflict: images of Antarctica in Australian literature'. In CA Cranston and Robert Zeller, eds, *The littoral zone: Australian contexts and their writers*. Rodopi, Amsterdam, pp. 261–89; Anthony Hassall (1988) 'Quests'. *Australian Literary Studies* 13(4): 390–408.
19 Rodney James (2006) *Sidney Nolan: Antarctic journey*. Mornington Peninsula Regional Gallery, Mornington [Vic].
20 Brigid Hains (2002) 'The graveyard of a century'. In Tim Bonyhady and Tom Griffiths, eds *Words for country: landscape and language in Australia*. UNSW Press, Sydney, pp. 124–39.

of both anxiety and opportunity. There were concerns about the organic vitality of the race (especially in a young nation founded as a penal colony) and about the invigorating potential — but also degenerative effects — of the frontier. The harsh desert environments threatened regression but also offered renewal. 'To the white Australian imagination,' wrote Hains, 'the frontier was the place where civilization unravelled into wilderness — for good or ill.'[21]

There was cultural as well as political theatre in Antarctic life. When BANZARE voyage members had their group photo taken at Commonwealth Bay in 1931, Mawson insisted that they 'all dress up for it and make it look cold'.[22] Australians down south were journeying into the heart of another 'unclaimed' space, and testing and proving their national and racial qualities. To a settler people in an Aboriginal land there was an attractive moral simplicity about colonising an uninhabited continent, a true *terra nullius*. There was something redemptive about Antarctica's unalloyed whiteness.

…

And then, there is the silence calling.[23] In this final section, I want to consider the silence and the sounds of Antarctica. The American biologist David Campbell, in his lyrical book *The crystal desert*, described terrestrial Antarctica as 'the antithesis of the Amazon … It is like the silence between movements of a symphony'. In his effort to define the uniqueness of Antarctica, this scientist chose *sound* as his metaphor of difference. For David Campbell, Antarctica and the Amazon — the two primary sites of his biological fieldwork — are stunning opposites. The Amazon, he writes, is an inchoate green tapestry, an 'apex of earthly diversity'. 'Imagine', he says, 'there are more species of lichens, liverworts, mosses, and algae growing on the upper surface of a single leaf of an Amazonian palm than there are on the entire continent of Antarctica.' Antarctica, by contrast he explained, is 'parsimonious … it is biological haiku'. But of course, Campbell goes on to acknowledge that Antarctica and the Amazon, however different, are both on the same blue planet, and are interactive in fascinating ways. Antarctica, in all its implacable, silent majesty, is 'also a key to the diversity of the tropics'. It is the weather factory and the global engine of climate that, over millions of years, has 'driven speciation in the distant tropics'.[24] Thus simplicity and diversity, silence and symphony, are connected; they are one.

---

21 Brigid Hains (2002) *The ice and the inland: Mawson, Flynn, and the myth of the frontier*. Melbourne University Press, Melbourne, p. 5.
22 Stuart Campbell, Diary, Mitchell Library, Sydney, Microfilm CY 4317, 5 January 1931.
23 The brilliant title of Tim Bowden's Antarctic history (1997) is *The silence calling: Australians in Antarctica 1947–97*. Allen & Unwin, Sydney.
24 David G Campbell (1993) *The crystal desert: summers in Antarctica*. Minerva, London, p. 51, and (2005) *A land of ghosts: the braided lives of people and the forest in far western Amazonia*. Rutgers University Press, p. 12.

Silence is one of the most common metaphors of Antarctic life and experience, and many of these papers explore it. It seems a paradox that the 'howling wilderness', or *The home of the blizzard* as Douglas Mawson called his foothold on the continent of ice, should be known for its silence. But, of course, the two *are* related as David Campbell knew, for the silence comes between the movements of the symphonic wind. Silence is a period of non-wind, and the power of silence is heightened by the memory of the blizzard. Indeed, it is the aftershock of wind that can give silence its resonance. Mawson himself put this very well. Listen to his words from *The home of the blizzard* as he seeks to analyse the experience of sound in Antarctica — he does so as a scientist (Mawson was always *first* the scientist) but there is also more than a little bit of the poet in him:

> The climate [at Commonwealth Bay] proved to be little more than one continuous blizzard the year round; a hurricane of wind roaring for weeks together, pausing for breath only at odd hours. Such pauses — lulls of a singular nature — were a welcome relief to the dreary monotony, and on such occasions the auditory sense was strangely affected. The contrast was so severe when the racking gusts of an abating wind suddenly gave way to intense, eerie silence that the habitual droning of many weeks would still reverberate in the ears. At night one would involuntarily wake up if the wind died away and be loth to sleep 'for hunger of a sound'. In the open air the stillness conveyed to the brain an impression of audibility, interpreted as a vibratory murmur.[25]

Mawson is here talking of the contrast between sound and silence, and about the auditory memory of wind. But during his two years at Commonwealth Bay, he learned that there was another source of distant droning, of muffled roaring. It was not just the *memory* of wind that was ringing in his ears. Mawson and his men gradually realised that, on the rare days when their own hut by the bay was becalmed, the ferocious katabatic wind continued to blow as usual about a thousand feet above them. As Mawson put it, 'So we came to realize that when a calm fell upon the Hut, the wind had merely retired to higher elevations and hung over us like the sword of Damocles, ready to descend at any moment.'[26] This was the source of 'an incessant, seething roar' that they heard so constantly.

No continent is more dominated by wind than Antarctica. At Commonwealth Bay, the meteorologist Cecil Madigan left memorable descriptions of his work recording a continental weather pattern ruled by wind. In 1912, complete weather observations were taken every six hours. All data was entered in

---

25 Douglas Mawson (1996) *The home of the blizzard* [originally published in two volumes in 1915]. Wakefield Press, Adelaide, p. 77. Some of the poetics were contributed by the expedition doctor Archibald McLean, with whom Mawson collaborated in the writing of the book.
26 Mawson (1996) *The home of the blizzard*, p. 78.

pencil in a meteorological day book, and 15 of these 100-page books were filled. Visiting the anemometer was, admitted Madigan, 'physically a fairly severe undertaking, presenting considerable difficulty in the mere finding of it'. He goes on to explain:

> After some practice the members of the expedition were able to abandon crawling, and walked on their feet in these 90 mile torrents of air, 'leaning on the wind'... I found that in a 90-mile wind, if I faced it and kept the body straight, I could touch the ground in front by extending an arm.[27]

Mastery of this 'hurricane-walking', as they called it, became an essential meteorological accessory. Just as the silence would roar in people's ears, and just as they would wake up when the blizzard died, so did people fall over when the wind stopped.

I have been depicting silence as a function of wind, silence as an absence. But silence itself has a texture and a timbre; it can roar in one's ears all on its own. The silence is palpable in Antarctica. It is a presence, not merely an absence. Carsten Borchgrevink, leading the first party to winter on the land in Antarctica, wrote in 1899 that 'The silence roared in our ears, it was centuries of heaped-up solitude.'[28] The American explorer Richard Byrd wrote in his diary in December 1928, after his first night on the continent, that 'It is as quiet here as in a tomb. Nothing stirs. The silence is so deep one could almost reach out and take hold of it.' American nature writer, Barry Lopez, when visiting the dry valleys, described 'a silence dense as water'.

And sometimes the silence could be exhilarating. Byrd's geologist, Laurence McKinley Gould, wrote in praise of the Antarctic silence:

> When there is no wind this is a land of unparalleled quiet. But it is a different quiet than one feels back home. I have stood in the woods at home when the world seemed dead. There was no kind of sound. But in that world where a variety of sound was the rule rather than the exception such a silence was oppressive if not ominous. Not so here — this is a land of silence. One stands in the midst of it without any feeling of oppressiveness. It is an expanding sort of silence. It is inviting. It is the natural state here and I like it — I have come to feel at home in the midst of it.[29]

---

27 Cecil T Madigan (1929) 'Tabulated and reduced records of the Cape Denison station', 'Adelie Land'. In *Australasian Antarctic Expedition 1911–14, Scientific Reports, Series B, vol IV, Meteorology*. Alfred J. Kent, Government Printer, Sydney, p. 20.
28 Janet Crawford (1998) *That first Antarctic winter*. South Latitude Research Ltd, in association with Peter J Skellerup, Christchurch, p. 112.
29 Laurence McKinley Gould (1931) *COLD: the record of an Antarctic sledge journey*. Brewer, Warren & Putnam, New York, p. 65.

In 1934, on his second expedition, the American aviator Richard Byrd tried an awesome, dangerous and near-fatal experiment on himself. For four dark months of the polar winter, he lived alone at the Bolling Advance Weather Base on the Ross Ice Shelf at 80° S. He found the silence of the Barrier enthralling:

> I have never known such utter quiet. Sometimes it lulled and hypnotised, like a waterfall or any other steady, familiar sound. At other times it struck into the consciousness as peremptorily as a sudden noise. It made me think of the fatal emptiness that comes when an airplane engine cuts out abruptly in flight. Up on the Barrier it was taut and immense; and, in spite of myself, I would be straining to listen — for nothing, really, nothing but the sheer excitement of silence.[30]

Morton Moyes, a meteorologist on Mawson's 1911–14 expedition, spent nine weeks alone in Queen Mary Land in 1912–13, awaiting the return of sledging parties. He documented the silence in his diary. November 7: 'All alone here now and the silence is immense.' December 20: 'The Silence is so painful now that I have a continual singing in my left ear, much like a Barrel Organ, only it's the same tune all the time.'[31] When his companions returned and broke the silence, Morton Moyes stood on his head for joy.

Returning penguins could bring similar pleasure. Charles Laseron, one of Mawson's expeditioners, wrote: 'No longer, when it was calm, did the ears throb with the silence, the raucous cries of the penguins filled the air to the exclusion of everything else'. He elaborated on this weird sensation of his ears *throbbing* with silence:

> In the middle of lunch we all become aware of something strange. Our ear-drums commence to throb as with a great noise. Somebody speaks and his voice cracks like a whip on the stillness. For the wind has stopped, and, accustomed as we are to its howl, the silence can literally be felt. For a while we speak almost in whispers, our heads are ringing and we feel very uncomfortable … And the intense, utter silence — it seems as if the whole world is dead. The tinkling of a piece of ice falling in the distance rings out like a thunder-clap.[32]

Louis Bernacchi, the Tasmanian scientist on Borchgrevink's expedition, looked inland across the continent from Cape Adare and this is what he saw:

> The silence and immobility of the scene was impressive; not the slightest animation or vitality anywhere. It was like a mental image of our globe in its primitive state — a spectacle of Chaos.

---

30 Richard Byrd (1938) *Alone*. Putnam, London, p. 120.
31 Morton Henry Moyes, Diary, Mitchell Library, Sydney, ML MSS 388/1, CY 3660.
32 Charles Laseron (1947) *South with Mawson*. Australasian Publishing Company, Sydney, p. 78.

> Around us ice and snow and the remnants of internal fires; above, a sinister sky; below, the sombre sea; and over all, the silence of the sepulchre![33]

Bernacchi felt that he was looking not just at ice-age Earth, at his world in the deep past of the Pleistocene, but also at the bleak future of his planet, spinning cold in space.

We can see that some of these metaphors of silence are those of death — 'the silence of the sepulchre', 'this everlasting silence'. This silence is not that between the movements of a symphony, but comes at its end. Antarctica sometimes seems to provide an experience of life on Earth before and after us, even an experience of Earth before and after Life itself.

The Antarctic silence was the space within which other, surprising sounds could be heard — the beating of one's heart, perhaps, or the thump of your very own pulse in your temples. It was said that Frank Wild had such a strong heart and booming chest that, if you happened to share a sleeping bag with him, you would be kept awake all night by the beating of his heart. Frederick Cook, the doctor on the Belgian Antarctic Expedition of 1897–98, the first to winter in Antarctica, speculated that the sun seemed to provide something that steadied the human heart. The absence of the sun, he reported, registered in the internal disorder of his fellow expeditioners. Mitral murmurs became audible, resounding loudly in the silence of the polar night.

And what of the peculiar rhythm and ache of the continent of ice itself? In 1987, Greenpeace established a World Park Base on Ross Island, and Gudrun Gaudian, the only woman staying for the winter, relished what she called the 'vast, white silence' of the place. Sometimes the only sound she could hear in the autumn was the creaking of the thickening ice in the bay as the tide moved beneath it: 'It makes an eerie sound, just like an old door in a secret castle being opened very slowly.'[34]

When I visited Antarctica, I yearned to hear the ice creak and to escape the throb and thrum of engines — even the ship at rest, at anchorage, was constantly drumming, cranking and sighing in order to sustain the community on board. The station hummed with its own technology. At McMurdo in high summer, the only thing that distinguishes night and day is a slowing of the pace and a slight diminishing of machine noise.[35]

---

33 Louis Bernacchi (1901) *To the South Polar Regions: expedition of 1898–1900*. Hurst & Blackett, London, p. 78.
34 Gudrun Gaudian, 29 March 1987, in John May (1989) *The Greenpeace book of Antarctica*. Child & Associates, Frenchs Forest, NSW, p. 164.
35 Bill Green (1995) *Water, ice and stone: science and memory on the Antarctic lakes*. Harmony Books, New York, p. 50.

Introduction

In Werner Herzog's wonderful film about Antarctica, *Encounters at the end of the World* (2007), one of his 'professional dreamers' talks beautifully about 'the rumble of the iceberg'. Douglas MacAyeal, a glaciologist, waxes lyrical about B15, the great berg he is studying, and he says: 'I can feel the rumble of the iceberg. I can feel the change, the cry of the iceberg as it's screeching and as it's bouncing off the sea bed, as it's steering the ocean currents, as it's beginning to move north. I can feel that sound coming up through the bottoms of my feet.'

And then Herzog introduces us to Regina Eisert, a physiologist living on the sea ice and studying Weddell seals. She says:

> It's the quietest place. When the wind is down or there's no wind, it wakes you up in the middle of the night. And if you walk out on the ice you hear your own heart beat, that's how still it is. And you can hear the ice crack, and it sounds like there's someone walking behind you but it's just the ice, these little stress cracks moving all the time. And you can hear the seals call and it's the most amazing sound, really inorganic — it sounds like Pink Floyd or something — they don't sound like animals.

It is that ocean under the ice — 'the world under the frozen sky', as Herzog calls it — which becomes the poetic heart of the film. People speak of entering that world as 'going down into the cathedral'. One of the film's quirkiest images is that of three scientists lying on the sea ice listening to the music of the underworld, ears pressed to the frozen surface of the ocean. The camera lingers long on this spectacle. The people are prone as if in prayer, and they are alert, their every sense attentive to sound.

That image of humans thoughtfully in thrall to another world will serve for me as a beautiful symbol of the conference. Art and science are indistinguishable in the contemplation of wonder and the quest for understanding. This is what we are doing here together — pressing our ears to the ice, tuning into Antarctic sounds, and ultimately taking the heartbeat of the planet.[36]

---

36 In sections of this paper, I have drawn on my 2007 book *Slicing the silence: voyaging to Antarctica* (UNSW Press, Sydney), and my contributions to the edited collection of Haward and Griffiths (2011) *Australia and the Antarctic Treaty system*.

Mawson's musings and Morse code: Antarctic silence at the end of the 'Heroic Era', and how it was lost

Mark Pharaoh[1]

Douglas Mawson's *Aurora* Expedition was a multi-base venture operating due south of Australia. Mawson's prior polar experience — which led to his thoughts on Antarctic phenomena — encouraged him to counter environmental extremes with technology. To overcome the isolation of his bases, wireless telegraphy was employed from 1912, and communication with Australasia developed.

The Morse code message below was an early 'success'. In more senses than one, the silence of Antarctica has remained 'broken' ever since.

.-- . .- .-. . ... --- .-. .-. -.-- ..-. --- .-. .-. --- --- .-. .-.. .- ... - ... .-. --- -.

This chapter explores the effects of sound in the Antarctic (outside and inside the winter quarters), and discusses what sound vs silence might have meant in terms of a sense of isolation in what was historically, a fascinating technological transition between two eras.

Douglas Mawson (1882–1958) was involved in three separate Antarctic expeditions, in different capacities:

- on the *Nimrod* expedition (1907–09) as physicist;
- on the *Aurora* expedition (1911–14) as supreme commander, having organised and raised the funds for it, as well as commanding the principal continental base;
- on the *Discovery* expedition (1929–30; 1930–31) as commander, again having played the dominant role in establishing what was in this instance only a ship-based venture.

Only the first two expeditions are of interest here — the northern party of the *Nimrod* expedition, and (more extensively) the operations at the 'Main Base' of the *Aurora* expedition.

---

1 Mr Mark Pharaoh, Senior Collection Manager, Australian Polar Collections, South Australian Museum, GPO Box 234, Adelaide, SA 5001, mark.pharaoh@samuseum.sa.gov.au.

Figure 1. 'Listening to nice things about himself'.

Source: *The Bulletin*, 19 March 1914.

We can categorise silence and sound in the following ways:

- Mawson's musings on Antarctic sounds, etc (outside);
- Morse code wireless-related matters (inside); and, in passing,
- other technological noises inside the hut: a range of sounds aside from wireless.

Within this broad spectrum ranging from Mawson's musings to Morse code, the following subjects stand out:

Mawson's musings (outside)	Morse code (inside the Main Base hut)
poetry (improvised)	wireless-related sounds
relating to sledging	end of 'Heroic Era'?
relating to blizzards	first wireless message

It would be interesting also to briefly consider what other sounds perhaps echoed around the huts of these expeditions that competed with Antarctic silence. Other technological noises heard inside the hut (but not discussed further in this paper) included acetylene lighting in operation, music playing (gramophone, improvised band), air-tractor engine running, lathe operating, welding ('thermiting'), and the tide gauge clock — warmed at night inside![2] So aside from noises emanating from animal life and the elements, silence is not all pervading.

The following text written by Mawson is from the copy of *The home of the blizzard*[3] presented to his old *Nimrod* companion, Tannatt William Edgeworth David. This adaptation — reproduced in the frontispiece of *The silence calling*[4] by Tim Bowden (who took his book title from this poem) — ends with 'Apologies to Service D.M.'. The corresponding sections of Mawson's adaptation and the original Service version shown here side by side illustrate the changes Mawson made (from words shown in italics in Service's version).

Mawson's version	Service's original version
To that lone land where bravely you endured	To that lone land *that haply you forsook*
And if perchance you hear the silence calling,	And if perchance you hear the silence calling
The frozen music of star-yearning heights,	The frozen music of star-yearning heights,
Or, dreaming, see the seines of silver trawling	Or, dreaming, see the seines of silver trawling
Across the ship's abyss on vasty nights,	Across the *sky's* abyss on vasty nights,
You may recall that sweep of savage splendor,	You may recall that sweep of savage splendor,
That land that measures each man at his worth,	That land that measures each man at his worth,
And feel in memory, half fierce, half tender,	And feel in memory, half fierce, half tender,

---

2 'The most chronic sufferer throughout the vicissitudes of temperature was the clock belonging to Bage's tide-gauge. Every sleeper in the hut who was sensitive to ticking knew and reviled that clock. So often was it subjected to warm, curative treatment in various resting-places that it was hunted from pillar to post. A radical operation by Correll — the insertion of an extra spring — became necessary at last.' Douglas Mawson (1915) *The home of the blizzard*. William Heinemann, London, vol. 2, pp. 171–2.
3 Douglas Mawson (1915) *The home of the blizzard*. William Heinemann, London.
4 Tim Bowden (1999) *The silence calling*. Allen & Unwin, Sydney.

The brotherhood of men that know the South.	The brotherhood of men that know the *North*.

The original poem, *L'Envoi*,[5] from *Ballads of a Cheechako* (1909)[6] — was written by Robert Service, the 'Canadian Kipling'. Mawson probably made these changes only to make the text more relevant to David's (and his own) experiences. But the lines 'If perchance you hear the silence calling, The frozen music of star-yearning heights,' to me raise the question: did these evocative words draw Mawson to this poem? Did they speak powerfully to him, even if in a near silent way? All that can be said conclusively was that Service was noted as being a great favourite of many of the men — including Mawson — on these earlier expeditions.

While this question will otherwise have to be left unanswered, there are a few examples of Mawson's thoughts which implicitly refer to (in this case, the absence of) distracting sounds, while outside sledging in Antarctica: 'At times during the long hours of steady tramping across the trackless snow-fields, one's thoughts flow on a clear and limpid stream, the mind is unruffled and composed'. This diary entry dates from the end of *Nimrod* Expedition.[7]

Another example relating to exterior sounds is also from his diaries: 'Snow could be seen pouring over the "Barrier"… [and was] the main cause of the seething roar, but it was mingled with an undernote of deeper tone from the upland plateau — like the wind in a million tree-tops'.[8]

This last example is from Mawson's *Aurora* expedition, a longer expedition to this treeless continent, which brings us to the subject of the sounds inside Main Base, specifically those involved with wireless telegraphy.

The wireless masts dominated Cape Denison, even in states of incompletion. They served roles beyond that of wireless telegraphy. Flags flown from the masts were a signal to the ships off the coast, their stays were guides in blizzards, and the varying degrees of completion were a message to the men as to the happenings around the base. Mawson's expedition pioneered the use of wireless telegraphy down south, but not without many setbacks.

Officially, wireless operations began relatively late in 1912: 'Sept 30, aerial was at such a height as to give hope that long-distance messages might be despatched … The [Buzzacott] engine started and gradually got up speed in the dynamo.

---

5   One or more detached verses at the end of a literary composition, serving to convey the moral, or to address the poem to a particular person (orig. employed in old French poetry); a conclusion or result.
6   A cheechako is 'a person newly arrived in the mining districts of Alaska or northwestern Canada', Oxford Dictionaries, 'cheechako', http://oxforddictionaries.com/definition/american_english/cheechako, accessed 9 June 2014.
7   Fred Jacka and Eleanor Jacka (1988) *Mawson's Antarctic diaries*. Allen & Unwin, Sydney, p. xxxv.
8   Mawson (1915) *The home of the blizzard*, vol. 1, p. 113.

The sharp note of the spark rose in accompanying crescendo and, when it had reached its highest pitch, Hannam struck off a message.'[9] Was it heard by anyone? No response came that year.

A fortnight later, on 13 October 1912, one mast blew down. No further wireless contact was achieved until early 1913, when it was 'possible for Jeffryes to "hear" Wellington, Sydney, Melbourne and Hobart, and once he managed to communicate directly with the last-named. Then there were numerous ships passing along the southern shores of Australia or in the vicinity of New Zealand whose "calls" were audible … occasionally the "chatter in the ether" was so confusing that Sawyer, at Macquarie Island, would signal that he was "jammed".'[10]

This reference to the 'chatter' over the wireless suggests that their silence was already lost, even if only at times. But Mawson revealed a more obvious sense in which the notion of Antarctic silence does not fit with the reality of life at Main Base in 1913, in a related passage concerning the practical difficulties of carrying out wireless receiver work. During this work:

> So many adventitious sounds had to be neglected; the noise of the wind as it swept by the Hut; then there was the occasional crackling of 'St. Elmo's fire';[11] the dogs in the veranda shelter were not always remarkable for their quietness; while within the Hut it was impossible to avoid slight sounds which were often sufficient to interrupt the sequence of a message; … when the aurora [Australis] was visible, signals would often die away … Jeffryes would sometimes spend the whole evening trying to transmit a single message … [It was] found easier to transmit and receive wireless messages between certain hours.[12]

The significance of wireless telegraphy: The end of an era

Some significant early expeditions to Antarctica were those of Scott (1910–13, *Terra Nova*), Mawson (1911–14, *Aurora*), Shackleton (1914–16, *Endurance/Aurora*), Rymill (1934–37, *Penola*) and Ellsworth/Wilkins (1935–37, *Wyatt Earp*).

---

9   Mawson (1915) *The home of the blizzard*, vol. 1, p. 153.
10 Mawson (1915) *The home of the blizzard*, vol. 2, p. 137.
11 Electrical weather phenomenon in which luminous plasma is created by a coronal discharge originating from a grounded object in an atmospheric electric field. St Elmo's fire is named after St Erasmus of Formiae (St Elmo, Italian for St Erasmus), patron saint of sailors.
12 Mawson (1915) *The home of the blizzard*, vol. 2, pp. 136–7.

In their classifications of eras or periods of Antarctic expeditions, Law (1957) and Fisher and Fisher (1958) put the end of the heroic era at 1916 and 1922 respectively (see Table 1). In other words, these authors included Mawson's 1911–14 expedition in the heroic era rather than their later mechanised or development era, though it is worthy of comment that Law and the Fishers don't agree with each other on when this next era should start, indicating just how subjective the precise establishment of such eras can be.

Table 1. Traditional and proposed new classification of Antarctic eras.

Law (1957)	Fisher and Fisher (1958)	This chapter
Heroic era 1900 to 1916	Heroic era 1890s to 1922	Heroic era 1900 to 1913
Development era 1918 to 1939	Mechanised era 1923 onwards	Mechanised/technological era 1914 onwards
Mechanised era 1944 to 1958		

I suggest that a new Australian (post-Phillip Law) interpretation, based on the significance of the wireless communications, adds to our understanding of Antarctic history. This new division for the heroic era ends in 1913, after Scott's last expedition, when wireless was now a reality, and the traditional silence or lack of communication with the outside world that so characterised any ventures over the Antarctic winter was broken.

The end of this era, and beginning of the Mechanisation (Technological) Era then follows — or in other words, the end of silence ...

Given the importance of wireless, it is interesting to know what was the first wireless telegraphy message from Antarctica to the outside world. While the official record provides one answer to this, one of the expeditioners, Charles Laseron, in his account of the venture provides the following unofficial answer relating to a period early on when the men were experimenting with the new technology, having set it all up:

.-- . .- .-. . ... --- .-. .-. -.-- ..-. --- .-. .--. --- --- .-. .-.. .- ... . .-. --- -.

'We are sorry for poor Laseron.'

So it would appear that

> Few mutilated messages reached Australia, but of this we knew nothing at the time [September 1912], as no answers came through.
>
> Probably Hannam or Bickerton, practising Morse, did not realise that their effort was actually going over the air ... Some would-be effort of humour on my part ... The secretary of the expedition, fortunately

decided to wait for further particulars before informing my family. When the *Aurora* finally picked us up [early in 1913] he was on board, and almost his first words were, "How is Laseron?".'[13]

A .-	B -...	C -.-.	D -..	E .	F ..-.	G --.	H	I ..	J .---	K -.-	L .-..	M --
N -.	O ---	P .--.	Q --.-	R .-.	S ...	T -	U ..-	V ...-	W .--	X -..-	Y -.--	Z --..

Figure 2. A morse key.

Source: Author's own research.

Conclusion

Like many Antarctic veterans, Mawson became sensitive to this unique, largely unknown environment, and this included how sound was at times experienced there. Focusing here particularly on the first two expeditions he was a member of, it is clear he was articulate enough to attempt to identify and compare some of these impressions, revealing for a time something of a Mawson-like poet.

While it can be useful to distinguish between sounds inside Winter Quarters and those outside, this paper has primarily explored something of the range of audio experiences to be encountered inside — when the incessant noise of blizzards did not fully intrude into this cacoon. It can be argued that an examination of these sounds reveals the surprising presence of machines and other technologically advanced equipment. Mechanisation at Main Base in 1912–13 centred on the attempts to establish — and then maintain — wireless telegraphy with the outside world. When contact was first made, despite being almost accidental, the impenetrable silence of Antarctica was broken forever.

Given the irreversible consequences of this momentous break with the past (which had been characterised by year-long isolation with no word from civilisation), a case can be made for a revision of the traditional division of Antarctic historical eras, with the ending of the heroic era being pushed back to 1912 when 'Laseron's' message got through. Coincidentally, this was the same year that Robert Scott's South Pole Party all died, even if it would take until 1913 for this to be known by the outside world, the lengthy delay being in part due to the absence of wireless on his expedition.

---

13 Charles F Laseron (1947) *South with Mawson*. Australasian Publishing Company, Sydney, p. 81.

Thulia: a Tale of the Antarctic (1843): The earliest Antarctic poem and its musical setting

Elizabeth Truswell[1]

Thulia: a Tale of the Antarctic is a long narrative poem written by James Croxall Palmer, assistant surgeon to the United States Exploring Expedition of 1838–42. The poem was first published in 1843, shortly after the completion of that epic and controversial voyage.

I suggest that this represents the first poem about Antarctica as we know that continent in its essentially modern sense. Coleridge's *Rime of the Ancient Mariner* obviously has strong claims to priority in the poetry of the extreme southern regions, because it was first published in 1798, after, and probably inspired by, James Cook's second voyage of 1772–75. But when Coleridge's poem appeared there was little sense of a substantial continent. In the *Rime* Antarctica is implied — an icy and a terrifying presence — rather than mentioned. While Cook was the first to penetrate southward below the Antarctic Circle, and, in his lengthy and well-documented voyage, to circumnavigate the polar continent, he did not discover it in any spatial sense. Indeed, he was aware himself of the limitations of his achievement in terms of his commission to search for the near-legendary Southern Continent. In his *Journal*, Cook wrote, 'I had now made a circuit of the Southern Ocean in a high latitude and traversed it in such a manner as to leave not the least room for the Possibility of there being a continent, unless near the Pole and out of the reach of Navigation ... That there may be a continent or large tract of land near the Pole, I will not deny'.[2]

Other voyagers followed in the early part of the 19th century. They were largely sealers and whalers, some of whom had a scientific as well as a commercial bent. But their footholds were tenuous, their sightings fragmentary and disconnected. It was not until the United States Exploring Expedition in 1840 traversed some 2,400 kilometres of ice-bound coastline that the presence of something akin to a major continent was established in the region of the South Pole.

My encounter with James Palmer's poem comes from my own experience of Antarctica. I have been writing an account of voyaging with the Deep Sea

---

1 Dr Elizabeth Truswell, Visiting Fellow, Research School of Earth Sciences, The Australian National University, Canberra ACT 0200, etruswell@aapt.net.au.
2 1 February 1775. James Cook (2003) *The Journals. Prepared from the original manuscripts by JC Beaglehole for the Hakluyt Society, 1955–67*, edited by Philip Edwards. Penguin, London, p. 414.

Drilling Project, which from the 1970s has sought to establish the history of the Antarctic icecap and the associated climatic changes. In the course of that project, in search of geological evidence for the oldest ice, a site was drilled into the ocean floor, close to the edge of Antarctica, lying off the region known as the Knox Coast. In searching for the origin of that name, I discovered that it was named for a member of the US Exploring Expedition, a 'Passed Midshipman' named Samuel Knox, who was the first to command the schooner *Flying Fish*.[3] This led me to look much more deeply into that controversial expedition, which was when I came across the poem.

The United States Exploring Expedition of 1838–42 was America's attempt to catch up with what were known to have been, or about to be, expeditions to the south launched from Europe — expeditions such as that of the British under the command of James Clark Ross in *Erebus* and *Terror*, and the French under Dumont d'Urville, with *Astrolabe* and *Zélée*.

The US Exploring Expedition (often referred to — but without affection — as the Ex.Ex. or the Wilkes Expedition) had a long and difficult birth, but was eventually approved by President John Adams, and Lieutenant Charles Wilkes was selected as Commander. Wilkes was certainly not the first choice, and possibly not the best, as subsequent events were to prove. The expedition's aims were many and diverse: to seek new territories in the South Seas, to protect US sealing and whaling industries, to look for new opportunities for commerce, to assert American power, and to undertake scientific research in a wide range of disciplines.

The expedition consisted of six vessels, aptly described as 'oddly assorted'. The flagship was the USS *Vincennes*, a sloop-of-war of the US Navy. Other large vessels were the *Peacock*, also a sloop-of-war; the brigantine *Porpoise;* the clumsy sailer *Relief*, which served as a supply ship; and bringing up the rear of the squadron, two tiny vessels, the *Flying Fish* and the *Sea Gull*, both former New York pilot boats. These last were certainly small, and ill-equipped for dealing with the rigours of Antarctic waters. The *Flying Fish* was a sloop of a mere 96 tons, often with a crew of less than ten.

Indeed, none of the vessels of the expedition had been modified to deal with the expected conditions. None had the double-planked hulls, the sturdy oaken keels and waterproof decking that had been fitted, for example, to the vessels of the British expedition under James Clark Ross.

Some nine scientists were appointed to the expedition. Wilkes had significantly reduced this number from a larger contingent originally proposed. The civilian

---

3   Nathaniel Philbrick (2003) *Sea of glory: America's voyage of discovery, the US Exploring Expedition 1838–1842.* Viking, New York.

scientific corps eventually consisted of naturalists, a botanist, a mineralogist-geologist, taxidermists, and a philologist or linguist. Wilkes elected to undertake the surveying and hydrography himself. The one member of this party who eventually enjoyed scientific fame was the geologist James Dwight Dana, who is essential to the present story. The Assistant Surgeon to the expedition was one James Croxall Palmer. The scientists — the 'scientifics' — didn't rate very highly with Wilkes. None of them were actually included in the Antarctic parts of the venture — they were kept apart and allowed to work in the Pacific.

The expedition left from Norfolk, Virginia, on 19 August 1838. The vessels sailed across the Atlantic to Madeira and the Cape Verde Islands, and then recrossed that ocean to voyage down the coast of South America, eventually to shelter in Orange Bay, on the southern coast of Tierra del Fuego. From there — with the assemblage of ships divided into two — they were to make the first attempt into the Antarctic. Their timing for this venture was poor, as the brief summer season was nearing its end. The aim was to achieve 'furthest South' — to venture further than either James Cook in 1774, or the sealing captain James Weddell in 1823. The *Peacock* and the tiny *Flying Fish* took the route in search of Cook's record — Cook's *ne plus ultra*, which lay to the west of the Antarctic Peninsula. The *Porpoise* and the *Sea Gull* followed Weddell's route to the east, but were driven back by impenetrable ice.

The *Flying Fish* almost reached Cook's most southerly point — but, reaching 70° S latitude, fell just a degree short. The *Peacock* and the *Flying Fish* were separated, and the *Flying Fish* crew in particular faced a battle against ice and storms — with huge seas, giant icebergs and ice floes — losing most of the sails and masts in the tumultuous conditions. Eventually they struggled back to Orange Harbour. The other small sloop, the *Sea Gull*, was lost forever in severe storms when the vessels of the expedition were leaving that refuge on the next leg of their voyage.

The remaining ships of the Ex.Ex. sailed into the Pacific, and carried out surveying, scientific and ethnographic studies of a multitude of oceanic islands. Then, from a base in colonial Sydney, they made another attempt on the Antarctic, sailing south on 26 December 1840, at the height of the southern summer. After encountering the ice-bound margin of East Antarctica, the vessels turned westwards and traversed some 2,400 kilometres of that hazardous coast.

The sighting of land was reported on several occasions — some of the sightings were controversial, poorly recorded in the ship's log and subsequently contested — and no landings were made. Later explorers, including Douglas Mawson, were dismayed to find that in places Wilkes' calculations had been in error by over 100 kilometres in latitude, due probably to the phenomenon of 'looming', where the refraction of light makes it possible to see objects lying far below the horizon. Nevertheless, where Wilkes had been able to get closer to the coast, his sightings were accurate, his measurements of longitude remarkably sound. Before retreating northwards at the long glacier they called 'Termination Tongue' — now considered part of the Shackleton Ice Shelf — Wilkes felt justified in claiming to be the first to establish Antarctica as a major continent, rather than isolated and disconnected islands. The legacy of the voyage was long-lasting; mariners around the world used many of Wilkes' charts for more than a century.

The magnitude of the achievements of the Ex.Ex., however, tended for some years to be overshadowed by the court martial brought against Wilkes by his subordinates, on the grounds of ill treatment of his junior officers. While these accusations were not upheld, and the claims of the officers were eventually dismissed, the doubts raised by the court martial lingered, and explorers such as James Clark Ross refused to accept the findings of Wilkes' survey.

The fate of the *Peacock*

The expedition returned to the US, in fulfilment of its commission to map part of the northwestern coast of North America — the region around the mouth of the Columbia River. There, the large ship *Peacock* foundered on a sand bar at the mouth of the river, and was lost, broken up by the waves. The crew, miraculously, was saved.

James Croxall Palmer and the poem *Thulia*

On board the *Peacock* at this stage was James Croxall Palmer (1811–1883), appointed then as Assistant Surgeon to the expedition. Palmer was a thoroughgoing medical man. He later served in a variety of vessels, and was involved in naval battles of the American Civil War. Subsequently, he enjoyed a distinguished career as head of a number of naval hospitals, eventually becoming Surgeon General of the US Navy.

Figure 1. James Croxall Palmer.

Source: Photograph reproduced by permission of the US Bureau of Medicine and Surgery.

Along with other officers, Palmer had kept a meticulous record of the events of the voyage in his journal. That journal was lost in the shipwreck, but Palmer was able to recall, in fine detail, the events, not only of the *Peacock*, but many of the struggles that had beset the other vessels.

Palmer was also a poet. In 1843, just a year after the completion of the Ex.Ex. expedition, he published the epic poem that he had begun during the Antarctic venture — this he called *Thulia: a Tale of the Antarctic*. In the poem, the tiny vessel *Flying Fish* becomes *Thulia* — a reference to Thule, an island in antiquity, or any far-off region beyond the borders of the known world, though the term has historically had a northern connotation. Palmer dedicated the volume to Lieutenant William M Walker, commander of the *Flying Fish* during its struggle to reach the sought-after furthest South. (It should be noted that Walker's command of the *Flying Fish* was a temporary assignment as Wilkes, ever concerned that cabals might be developing against his leadership, frequently changed the officers in command of the ships of the expedition. Samuel Knox first commanded the vessel). In the preface to *Thulia*, Palmer offered the following explanation:

> The following poem is a true story of the incidents more minutely detailed in the Appendix, to which the reader is referred for a narrative prepared for the journals of the *Flying Fish*. It unfortunately happened that these journals, which had been collected on board the U.S. Ship *Peacock*, were lost with that vessel at the mouth of the Columbia: so that the account which I wrote only for the gratification of a few friends, has become the sole remaining history of a highly interesting adventure.[4]

The poem itself is a long, book-length epic in characteristic ballad form, most of it in four-line stanzas with a simple *a-b-a-b* rhyme pattern. The volume is illustrated with 12 engravings, contributed by the expedition's able young artist, Alfred Agate.

Palmer may well have been aware of the *Rime of the Ancient Mariner*, but he was certainly no Coleridge! There is, as might be expected, a mix in the poem of high adventure, vivid imagery, idealism, terror, and a longing for the softer climes of home. There is too a clear theme of patriotism — the search for glory in the name of America.

The language of the poem is essentially simple, populist perhaps. It oscillates between a form of reality about nature, and a simple romanticism. According to the American scholar William Lenz, Palmer uses 'simple, familiar literary forms to domesticate the Antarctic'.[5] The landscape it describes lacks the ominous presence of the supernatural, so evident in Coleridge's epic.

Within *Thulia* there are some separate poems. These seem to sit oddly, interrupting the flow of the ballad. *The Antarctic Mariner's Song*, for instance, is one such, with its theme of national glory. *The Bridal Rose* is another poem, a story of romantic love based on an 'adventure' on board the *Peacock* (presumably in the Pacific). This lack of unity in the poem's structure, as noted by Lenz, may reflect the occasional nature of the composition, and the difficulty that Palmer had, perhaps, as a non-professional writer, in sustaining a long work.

4　James Croxall Palmer (1843) *Thulia: a tale of the Antarctic*. Samuel Colman, New York, p. 9.
5　William E Lenz (1995) *The poetics of the Antarctic: a study in nineteenth century American cultural perceptions*. Garland Publications, New York, p. 64.

With its publication in 1843 — some said in time to catch the Christmas market — this poem was in fact the first narrative of the voyage to appear in print after the return of the expedition. The notes and appendix to the poem support the verses with a remarkably full description of the quest for furthest south.

Wilkes had appropriated for himself the writing of the official account of the expedition, drawing both on his own journals and on those of his officers. His five-volume narrative of the voyage was published with funding by the US Congress in 1844, two years after the end of the expedition, and just one year after the publication of *Thulia*. Palmer's epic poem thus neatly pre-empted his commander's effort; its quick publication suggests that it slipped under his radar. It may be that Wilkes did not recognise it for what it was — and thought it to be just a romantic poem, rather than a revealing story describing significant parts of the expedition's voyage.

Palmer published a second edition of the poem in 1868, when he was head of the naval hospital in Brooklyn, New York.[6] This he titled *The Antarctic Mariner's Song*. Some new poems were added in this second version, including a rollicking sea-shanty, *The Air from the Icebergs*, detailing an event in which the rudder of the *Peacock* was splintered and almost lost in a rear-end collision with an iceberg during the long voyage around the coast of Antarctica.

Sentimentality characterises some of the newly added poems; *Monody*, for example, reflects on the death of a child whose father is away on the exploring expedition. Other verses in this edition are more introspective, perhaps viewing the experience of the voyage from the perspective of 25 years. In this edition, Palmer also made many minor changes to the wording of the original stanzas of *Thulia*. He carried out extensive 'tinkering', substituting some words and changing word order.

There are minor differences too in the illustrations; one engraving, *The ice islands,* has been added, with its emphasis on the human presence in a landscape that overwhelms. Others, particularly those that focus on details of life on board the vessels, have been enlarged to occupy a greater prominence.

The following extracts give a brief overview of the language, structure, and themes of *Thulia*. First, the narrative verses give the Antarctic setting, and the former role of the tiny *Flying Fish* as a pilot boat on the Hudson River.

> I.
> Deep in a far and lonely bay,
> Begirt by desert cliffs of snow,
> A little bark at anchor lay,

---

[6] James Croxall Palmer (1868) *Antarctic mariner's song.* Van Nostrand, New York.

In southern twilight's fiery glow.

Too frail a shell — too lightly borne
Upon the bubble of a wave,
To face the terrors of Cape Horn,
Or stern Antarctic seas to brave.

In other days she loved to glide
O'er Hudson's bosom bright and still;
And float along the tranquil tide,
By craggy steep and sloping hill.

Now, like a land-bird, blown away
By tempests from its happy nest,
She flies before the whirling spray,
To seek this dreary place of rest.

From time to time, a clearly patriotic theme comes through — never more strongly than in *The Antarctic Mariner's Song*, from which the following verses are taken:

I.
Sweetly, from the land of roses
Sighing comes the northern breeze;
And the smile of dawn reposes,
All in blushes, on the seas.
Now within the sleeping sail,
Murmurs soft the gentle gale.
Ease the sheet, and keep away:
Glory guides us South today...

IV.
Circled by these columns hoary,
All the field of fame is ours;
Here to carve a name in story,
Or a tomb beneath these towers.
Southward still our way we trace,
Winding through an icy maze.
Luff her to — there she goes through!
Glory leads, and we pursue.

Between two icebergs gaunt and pale,
Like giant sentinels on post;
Without a welcome or a hail,
Intrude they on the realm of Frost.

> In desolation vast and wild,
> Outstretched a mighty ruin lies:
> Huge towers on massy ramparts piled:
> High domes whose azure pales the skies.

Although some of Palmer's images verge on the gothic ('giant sentinels', 'huge towers' and 'massy ramparts', for instance), 'they carry no metaphysical threat, invoke no curse or dread, conjure up no spiritual horror as in Coleridge, Shelley or Poe. They are in fact comfortably familiar literary images'.[7]

The appendix to the poem is in part notes to the text, explaining the realities of some of the poetic references, and including the very real accounts of the voyage. In this, Palmer confesses the difficulty he has with the Romantic and the Real.

It is clear from this that Palmer is negotiating the demands of poetry, travelogue and scientific reporting. The notes before the appendix offer scientific explanations for some of the romantic images in the poetry. In these Palmer mixes poetic expression and science — he seems to be driven by a need to explain himself — to validate the poetry with contemporary science. He thus seems to be vacillating between his roles as a poet and as a member of a huge scientific expedition.

Selected verses demonstrate this mix of romance and reality.

> O'er mounds of vapour daily rolled,
> Huge castled clouds are towering high,
> Confronting with the billows bold,
> That dash defiance to the sky.
> (Palmer 1843, p. 21)

> And with the roving albatross,
> The sheath-bill flickers round and round;
> And petrels hop the foam across,
> Where lightest janthine might be drowned.

> (Palmer 1843, p. 23)

In these verses the scientific observations creep in. The line 'Huge castled clouds are towering high' comes from the journal of Captain Fitzroy of the *Beagle*, who reported that these clouds or *cumuloni* were peculiar to the waters around Cape Horn, and came up with the south-west gales.

---

7   Lenz (1995) *The poetics of the Antarctic*.

The second of the above verses is dense with biological references. First, a brief rollcall of bird life. After the albatross comes reference to the sheathbill — probably the Snowy Sheathbill of Antarctic waters and islands — then to the petrel, which could refer to any one of a range of species, but which are mostly distinguished by low flight skimming across wave surfaces, hence they 'hop the foam across'.

Then there is 'janthine' — surely a curious word in a romantic poem of this era. The reference here is probably to *Janthina janthina,* the fragile purple sea snail, often found washed up on southern beaches. This gastropod of the open oceans builds a little raft of bubbles to float on the sea surface; its shell colour is light above and dark below, so that sea-birds passing overhead find it difficult to detect, a fact that Palmer notes.

Lenz doesn't speculate on the relationships that Palmer may have had with the 'scientifics' of the expedition, nor do the journals of other expedition members offer enlightenment. Was his awareness of details of the science heightened by his interest in their discoveries? Did he feel that his link with a scientist already as eminent as, for example, James Dana, would help to legitimise his poetry? Given that Palmer would have shared an educated background with members of the scientific party, it is not unexpected that he would have chosen them as companions on the voyage, and been a party to the discussion of their scientific endeavours.

James Dwight Dana and the musical setting of *Thulia*

Not only does the original poem — the epic of *Thulia* — have claims to be the oldest Antarctic poem, it also includes what is probably the first Antarctic music. It is here that James Dwight Dana comes into the story. Dana, just a few years younger than Charles Darwin, had produced his *System of mineralogy* by the age of 24. Published to wide acclaim in 1837, this book is, amazingly, essentially still a standard text today, with more than 22 revised and reprinted editions. Dana's interests were wide-ranging. He joined the Ex.Ex. as a geologist and mineralogist, but eventually took responsibility for writing the reports on zoology, as well as those on geology, working on these for 13 years after the end of the expedition.[8] Included in his report on the Crustacea is the first

---

8   James D Dana (1846) *Zoophytes. United States Exploring Expedition,* vol. 7. C Sherman, Philadelphia; James D Dana (1849) *Geology. United States Exploring Expedition*, vol. 10. C Sherman, Philadelphia.

description of krill, the tiny shrimp-like organism that is the base of the food chain for a number of Antarctic ecosystems.[9] Scientifically, its name remains *Euphausia superba* Dana 1850.

Figure 2. James Dwight Dana.

Source: Painted by Daniel Huntington, 1858 (Wikipedia Commons).

In his life's work, Dana attempted grand geological syntheses. He wrote a treatise on the origins of coral reefs — basically expanding Darwin's understanding of them, showing that the volcanic islands with which reefs are associated occur in linear chains, reflecting the age progression of the islands. Much of this knowledge derived from his study of the islands of Hawaii. He established the geologic distinction between the composition and dynamics of continents and ocean basins, and the ways in which mountain belts — particularly those of North America — form about the ancient core of a continent. Among his awards

---

9   James D Dana (1852) *Crustacea. United States Exploring Expedition*, vols 13, 14. C Sherman, Philadelphia.

were the prestigious Copley Medal of the Royal Society, the Wollaston Medal of the Geological Society of London, and the Clarke Medal of the Royal Society of New South Wales. Contemporary scientists, including Darwin, heaped praise on Dana's head. Following his work on the Crustacea, but referring too to his work on corals and geology, Darwin wrote to Dana thus, 'I am really lost in astonishment at what you have done in mental labour. And then, beside the labour, so much originality in all your works!'[10] Alexander von Humboldt, too, referred to him as one of the greatest scientists of the age.

Dana spent three months in New South Wales while the rest of the expedition undertook the voyage to the edge of Antarctica.[11] The corps of civilian scientists was not to be involved in that part of the voyage, the imperious Wilkes having rationalised that there would be nothing in it to interest them. Wilkes, no doubt, was secretly relieved to be temporarily rid of the 'scientifics', who could not be subjected to his strict naval discipline.

Dana looked forward to his enforced stay in the Australian colony where he 'could gratify ... but partially, in a geological point of view, the curiosity which so strange a land may well excite'.[12] He was soon introduced to the Reverend WB Clarke, the 'father of Australian geology'. He travelled with Clarke to the Illawarra, where the two engaged in spirited debate about the origin of river valleys. Later, he explored the Hunter Valley, and made an insightful contribution to the then controversial issue of the age of the Australian coal measures.

He was a profoundly religious man, and wrestled with Darwin's views on the changing nature of species. He finally agreed with Darwin, much to Darwin's relief, but he did retain much of his religion. He remained a Christian, but a number of manuscripts show his struggle to reconcile a benign Creator with his own understanding of earth history.

Dana was a musician too: he played both the guitar and the flute, he wrote hymns and love songs. And he it was who set some parts of Palmer's poem to music. In *Thulia*, the settings for guitar of four verses of *The Antarctic Mariner's Song* were published in the original volume (see below).[13] But Dana's contribution to the life of the expedition was more than this; his compilation of a songbook — which apparently remains unpublished — contains more settings of Palmer's poetry, including the *Jolly Old Peacock*.

---

10   Charles Darwin, letter to James Dana, quoted in Louis V Pirsson (1919) 'Biographical memoir of James Dwight Dana 1813–1895'. *US National Academy of Sciences, Biographical Memoirs* 9: 41–92, p. 75.
11   Ann Mozley (1966) James Dwight Dana (1813–1895). *Australian Dictionary of Biography*, vol. 1, Melbourne University Press; available at http://adb.anu.edu.au/biography/dana-james-dwight-1953.
12   James Dana, quoted in Ann Mozley (1964) 'James Dwight Dana in New South Wales, 1839–1840'. *Journal and Proceedings of the Royal Society of New South Wales* 97: 185–91.
13   Palmer (1843) *Thulia: a tale of the Antarctic*, pp. 42–6.

Figure 3. Musical score: *Thulia* (1843).

Source: Palmer (1843) pp. 42–46.

Performance

It is impossible to know how the musical ballads would have been sung in the 1840s — nor how often, or who the audiences might have been. The poem itself, however, seems to have reasonably popular, and Lenz quotes a number of reviews in contemporary magazines.

In recent years, some of the songs have had a limited number of performances. In 1985 the Smithsonian Institute had some of them performed to commemorate the Wilkes Expedition, since artefacts from that expedition formed much of the original Smithsonian collections.

More recently, at an open day in 2009 held by the US Geological Survey, both the sea shanty *The Jolly Old Peacock* and parts of the *Antarctic Mariner's Song* were performed by a small group of musicians. According to the news article reporting this performance,[14] Dana's 56-page songbook included a full Nativity, the two Antarctic songs, and others about Oregon and his personal life. The 'lyrics' were those of James Palmer, and probably include some of the poems added in the *Antarctic Mariner's Song* of 1868. The songbook was never published, nor was it mentioned in the formal logs of the expedition. It is reported to have been held by the Palmer family until recently, when it was sold to a private collector. Access to the songbook was instigated by Alan Cooper, an emeritus geologist to the US Geological Survey, a musician himself, and well known to Australian Antarctic scientists. The notes on that performance say that the songs were performed in the 1840s style of the original music manuscripts. Charles Wilkes was the first to assert that Antarctica was a continent, taking upon himself as commander the defence of this claim in the narrative of the voyage.[15] There is a delicious irony then in the fact that the nature of that landmass should have been first revealed not by Wilkes himself, but by an assistant surgeon in the form of a romantic poem written during the voyage, and set to music by one of the distrusted 'scientifics'.

---

14 USGS News 13 May 2009, http:// www.usgs.gov/newsroom/article.asp?ID=2219.
15 Charles Wilkes (1844) *Narrative of the United States Exploring Expedition during the years 1838, 1839, 1840, 1841, 1842*, vols 1–5. C Sherman, Philadelphia.

Nankyoku no kyoku: The cultural life of the Shirase Antarctic Expedition 1910–12

Rupert Summerson[1]

Introduction

The austral summer of 2011–12 was the centenary of many significant milestones in Antarctic history: Amundsen's successful expedition to reach the South Pole, Scott's tragic demise, the arrival of Mawson's expedition in the Antarctic, and not the least is the only just remembered Japanese expedition to Antarctica under the leadership of Lieutenant Nobu Shirase.[2]

The Japanese Antarctic Expedition (1910–13) was a Japanese private expedition organised by Lieutenant Nobu Shirase and funded largely by donations. Like many of the other major expeditions of the so-called Heroic Era, it was only partially funded by the government. Until very recently, little was known about the expedition in the English-speaking world; apart from a handful of articles in journals and magazines and summaries derived from these same articles in general books about the Antarctic, there is very little detail. Until the publication in late 2011 of the long awaited translation of *Nankyoku-ki*, the official account of the expedition by the Shirase Expedition Supporters' Association, there was very little information about the expedition in English, the main source of information being Ivor Hamre (1933).[3] RA Swan contributed a short article 22 years later.[4] The Reader's Digest book on Antarctica included a section on the expedition, which seemed to be based largely on Hamre's article.[5] There is, of course, substantially more information in Japanese, though accessing this from Australia is very difficult. The bibliography of the expedition compiled by Chet Ross, which principally comprises sources in Japanese, is invaluable

---
1 Dr Rupert Summerson, PO Box 3853, Manuka, ACT 2603, rupert.summerson@bigpond.com.
2 In Japanese, people's names are given with the family name first, then given name. When translating names into English I have made the name order the same as in English, i.e. given name followed by family name.
3 Shirase Antarctic Expedition Supporters' Association, ed. (2011) *The Japanese South Polar Expedition 1910–12: a record of Antarctica*. Erskine Press and Bluntisham Books, Norwich; Ivar Hamre (1933) 'The Japanese South Polar Expedition of 1911–1912: a little-known episode in Antarctic exploration'. *Geographical Journal* 82: 411–23.
4 RA Swan (1955) 'Forgotten Antarctic venture: the first Japanese south polar expedition 1911–1912'. *Walkabout* 21 (August): 31–33.
5 Reader's Digest (1990) *Antarctica: great stories from the frozen continent*. Reader's Digest, Sydney.

in understanding what had been written about the expedition and some initial details about the cultural life of the expedition.[6] My correspondence with him led to some fruitful discoveries. Two recent PhD theses about the Shirase expedition, McInnes (2009)[7] and Stevenson (2010),[8] have become available to the general reader.

Main events of the expedition

The expedition left Tokyo on 1 December 1910. The ship, the *Kainan Maru* (*'Southern Pioneer'*), was a 204-ton, 30.5 m long, three-mast auxiliary schooner that had once been a fisheries supply vessel. Its captain was Naokichi Nomura, who was an experienced sailor. The first port of call was Wellington in New Zealand, which they reached on 7 February 1911. They departed Wellington on 11 February, heading south towards Antarctica, encountering ice near Cape Adare. It was already March and too late in the season to attempt to enter the Ross Sea. The ship therefore turned north and arrived in Sydney on 1 May 1911. There was considerable disappointment among expedition members about this setback but the expedition resolved to return to Antarctica the following summer. The expedition spent the winter at Parsley Bay, near Watson's Bay in Sydney, while the *Kainan Maru* was overhauled at Jubilee Dock in Sydney. Shirase despatched Keiichi Tada, the secretary of the expedition, and Captain Nomura back to Japan in May 1911 to raise funds and bring more dogs. Nomura returned in October 1911 with provisions and spare parts for the ship and Tada returned in November bringing 29 sledge dogs. On 19 November 1911 the expedition departed Sydney en route to Antarctica. The first iceberg was encountered on 11 December and they entered the pack ice the following day. They crossed the Antarctic Circle on 21 December at longitude 177° E (near Scott Island at the entrance to the Ross Sea). On 29 December they emerged from the pack ice into open water in the Ross Sea.

On New Year's Day 1912, an important day in the Japanese calendar, they were at 69°40' S. The mountains of the Admiralty Range, South Victoria Land, the first land they had sighted, came into view on 3 January 1912. Cape Adare was also sighted but they were unable to land there. On 4 January Coulman Island came into view and from there they steamed south-eastwards until the Great Ice Barrier, which is now called the ice front of the Ross Ice Shelf, came into view

---

6   Chet Ross (2010) *Lieutenant Nobu Shirase and the Japanese Antarctic Expedition of 1910–1912: a bibliography*. Adélie Books, Santa Monica CA.
7   Brendan Neil McInnes (2009) *The forgetting of a hero: the Antarctic explorer Shirase Nobu*. University of New England, Armidale, NSW.
8   William R Stevenson III (2010) *The spirit of adventure: Japanese exploration and the quest for the South Pole*. University of Hawai'i, Manoa.

on 10 January at latitude 78°10' S. They then continued sailing eastwards along the ice front, reaching their initial destination, the Bay of Whales, on 15 January 1912. The main landing party went ashore the following day and established a base camp. The five members of the 'Dash Patrol', including Shirase and Takeda, the chief scientist, departed from the base camp on 20 January taking two dog sledges. On 28 January the Dash Patrol reached their furthest point south at 80°05' S and from there they returned safely to base camp, arriving on 31 January. Meanwhile the *Kainan Maru* sailed eastwards and dropped two landing parties on 23 January to explore the Alexandra Mountains in Edward VII Land. Unfortunately they were not able to reach the summit or even the exposed rock because of a wide bergschrund below the outcrop.[9] Both parties safely returned to the ship on 24 January. The ship then continued eastwards to attempt to exceed Captain Scott's furthest east point during the *Discovery* expedition in 1902. The *Kainan Maru* reached 152° W on 26 January, 17.3 km further east than *Discovery*'s record. The ship was then turned round and headed back to the Bay of Whales to retrieve the main landing party.

On 3 February 1912 the ship was manoeuvred into place against the sea ice near a low point in the ice cliffs and by 10 am on 4 February most of the supplies and equipment had been loaded back onto the ship. The weather started to deteriorate rapidly and the men and six of the dogs managed to get back on board as the bay became ice-bound with an onshore wind. The ship made a narrow escape but 20 dogs were left behind. Shirase had hoped to make a final landing on Coulman Island but the bad weather continued and on 14 February a conference was held at which it was decided that enough of the aims of the expedition had been achieved, so the order was given to set course for New Zealand. The ship arrived in Wellington on 23 March. Shirase, Takeda and three others left the ship in Wellington to head home by mail steamer to make a report and make arrangements for the expedition's return. The *Kainan Maru* with the rest of the expedition finally arrived at Tokyo to a rapturous welcome on 20 June 1912.

Music on the Japanese Antarctic Expedition

Most if not all of the expeditions of the heroic era had some form of musical life:

> A gramophone with a large supply of records was, I think, our best friend. Of musical instruments we had a piano, a violin, a flute, mandolins, not forgetting a mouth-organ and an accordion. All the publishers had been kind enough to send us music, so that we could cultivate this art as much as we wished.[10]

---

9   A *bergschrund* is a permanent crevasse formed on mountain slopes in glacierised terrains by the moving ice pulling away from the fixed ice attached to the rock.
10   Roald Amundsen (1912) *The South Pole*. John Murray, London.

Meares has become enamoured of the gramophone. We find we have a splendid selection of records. The pianola is being brought in sections, but I'm not at all sure it will be worth the trouble.[11]

Sunday being quiet Scott read service while the officers and men grouped round the wheel. We seldom had service on deck; for Sundays became proverbial days for a blow on the way out, and service, if held at all, was generally in the ward-room. On one famous occasion we tried to play the pianola to accompany the hymns, but, since the rolls were scored rather for musical effect than for church services, the pianola was suddenly found to be playing something quite different from what was being sung. All through the expedition the want of someone who could play the piano was felt, and such a man is certainly a great asset in a life so far removed from all the pleasures of civilization. As Scott wrote in *The Voyage of the Discovery*, where one of the officers used to play each evening: 'This hour of music has become an institution which none of us would willingly forgo. I don't know what thoughts it brings to others, though I can readily guess; but of such things one does not care to write. I can well believe, however, that our music smoothes over many a ruffle and brings us to dinner each night in that excellent humour, where all seem good-tempered, though "cleared for action" and ready for fresh argument.'[12]

During the afternoon three Adélie penguins approached the ship across the floe while Hussey was discoursing sweet music on the banjo. The solemn-looking little birds appeared to appreciate 'It's a Long Way to Tipperary', but they fled in horror when Hussey treated them to a little of the music that comes from Scotland. The shouts of laughter from the ship added to their dismay, and they made off as fast as their short legs would carry them.[13]

The gramophone is wound and the record goes on. It is a band piece, beginning quietly, but accelerating to a stirring crescendo, in which the loud clash of cymbals comes faster and faster, to reach the climax in a resounding crash. Then the music dies away in a soothing melody. It is Mertz's favourite record, and peculiarly adapted to his personality. Long since it has become known as 'Mertz killing seals', and is very suggestive of his emphatic methods.[14]

---

11   RF Scott (1913) *Scott's last expedition*. John Murray, London.
12   Apsley Cherry-Garrard (1922) *The worst journey in the world*. Constable & Co Ltd, London.
13   Ernest Shackleton (1919) *South: the story of Shackleton's 1914–1917 expedition*. Heinemann, London.
14   Charles Francis Laseron (1947) *South with Mawson: reminiscences of the Australasian Antarctic Expedition, 1911–1914*. Australasian Publishing Co Pty Ltd, Sydney.

At the outset, it was hard to believe that the Shirase Antarctic expedition would be any different. The publication of a bibliography of the Shirase expedition was the stimulus for an investigation into whether the Japanese Antarctic expedition included some music.[15] Following some correspondence with the compiler of the bibliography, Chet Ross, I asked whether, during the course of his researches, he had encountered any mention of music being played on the expedition. He responded with an illustration from a book called *Yamato yukihara: Shirase Nankyoku tanken-tai* ('*Yamato snow plain in Antarctica: Shirase's expedition story*') by Sekiya Toshitaka (Figure 1). This book is the story of the expedition written for children, but Ross reassured me that the author was meticulous in representing the events of the expedition accurately, albeit in a form accessible to children. The illustration shows a scene on the foredeck of the expedition ship, the *Kainan Maru*, showing the crew lounging on the deck around a figure sitting cross-legged playing a *shakuhachi* (a Japanese end-blown bamboo flute). Nearby was a wind-up gramophone. No information was forthcoming about the musician, however.

Figure 1. Illustration from Toshitaka (2002) *Yamato yukihara: Shirase Nankyoku tanken-tai.*[16]

Note: The caption reads: 'We enjoyed sitting on the deck after washing, and listening to the records on fresh nights. It was a very long six months boat journey to Antarctica.' (translation courtesy of Noriko Sakai).

Source: Sekiya Toshitaka and Fukuinkan Shoten Publishers, Tokyo.

Despite the paucity of information about the expedition in English, it has been possible to compile a brief account of the cultural life of the expedition, in particular the music and poetry. The following are extracts from the English translation of *Nankyoku-ki*, the official record of the expedition.[17]

---

15 Ross (2010) *Lieutenant Nobu Shirase and the Japanese Antarctic Expedition of 1910–1912*.
16 Sekiya Toshitaka (2002) *Yamato yukihara: Shirase Nankyoku tanken-tai*. Fukuinkan Shoten, Tokyo.
17 Shirase Antarctic Expedition Supporters' Association (2011) *The Japanese South Polar Expedition 1910–12*.

> With one last long look and one last goodbye, they parted. Just then the sudden sad note of a shakuhachi trembled across the water, a note to rend the hearts of those we left behind as we set off on our long and lonely voyage.[18]

> That evening [20 December 1910] we all went up on deck in search of cooler air. As we stood around chatting and admiring the brightness of the moon the low notes of a shakuhachi rose from some far corner of the ship and played a harmony to the sound of the waves.[19]

> 29 December 1911. Having made a general survey of the activities on deck, Lt Shirase put Tada and Muramatsu in charge and settled down to enjoy some music on the gramophone.[20]

Kenjo Tsunabuchi's two-volume *Kyoku: Shirase Chūi Nankyoku tankenki*, about the Shirase expedition, was published in 1983.[21] *Nankyoku* (南極) is the Japanese word for Antarctica; its meaning is derived from *nan* (南), which means south (Kanji/Chinese), and *kyoku* (極), which means furthest extent or pole. *Kyoku* also has other meanings, including music (曲), though there is no etymological link between pole and music.

Tsunabuchi's book, which is not in Ross' bibliography, is a historical novel but both McInnes (2009) and Stevenson (2010) agree that it contained much useful information. According to McInnes it is 'a work very firmly based on the historical facts',[22] and Stevenson says that it 'stands as the farthest reaching and most intriguing account to date'.[23] First and foremost, it revealed the name of the shakuhachi player on the expedition, Keiichi Tada (多田恵一) (Figure 2).

---

18   Shirase Antarctic Expedition Supporters' Association (2011) *The Japanese South Polar Expedition 1910–12*, p. 54.
19   Shirase Antarctic Expedition Supporters' Association (2011) *The Japanese South Polar Expedition 1910–12*, p. 59.
20   Shirase Antarctic Expedition Supporters' Association (2011) *The Japanese South Polar Expedition 1910–12*, p. 112.
21   Kenjō Tsunabuchi (1983) *Kyoku: Shirase Chūi Nankyoku tankenki* ('Pole: Lt Shirase's Antarctic journey'). Shinchōsha, Tōkyō.
22   McInnes (2009) *The forgetting of a hero*, p. 51.
23   Stevenson (2010) *The spirit of adventure*, p. 38.

Figure 2. Members of the Japanese Antarctic Expedition on the deck of the Kainan Maru in January 1912. Keiichi Tada is circled in the back row.

Source: Shirase (1913) *Nankyoku-ki*.

Tada was the first person to be recruited to the expedition and was appointed as secretary, becoming Shirase's right-hand man.[24] When the expedition returned to Sydney after the failed first attempt to reach Antarctica in 1911, Tada and Captain Nomura returned to Japan to report on the expedition, raise funds for a second attempt and return to Australia with provisions, spare parts for the ship and 26 sledge dogs (the dogs taken on the first voyage had all died, except for one). Tsunabuchi records:

> Tada went to Okuma's house with Miura[25] after dinner and made Miura talk about the life in Sydney. After that, as Okuma asked, Tada played Shakuhachi for Mrs. Okuma and other ladies of high society. Okuma was satisfied with Tada's playing and named that shakuhachi *'kozasa-go'* which means little bamboo leaf. Tada wrote 'the moon is clear in the sky tonight, and we had tasteful night'.[26]

Tsunabuchi also mentioned that Murakami wanted to send Horiuchi instead of Tada, as Tada's behaviour was not good. But in the end Tada was sent from

---

24 Ross (2010) *Lieutenant Nobu Shirase and the Japanese Antarctic Expedition of 1910–1912*, p. 30.
25 There is some confusion about who Miura was and whether Kenjo meant Nomura, the ship's captain who returned to Japan with Tada to obtain more supplies.
26 Tsunabuchi (1983) *Kyoku: Shirase Chūi Nankyoku tankenki*, translation by Noriko Sakai.

Yokohama with 29 dogs. Tada fell out with Shirase at some point and was relegated to the position of assistant naturalist during the second summer. Ross suspects that the falling out may have had something to do with Tada writing an article for a magazine in Tokyo, without Shirase's knowledge, when he returned there during the winter in Sydney.[27] There is very little mention of him in *Nankyoku-ki*.[28] It is notable also that no mention is made of who played the shakuhachi the three times it is mentioned in *Nankyoku-ki*. Tada left the ship immediately it arrived in Yokohama and took no part in the return celebrations in Tokyo. He wrote four books about the expedition,[29] two of which were published before Shirase's own account, one and two months respectively after the expeditions return. In 1915 he published his autobiography,[30] which includes a photograph of him looking very much at ease with Count Okuma.[31] Late in life he published another book about the Antarctic expedition.[32]

It has not yet been possible to determine what pieces of music Tada played or what was played on the gramophone. Tada's books are now very rare, even in Japan, which, compounded by language difficulties, makes it very difficult to find a copy. There is, however, a glimmer of light into this as yet dark corner of the expedition. Tsunabuchi describes an incident soon after the expedition left Tokyo at the beginning of the expedition.[33] It was the first time that they had a Japanese-style hot bath since they left Japan. For Japanese people taking a bath is really important so they felt that it was a special occasion. After the bath they enjoyed a nice meal with fresh seafood. Everyone was happy, they listened to some 78 rpm records on the gramophone and started singing songs, including the expedition's song that Tada had composed (see below). Takeda asked Tada to teach him to sing *Hakata-bushi* (*bushi* is a common suffix for Japanese folk songs and means something like melody[34]), thus *Hakata-bushi* means melody – or song from Hakata). Takeda thought that it was funny as he was from Hakata and Tada was born in China (which was common at that time). That this was a real incident, not one made up by Tsunabuchi, is confirmed in *Nankyoku Tanken Nikki* (Antarctic Expedition Diary), written by Tada and published in 1912.[35]

Hakata was a trading port on the west coast of Japan on the island of Kyushu in Fukuoka Prefecture. It was absorbed into Fukuoka City in the late 19th century

---

27 Ross (2010) *Lieutenant Nobu Shirase and the Japanese Antarctic Expedition of 1910–1912*.
28 Shirase Antarctic Expedition Supporters' Association (2011) *The Japanese South Polar Expedition 1910–12*.
29 Keiichi Tada (1912a) *Nankyoku tanken shiroku* ('*The authentic account of the Antarctic Expedition*'). Keiseisha, Tokyo; (1912b) *Nankyoku tanken nikki* ('*Antarctic expedition diary*'). Maekawa Bunoeikaku, Tokyo.
30 Keiichi Tada (1915). *Shokon* ('*The Scar*'). Ibuki Shobou, Tokyo.
31 Ross (2010) *Lieutenant Nobu Shirase and the Japanese Antarctic Expedition of 1910–1912*, p. 35.
32 Keiichi Tada (1958) *Nankyoku tanken jitsuroku* ('*The true record of the Antarctic Expedition*'). Kainan Shuppan Kyokai, Tokyo.
33 Translation by Noriko Sakai.
34 David W Hughes (2008) *Traditional folk song in modern Japan*. Global Oriental, Folkestone, UK.
35 Tada (1912b) *Nankyoku tanken nikki*.

and is now a ward in that city (Wikipedia). There is a strong tradition of folk song (*min'yō*) in Japan: *Min'yō wa kokoro no furusato* ('Folk song is the heart's home town').[36] In any one *buraku* (hamlet) in early modern (*Meiji* era) times, a community might know more than 100 songs, which might be classified into songs for a number of different events such as festival songs, work songs, party songs, children's songs, etc. *Hakata-bushi* is a romantic song about a young woman dressed wearing a Hakata *obi* (the broad sash worn round the waist over the *kimono*). She walks gracefully, like a willow, and the moon rises over pine trees. Like many *min'yō* this song extols some of the virtues of the town, village or district in question. It is likely that many, if not most, of the expedition members would have known songs from their home towns and that these would have been sung at various times during the expedition.

Expedition songs

'Our route took us over the Kaji-bashi (bridge), through the Tatami district, and down Shindoro street … with the crowd still singing the expedition's song as they went.'[37] The song, composed by Kamiya Fusen,[38] was sung at the departure of the expedition and at its return. As McInnes notes, the *biwa* is a traditional Japanese musical instrument, closely related to the Chinese *pipa*. Its closest Western counterpart is a lute. The title *Tanken Biwa Uta* ('Expedition *Biwa* Song') implies that it was composed to be accompanied on the *biwa*. Given that the *biwa* is quite a soft instrument, it seems a curious choice for what seems to have been intended as a rousing song for massed voices.

Tanken Biwa Uta ('Expedition Biwa Song')

> With no time for resting on the tiller, they part the waves that reach the sky,
> Through the scorching heat that brings the *Kuroshio* to a boil,
> They sail beyond the equator
> Relentlessly onwards, on to the south,
> Through the frozen seas,
> Beneath Mount Erebus, rising 4000 *shaku* into the sky.
> How we anticipate the high spirits of the men as they go ashore,
> Carrying the hopes of the Japanese people
> To that place yonder where the silent, endless

---

36 Hughes (2008) *Traditional folk song in modern Japan*, p. 1.
37 Shirase Antarctic Expedition Supporters' Association (2011) *The Japanese South Polar Expedition 1910–12*, p. 237.
38 McInnes (2009) *The forgetting of a hero*, p. 244.

World of Silver lies.

Men! Crest those waves on your way to the Southern Hemisphere!
On, to the very ends of the Earth, never resting until you reach the Pole!
Where you will raise our flag, your sincerity burning for a thousand years!
Not knowing the way, you drag your sledges across the immense ice-fields through ways uncharted,
Valiantly determined even at risk of life
To overcome the countless hardships and scale the soaring peaks of ice.
At the very point of the Earth's axis,
To the brilliant glow of our Sovereign's majesty,
At the raising of the *Hinomaru*
Your cheers will rend the skies,
And your shouts of triumph never die.
Truly, a courageous and heroic venture!

Tsunabuchi records a different song, however: *Nankyoku Tankentai Taika* ('The song of the Antarctic expedition team'), which he infers was written by Tada but may, in fact, have been written by Kenju Ōwada, 'a famed poet and lyricist'.[39]

Nankyoku Tankentai Taika ('The song of the Antarctic expedition team')

So, our destination is the great ice field in the South at the end of the earth's axis.
Our ship is the famous *"Kainan"* (*Southern Explorer*), loaded with an important mission.
There is no need to fear the many hardships that may come to us in moving through the ocean.
Many difficulties will come to us as we follow the mountains and rivers, but we need not worry.
Our team bears the hopes of seventy million of our compatriots.
Our team will go forward with the eyes of our country on us.
Let's go bravely and put the sails up in the sunrise.
Let's move forward without looking back, with our sleek dogs in attendance.

(*translation by Noriko Sakai*)

---

39 Stevenson (2010) *The spirit of adventure*, p. 145.

There are a number of questions about the second song. Again, was it a fictional device by Tsunabuchi? There are so many differences between it and Kamiya Fusen's song that it is not possible to be sure that they are not two translations of the same song. Tsunabuchi was familiar with both Shirase's and Tada's books[40] so he must have known of Kamiya Fusen's song. Perhaps Tada made up the words, or perhaps misremembered the words from the departure of the expedition. Or perhaps Tada wrote a new song for an as yet unknown reason. Without new information this will have to remain a mystery.

Poetry on the Japanese Antarctic Expedition

The tradition of poetry writing in Japan extends into the distant past; the publication of the first anthology of poetry, the *Manyōshū*, was in the 7th century. Poetry has been, and still is, a vital part of Japanese culture. It reached its most highly developed form in the Emperor's court but it was by no means restricted to the court — the *Manyōshū* includes poems written by people from all walks of life.[41] It was expected that every warrior would be as skilled with the brush as with the sword. Even that most famous of Japanese swordsmen, Miyamoto Musashi (1584–1645), was well-versed in the arts of the brush. This tanka is said to have been composed by him (to a young woman):

> When it comes to love
> Don't write letters
> Don't write poems
> For even a single penny
> Watch your money carefully.[42]

Poetic forms tended to be short with *waka*, now known as *tanka*, forming the core form of the poetic repertoire until Matsuo Bashō elevated the *hokku*, the opening verse of a *renga* (linked verses), to what we now know as *haiku*, as a serious poetic form, in the latter half of the 17th century.[43] The structure of *waka* is simple: five lines with the syllabic structure of each line as follows: 5-7-5-7-7 giving a total of 31 syllables. Haiku have 17 syllables with the structure 5-7-5. The *waka* was predominantly a courtly form with a restricted range of acceptable themes, principally love and the natural world, especially the changing seasons.[44] There are many wonderful books of Japanese poetry

---

40 McInnes (2009) *The forgetting of a hero*, p. 47.
41 Hiroaki Sato and Burton Watson (1981) *From the country of eight islands: an anthology of Japanese poetry*. Anchor Press/Doubleday, New York.
42 William Scott Wilson (2004) *The lone samurai: the life of Miyamoto Musashi*. Kodansha, Tokyo, p. 95.
43 Makoto Ueda (1982) *Matsuo Bashō*. Kodansha, Tokyo.
44 Steven D Carter (1991) *Traditional Japanese poetry: an anthology*. Stanford University Press, Stanford CA.

— those already mentioned, to which could be added Kenneth Rexroth's *One hundred poems from the Japanese*.[45] Daisetzu Suzuki discusses the important role Zen has in Japanese culture and how this is reflected in its poetry.[46]

Given the importance of poetry in Japanese cultural life, therefore, it is not surprising that some poetry was composed during the expedition to Antarctica. It is also not surprising that Shirase, the son of a Buddhist priest, also wrote poetry. Tsunabuchi quotes three haiku by Shirase, but he may have written many more. None are mentioned in *Nankyoku-ki* but that was intended to be a report, whereas his personal account of the expedition, *Nankyoku Tanken*, has not yet been translated into English.

Haiku by Shirase:

> On deck
> cutting my nails
> this lengthy leisure

> Storm over,
> people are exercising
> the sledge dogs

> The sledge dogs
> leap around the deck
> wagging their tails

> (*translation by Amelia Fielden*)

Tada was, by contrast, much more prolific and, frankly, a much better poet. Six tanka were reproduced in *Kyoku: Shirase Chūi Nankyoku tankenki*.[47]

Tanka by Tada:

> As the ship sailed
> Silently through the ocean
> Under a clear moon,
> I think the Dragon's Palace
> Must be something like this

> In the mild spring
> Of my hometown far away
> The flowers
> Will be blooming

---

45   Kenneth Rexroth (1964) *One hundred poems from the Japanese*. New Directions, New York.
46   Daisetz T Suzuki (1959) *Zen and Japanese culture*. MJF Books, New York.
47   Tsunabuchi (1983) *Kyoku: Shirase Chūi Nankyoku tankenki*.

Birds will be singing

A clear moon
A peaceful passage
Over the beautiful sea …
Midnight and
No-one is stirring

Sky, water, water,
More sky … despondently
I watch
The moon shining brightly
On the plains of the sea

Ah … the plum trees
Will be in full bloom now
Around my home town —
Here no flowery hues
Colour the waves

Looking back
Looking back again
Looking back
All I'll see are mountains
And mountains of snow

(*translation by Amelia Fielden*)

I do not know the order in which these poems were written but there seem to be three themes in these poems. The first is wonder at the new scenes Tada is witnessing, as exemplified by the first and third tanka. The second theme is homesickness: the second and fifth tanka. The third theme is more difficult to pin down and relates to the fourth and sixth tanka. Repetition is used in both of these: 'Sky, water, water … More sky' and 'Looking back' repeated three times. It as if he wanted to drive these scenes into his memory. Although he is despondent in the fourth tanka he is still able to enjoy the moon shining brightly. In the last tanka he realises that he will never see Antarctica again and despite the desolation of its landscapes it is a place he will never forget.

Concluding remarks

Written material relating to the Shirase expedition is scarce. Only one of the primary sources for the expedition has been translated into English. Most of the others have been out of print for decades, if not nearly a century. It is clear that the Shirase expedition had a rich cultural life with music, song, poetry forming an important part of its daily activities. To date only a very small fraction of that material is accessible. The publication of the translation of *Nankyoku-ki* has opened a window into the life of the expedition, revealing not only a record of amazing seamanship by Captain Nomura and the crew of the *Kainan Maru*, Shirase's tenaciousness in organising and leading the expedition and the courage of them all, but also insights into Japanese responses to the natural world of Antarctica and an appreciation of its beauty. Let us hope that more translations will follow.

Thanks to Shirase's determination and despite the lack of official support, Japan became a member of that 'club' of nations with a long history of Antarctic exploration. It contributed to the International Geophysical Year in Antarctica (1957–58), it was one of the original signatories of the Antarctic Treaty in 1960 and has remained engaged in Antarctica ever since. It would be fascinating to hear more about Japanese cultural life in Antarctica today.

Acknowledgements

I would like to thank the following people for their help with this project: Chet Ross, especially for sending me the illustration of the shakuhachi player on the deck of the *Kainan Maru* which confirmed that the Shirase expedition had a musical life; Noriko Sakai and Moko Eade, for their help with translating Japanese texts; Amelia Fielden, for translating Tada's and Shirase's poems; Pat Millar, for obtaining copies of McInnes's and Stevenson's theses; and Dr Riley Lee for helping me to learn to play *Hakata-bushi*. Hilary Shibata at the Scott Polar Research Institute provided invaluable feedback on an earlier draft of this paper.

The first published music from Antarctica? Captain Doorly's piano and its roots in older traditions of polar exploration and an imperial guilty conscience[1]

Jeff Brownrigg[2]

This chapter examines the roots of the first music known to have been composed in Antarctica or as a part of voyage to that region. It traces the souring of enthusiasm for polar exploration following the disastrous Franklin Expedition to discover the Northwest Passage in 1846, as more than a score of missions set out to discover what happened to Franklin and his men. Britons (and the world) followed the emerging story of Franklin's fate with growing incredulity and horror. The conclusions of searchers included well-supported charges of cannibalism and perhaps even murder, clear evidence of what appeared to be the utter degradation of British sailors as they faced annihilation.

Franklin has, of course, strong associations with Australia, and the ships he used on his last, fatal quest had been some of the first European vessels to venture into Antarctic waters in the first decades of the 19th century. Their loss generated a minute examination of sailors' lives and property. What had the desperate men selected to carry with them as they trudged away from their beset ship? What was life on board like? How were physical, psychological and spiritual needs met in resourcing journeys that might take years?

There is a curious relationship between the perception of the provision of music for Arctic and Antarctic expeditions. We know little of the musical lives of sailors on these ships, beyond the evidence of song, diary entries and the occasional painting. As it happened, music written on the support ship for Robert Scott's first Antarctic expedition was published in Melbourne. It was music that grew out of the need to re-establish a suitably wholesome, hearty and heroic spirit after the horror of Franklin's demise and what was seen at the time as nothing less than the decline of civilisation.

---

1   This paper was presented at the Antarctica and Music conference with a recital in which the Australian Rugby Choir gave a fine performance of these songs, reproducing the hearty spirit of the men who sang in the wardroom of the *Morning* in 1902.
2   Dr Jeff Brownrigg, Cultural Heritage Studies, Locked Bag 1, University of Canberra, ACT 2601.

The British architects of polar exploration, principally Sir Clements Markham (Figure 1), imagined that the race to the South Pole might divert attention from the Arctic debacle and re-establish British pride and confidence in its Navy. A primary force who drove Scott's endeavour to be the first to reach the South Pole, Markham counselled that sledding dogs should not replace human effort, a costly and fatal error in what stands in relation to Arctic exploration as a counterbalancing Antarctic tragedy.

Figure 1. Sir Clements Markham, perhaps the most important link between Arctic and Antarctic polar exploration. As a young man he searched for Franklin. In later life he initiated and supported British polar expeditions in the first decade of the 20th century.

Source: Private collection.

Life-and-death decisions, ill-informed and brilliant judgements were part and parcel of the administration of dangerous adventures in hostile places, but some decisions were essentially benign. The campaign orchestrated by Markham saw the piano situated as a special implement of the polar explorer. Markham personally acquired an instrument for the supply ship *Morning*. Why was this?

There is nothing new in making a claim that the British Empire rose steadily in self-confidence and self-belief as the 19th century progressed. Just how these things manifested themselves in behaviour, bearing and action cannot be effectively scrutinised in a single strand of economic, or social, military or cultural history or any other sort of interrogation of the past.

Authority and purpose were reflected in a swaggering assertion of Britain's place, reflected as much in the music of composers such as Edward Elgar, or Parry, as anywhere else and fulsomely present in the singing of the Australian bass-baritone Peter Dawson, as 19th century mannerisms, ideas and enthusiasms carried over into the early 20th century. For 50 years after 1890, Empire ballads, like the grand orchestral statements of imperial pomp and circumstance, filled with energy and assertiveness, spilled from horns of innumerable gramophones and phonographs, providing a new twist upon the idea of the sun never setting; somewhere on earth people were listening to music that was quintessentially British. And yet, music, and sound more generally, remains at best an irregular component of the study of cultural heritage. Historians and others who write about the past are generally ill-prepared to discuss what is probably the most pervasive art form, after those things that are the component parts of speech as purveyors of memory in prose and verse narratives. Language — and English in particular — is steadily conquering the world since, at least, the accession of Queen Victoria.

Music, too, could colonise, in addition to all of those other things it did — evoking and sustaining the past, identifying what Britishers had in common, speaking to shared core values and inculcating attitudes and values among peoples who were neither Anglo nor Celtic. After the 1890s, the great anthems and musical narratives of the Empire proudly suggesting an ascendant order were performed in most places where English was heard, underpinning a sense of belonging, a sense of the power of the whole imperial organism while almost inadvertently demonstrating the unifying capability of words and of melodies.

There were, of course, occasional dents in the otherwise pristine breastplate of ascendency. The Mardi, for example, inflicted one of these in the Sudan and many young Englishmen wearing scarlet jackets and bright brass buttons died against the austere, black background of the Khyber Pass, causing another blemish. An earlier incident — we might say 'defeat' — the loss of the Sir John Franklin's expedition to discover the Northwest Passage in late 1840s, was delivered by nature rather than a human foe and it shook Victorian Britain, sending a ripple of anxiety around the globe. But any shakiness in the steady, guiding hand of the *Pax Britannica* was temporary, though Britons would never quite forget the tragedy. Franklin, looking for a sea route from the Atlantic to the Pacific,[3] had disappeared, leaving a scattering of traces that appalled readers

---

3   The idea had a long history. It was a notion dabbled in by explorers such as Giovanni Caboto (John Cabot) working under the patronage of Henry VII, Elizabethan adventurer Martin Frobisher, and James Cook who

of the *Times* in the early 1850s when the first shocking stories of the expedition's fate found their way into the comfortable Victorian parlours. His ships were equipped with technologies as innovative and 'modern' as gizmos developed to support life during space travel.

At some time after the 1850s a song, sometimes said to be the work of Jane Franklin (Franklin's widow), touched a chord in the British heart and remains in popular music today.[4]

> To Baffin's Bay where the whale-fishes blow,
> The fate of Franklin no man may know.
> Ten thousand pound would I freely give
> To say on earth that my Franklin do live.

But Franklin remained lost, his fate buried not so deeply beneath the snow and ice of Baffin Bay. More than ten thousand pounds was expended on desperate, essentially fruitless rescue attempts in the decade following his disappearance. The Arctic offered up tantalising hints of a story and continues to do so. Missions seeking to discover what had happened to Franklin's ships *Erebus* and the *Terror* and the couple of hundred souls who sailed in them have continued to the present day. What the scattered clues suggested was a desperate battle for survival against the odds, and the abandonment of civilised values; the degradation of human beings who, under the most extreme stress and challenged by hostile elements that dictated their fate, abandoned long-held moral precepts. The very suggestion of cannibalism besmirched the English character.

Andrew Lambert, in a recent account of Franklin's life (and death), wrote in 2009:

> [Franklin] did not live to witness the last days of his expedition, when the veneer of civilisation lifted to reveal primeval savagery, darkness and despair.[5]

All of Franklin's men died, many, perhaps most, having been reduced to eating their fellows in a desperate attempt to survive, butchering dead companions to obtain a portable food source which they carried until they too dropped. But an unspoken question haunted these revelations. Had British servicemen been driven to murder by desperate hunger? The very thought compounded the revulsion.

---

looked to the North and South Poles, albeit briefly.
4   See, for example, the version by the folk-rock group Fairport Convention from the late 1960s.
5   Andrew Lambert (2009) *Franklin: tragic hero of polar navigation*. Faber, London, p. 350.

The first published music from Antarctica?

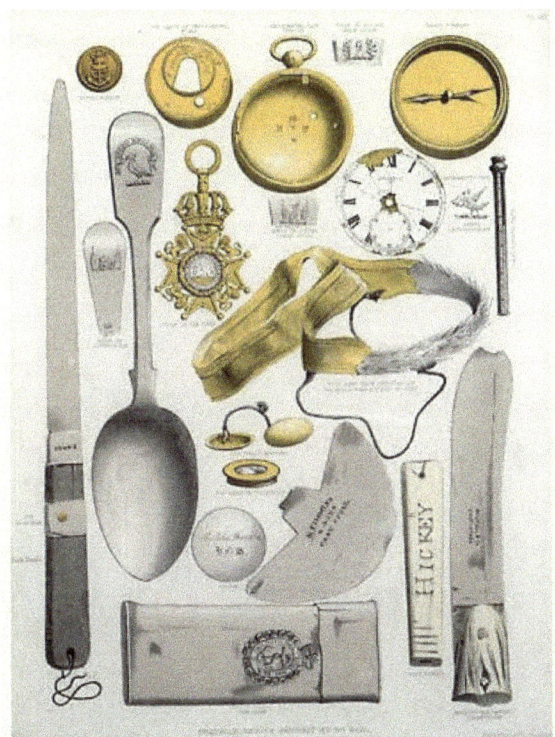

Figure 2. Relics of the Franklin Expedition collected by Dr John Rae in 1853–54 as published in 1855. Many of the items were identified as the property of particular crew members, including Franklin's medallion, clearly visible in the only surviving, somewhat ghostly, photograph of Sir John taken on the eve of his final voyage.

At first such stories were discounted; even Charles Dickens, a potent force at the cutting edge of popular culture, questioning the descent into unspeakable horror that ran counter to the accepted understanding of what it was to be civilised. Franklin's men, Dickens wrote, were:

> The flower of the trained English navy ... it is the highest degree of improbability that such men would, or could, in any extremity of hunger, alleviate the pains of starvation by this horrible means.[6]

Finally, an incredulous Dickens blamed the Inuit from whom graphic accounts of the last days of Franklin's men had been collected. These accounts were progressively augmented as new expeditions brought back eyewitness accounts

---
6   Lambert (2009) *Franklin: tragic hero of polar navigation* pp. 250–2; Martin W Sanders (2006) *Resolute*. Sterling, New York, p. 140; Owen Beattie (1987) *Frozen in time: the fate of the Franklin Expedition*. Bloomsbury, London, p. 60.

of the dreadful events of 1846–48. There were stories of the dismemberment of corpses, tales supported by a few human bones showing clear evidence of butchering.

In 1987 Owen Beattie exhumed the frozen bodies of three of Franklin's luckier men who had died from a combination of tuberculosis and lead poisoning early in the voyage (1846) and who were buried in frozen ground. Beattie determined that conditions dangerous to health were unwittingly exacerbated by new technology. Tuberculosis was made more virulent in the damp warm atmosphere of the claustrophobic spaces aboard Franklin's damp, centrally heated ships. Beattie concluded that canned provisions, first widely used during the Napoleonic wars, had leached lead from inefficient soldering into preserved food.[7] Franklin and his men were, in effect, killed by their food and accommodation. This was supported by research in the late 20th century. Officers on better rations, and hence higher doses of lead, almost certainly suffered impaired reasoning. In 1987, filling out the background of his autopsies by mirroring something of the dismay felt in the 1850s, Beattie wrote:

> Even today the stories are so abhorrent that they can hardly be believed. The Inuit reported finding boots filled with cooked human flesh, flesh that had been boiled. 'Some bones had been sawed with a saw; some skulls had holes in them,' Hall [writing after his 1869 search] wrote. Other bodies found nearby had been carefully stripped of flesh.[8]

Subconsciously, perhaps, Beattie nursed an idea that lead poisoning had caused behaviour that in different circumstances might have been kept in check. Polar exploration, however, was inherently dangerous, its extreme conditions capable of causing civilisation as it was understood to collapse.[9] Starvation leading to cannibalism was, of course, not unknown in the 19th century. Théodore Géricault's painting 'Raft of the Medusa' (painted in 1818–19) illustrates an event in French naval history in which shipwrecked sailors adrift in the Atlantic were forced to eat each other. Understanding the risks involved in polar exploration might have led to adequate, meticulous preparation, but Fate could also deliver the unexpected, as it did in the American space program on 28 January 1986 or high in the Andes in 1973.[10]

---

7 Beattie (1987) *Frozen in time*, pp. 156–63.
8 Beattie (1987) *Frozen in time*, p. 60.
9 In the late 1820s Franklin had been involved in an expedition in the Arctic in which men had starved to death, and, it was said, had been reduced to cannibalism. Franklin became known as 'the man who ate his boots' but this might not have been the whole story. If cannibalism occurred, it remained a closely protected secret.
10 After an airplane crash in the high Andes a South American soccer team survived by eating flesh from those who died in the accident. The incident generated a book and film, both called *Alive*.

As early as 1854 (in a letter to the Secretary of the Admiralty), Dr John Rae formally broke the news of 'a fate terrible as imagination can conceive'.[11] In 2009 historian Andrew Lambert concluded that lamentation for the loss of Franklin and his crew was transformed into deep repugnance. Such was the outcry at the thought that Englishmen, regardless of the duress they experienced, might eat each other, that the public needed a distraction. Polar exploration was instantly tainted and settled, for a time, on a pragmatic, discreet back-burner.

The saga of the Franklin rescue missions (there were 25 expensive major expeditions up to 1880) lingered after the 1850s as the chance of finding survivors — perhaps living with the Inuit — diminished, the vaguest hope dwindling in the face of accumulating evidence.

Figure 3. Painting by Sir Edwin Landseer, 'Man Proposes, God Disposes' (1864), often considered to have been influenced by the fate of the loss of Franklin's expedition to find the North West Passage.

But while desire for an accurate picture of what had happened remained after the passionate searches had all but concluded by the 1880s, the Franklin legend was transformed and sanitised in the 1890s by moving the focus of polar interest to the South Pole. Organisations such as the Royal Geographical Society, sponsoring research on what were perceived as the Earth's last frontiers, looked for a new spin that might encourage the necessary forgetfulness of what had been, something that invigorated enthusiasm for the heroic quest of figures who could be made as powerfully attractive to the public imagination as the courtly, chivalric characters of Tennyson's poems or those in the novels of Sir Walter Scott.

---

11 Letter dated 29 July 1854 from John Rae to the Secretary of the Admiralty. In McGoogan, Ken, ed. (2012) *The Arctic journals of John Rae*. Touchwood Editions, Canada, p. 240.

Dr John Rae had been second in command to John Richardson in a 1848 expedition to find Franklin. In 1853 he discovered a variety of relics and more importantly, testimony of the indigenous people of the region, often horrible and graphic in their detail. Rae was generally ridiculed in the UK. However, cannibalism and polar exploration remained linked into the 20th century when Mawson's survival seemed to some to have been effected by eating a comrade.

Lambert argues that 'the Antarctic provided a perfect replacement to wipe the Arctic' and, presumably, behaviour Victorians most often attributed to 'savages', 'from the national memory'.[12] Civilisation, in the words of Lord Tennyson (Poet Laureate for much of the time that the 'find-Franklin' expeditions were actively engaged in the search), would be best served and demonstrated beyond doubt by further excursions into the dangerous places; forays in the home of blizzard or the polar bear. The human spirit would prevail regardless of the infirmities of humanity or its previous misadventures. Tennyson, who was related to Franklin by marriage, had written in 1833 a poem that instantly inspired and endured even as details of the Arctic disaster were recovered and interpreted.

> 'Tis not too late to seek a newer world.
> Push off, and sitting well in order smite
> The sounding furrows; for my purpose holds
> To sail beyond the sunset, and the baths
> Of all the western stars, until I die.
> It may be that the gulfs will wash us down:
> It may be we shall touch the Happy Isles,
> And see the great Achilles, whom we knew
> Though much is taken, much abides; and though
> We are not now that strength which in old days
> Moved earth and heaven; that which we are, we are;
> One equal temper of heroic hearts,
> Made weak by time and fate, but strong in will
> To strive, to seek, to find, and not to yield.[13]

Doubtless Tennyson's verse was included among the 1,700 volumes that were packed into the ward room and other cabins of the *Erebus* in 1845. Tennyson was standard fare for the middle and late Victorians. Franklin's men, had they the time to read Tennyson on their final voyage, would have recognised themselves and the adventurous, inquisitive spirit the poet describes.

Tennyson's classical allusions were deeply resonant throughout the English-speaking world at the time, but the principal figure in packaging Franklin's story as a heroic adventure, albeit in the well-worn Tennysonian chivalric tradition, was Sir Clements Markham.

---

12 Lambert (2009) *Franklin: tragic hero of polar navigation*, p. 350.
13 These are the final lines of Alfred, Lord Tennyson's much anthologised poem 'Ulysses' (source http://www.bartleby.com/42/635.html, accessed 26 August 2014). Written in 1833, they were first published in his second volume of verse, *Poems*, in 1842.

The first published music from Antarctica?

Figure 4. Sir Clements Markham (front centre, with top hat) at the departure of the Robert Falcon Scott's ship *Discovery* in 1901. Scott, in his naval uniform is first of Markham's right. Next right is Lieutenant Engineer Skelton, the subject of vaudeville song at the Royal Terror Theatre, McMurdo Sound, 1902.

Markham had been there as the saga of the search for Franklin began, serving as midshipman on the *HMS Assistance* during the Royal Navy's major search in 1850–51. Later he was Secretary to the Royal Geographical Society from 1863 to 1888, becoming its President from 1889 to 1901. So 50 years after searching for Franklin, he played a crucial supportive role in the design and realisation of Robert Scott's first Antarctic expedition of 1901–1904 (Figure 4). His views on all subjects were accepted as informed by long experience even when his judgement was flawed or simply wrong. Dog sleds, for example, might have given Scott extra impulsion and he might have beaten Amundsen to the Pole. This is speculation, but discussions of Scott's failure often turn to his adopting the old ways; stout-hearted men hauling all that was needed for survival, much as the remnants of Franklin's party had manhauled supplies and the miscellaneous matter that littered the route of their doomed trek. Markham was possessed by the idea that Franklin's tragedy should not be repeated in the South. He turned his mind to the most minute details and inflicted them, brooking no opposition.

Searching for the model of an ideal polar explorer, Markham had written, in 1875:

> The most valuable qualifications for Arctic service are aptitude for taking part in those winter amusements which give life to the expedition during the months of forced inaction [etc.].[14]

Markham was 15 on 19 May 1845 when Franklin's ships had sailed from the Thames, so 30 years of observation must have nurtured in him the opinion that the long incarceration of 'wintering' near the poles should be accommodated with supplies that encouraged appropriate pastimes. The alleviation of

---

14   Lambert (2009) *Franklin: tragic hero of polar navigation,* p. 318.

boredom, banishment of anxiety and homesickness, and personal growth and development might all be addressed with appropriate provisioning. Markham's pronouncements, with Franklin's expedition clearly in his thoughts, ensured that a variety of musical instruments were included in the fitting out of Scott's ship *Discovery* and that of the supply vessel *Morning*. Franklin, too, had carried musical instruments; two hand-operated reed instruments (hand organs) which utilised folded, punched cardboard, not unlike the programs of holes on a paper roll provided 50 years later for Scott's pianola. (There was nothing particularly innovative or especially new about providing for the mental health of sailors who might endure months of relative isolation on long voyages even if they were not ice-bound.[15]) Music-making machines (hand organs and pianolas) allowed the musically unskilled to produce reasonable quality performances simply for listening or for accompanying singers. The *Erebus* and the *Terror* had 'encoded' performances of familiar tunes and also a selection of more than a dozen hymns, so body and soul were clearly catered for. Scott's expedition also had a harmonium (a reed organ, of the sort used in small churches).

Markham personally selected a piano for the *Morning* and it arrived just in time to be loaded.

Scott's party had been in Antarctica for a year (1901–02) when the first relief ship was despatched, and in that time a powerful interest in 'theatricals' had evolved in the group. Markham's philosophy concerning mental health was made tangible and Scott's men demonstrated their 'aptitude for Arctic service', albeit in the Antarctic.

During that first 12 months in Antarctica, members of Scott's team commandeered a local hut and established it as the 'Royal Terror Theatre', putting together plays, reviews and concerts, often attaching new words to well-known melodies. In one of these, a popular song by Marie Lloyd (a towering presence in English music hall and review) was transformed into a parody sharply focused on the *Discovery*'s first engineer, Reginald Skelton. The original was performed by Marie Lloyd — who had performed in Melbourne in May 1901 at the opening of the newly built Opera House at the same time as Markham issued final 'Instructions to the Commander of the Expedition' party. (*Discovery* sailed from the UK on 6 August.) An audience favourite from its first presentation in 1893, 'Oh Mister Porter' included the following catchy chorus:

> Oh Mr Porter, what shall I do?
> I want to go to Birmingham
> And they've taken me on to Crewe
> Take me back to London quickly as you can.

---

15 Cook was a masterly psychologist, and numerous expeditions of his time and later set up amateur music and theatricals to salve the tedium of containment on board ship.

Oh Mr Porter what a silly girl I am![16]

In the hands of Stoker Page — who wrote new words for the popular tune — the song gently poked fun at Skelton, recognisably an example of the lowly having a good-natured shot at their betters and certainly evidence of the sort of *esprit de corps* that Markham encouraged. (Skelton had overseen the building of *Discovery* in Dundee and had a 'parental' interest in the ship.) Scott's men also poked fun at the tedium of their routine duties.

> Oh Mr Skelton, what shall I do?
> You've sent me to the boiler
> When I'd rather be in the flue.
> Send me in the bilges as quickly as you can,
> Oh Mr Skelton, you're a very nice young man.[17]

The Antarctic audience found the imprecations of the humble stoker amusing, but the Royal Terror Theatre endured only a single season before it was required for storing sledges. Its reassignment saw the enthusiasm for amateur theatre dramatically wane.

Providing the words was one thing, writing words *and tunes,* another and it was there that the crew of the *Morning* extended what Scott's colleagues had started.

On 25 June 1902 the *Morning* left East India Dock in London to find Scott and to supply the British Antarctic Expedition, but just before the *Morning* sailed, a piano was delivered to the ship, a farewell gift from Sir Clements Markham following a suggestion from Second Executive Officer Edward 'Teddy' Evans, later Admiral Sir ERGR Evans KCB, DSO (and later still, Lord Mountevans).

If any part of the *Morning*'s remarkable history is recalled today, it is the surgery performed (at sea) on Markham's piano that has lingered in memory (Figure 5). Doorly's writings concerning the voyage (especially the books and pamphlet published in 1916, 1937 and 1943[18]) included a line drawing of the operation necessary to get the instrument below deck.

---

16 Marie Lloyd (1977) *Song book*. EMI 'The Music Makers' Series. EMI Music Publishing Ltd, London, p. 62.
17 Mike Pearson (2004) 'No joke in petticoats: British polar expeditions and their theatrical presentations'. *TDR*, 48(1) Spring: pp.44–59. The words of the song/parody are presented as a continuous line, p. 49.
18 The original edition (there has only been one) of *In the Wake* (ca.1937) is undated, but the title page includes a list of Doorly's publications including *The Songs of the 'Morning'* which was certainly published in 1943 in an edition that *is* dated (Gerald Doorly (1943) *The Songs of the 'Morning'*, Bread and Cheese Club, Melbourne). The copy used in research for the present article has a birthday inscription dated 16 July 44. This means either that the original edition was published after the date accepted in, for example, the entry in the *Australian Dictionary of Biography*, or that changes were made to the title page in a new edition in or about 1943. No copy of *Handmaiden of the Navy*, Doorly's history of the Merchant Marine, has been sighted.

Figure 5. 'Dissecting the piano.' Markham's last-minute gift was too large to be stowed below decks without considerable modification.

Source: Sketch from *The Songs of the 'Morning'* (1943).

In essence, the keys were removed, the legs supporting the keyboard also detached together with the protruding keyboard structure — the shelf that cradled the keys — was sawn off with a meat saw borrowed from the kitchen. Once below deck and safely in the tiny ward room, the instrument was reassembled and put to use.

Removing the piano to the ward room was effected in the first days of the voyage. It took 135 days for the *Morning* to steam and sail from the UK to New Zealand, and after three weeks in the 'Land of the Long White Cloud', several more weeks seeking *Discovery*. Time presented ample opportunity to use the instrument. Ships were survival capsules. This was true for Franklin as it was for Scott. Ocean voyages were perilous and an ice-bound ship a refuge at the hostile poles. In 1911 Shackleton's *Endurance* was finally crushed, as both the *Erebus* and *Terror* appear to have been in about 1848, but for a time each afforded shelter to stranded crew. Regardless of circumstances, voyaging or wintering in the ice, as long as the integrity of the fabric of the ship was not compromised, a piano was a useful piece of equipment.

Travelling or stationary, it was James Gerald Stokely Doorly who played the doctored piano more than his shipmates. Born in Port au Spain on 4 June 1880, Doorly's father was a clergyman who later became Archdeacon of Trinidad, where James Gerald went to school. Doorly was not, however, a highly trained musician.[19] His pianism was learned incidentally and he probably played by ear. He trained as a cadet in the merchant marine at Thames Nautical College, graduating as a gold medallist in 1897, learning seamanship and navigation as he was fitted out for command. During the Boer War he worked on troop and hospital ships, but in 1902 he was signed up as third officer on the steam yacht *Morning*, which was to resupply the National Antarctic Expedition already testing itself at McMurdo Sound on the Ross Sea.

Figure 6. The *Morning* trapped in ice. The image suggests the look of a photograph by Frank Hurley, who provided an image as the frontispiece in the same volume.

Source: From *In the Wake*, Gerald Doorly's reminiscences published by Robertson and Mullens Ltd, Melbourne.

---

19   It is not clear for example, if the 1916 version of the music for 'Southward' is in Doorly's hand. The 1943 version was written by a more experienced copyist but reproduces exactly the same notes. The formation of notes and clefs is more sophisticated. If Edith Harrhy assisted Doorly in 1943 then there is no evidence of her having made any alteration to the original 1916 published version of 'Southward'. RH Croll, in his introduction to *The Songs of the 'Morning'* (p. 5), wrote that 'Miss Edith Harrhy, the well-known Australian composer has most admirably scored the full series, bestowing on it that order which was necessary to complete the work And make it an harmonious whole'. Perhaps this means that the songs published in 1943 are Edith Harrhy's transcriptions of published and manuscript pieces composed by Doorly. If so, Harrhy seems to have practised minimal intervention.

By 1904 Doorly had gained his master's certificate, after which he mainly worked for the Union Steamship Company where his most notable accomplishment might have been his 1908 marriage to the owner-director's daughter. In 1917 he survived being torpedoed in the English Channel and in June 1925 he left the Union Steam Ship Company in New Zealand, taking up a position in the Port Phillip Sea Pilot's Service. Retiring from this job 20 years later, he lived in Melbourne until the early 1950s when he returned to New Zealand, dying in Wellington in 1956.

Although a couple of substantial prose works and occasional articles in newspaper and periodicals are his principal claim to fame, the seven songs of *The Songs of the 'Morning'*, published in 1943 though written 41 years earlier, are his most important legacy (Figure 7). His recollections, setting out his various adventures with hearty good humour, are not, I think, as significant as his songs. The songs were, in Doorly's words, 'written and composed in the Antarctic' and like his claim that they had 'never hitherto been published', this was more or less true. From Doorly's biographical writing it is clear that they were written at different times during the long, often tedious voyage of the *Morning* between 1902 and 1904.

Figure 7. Cover of *The Songs of the 'Morning'*. This was probably the first published music written as the direct result of Antarctic polar exploration, and during it. Others as early as Cook's voyages might have played the fiddle and flute or sung, but there is no evidence of composition reflecting the experience of these activities in Antarctic waters.

Source: Published by the Bread and Cheese Club, Melbourne, 1943.

As the *Morning* steamed and sailed south in 1902, Chief Engineer JD Morrison provided words for 'Southward' (1), which Doorly set to an original melody. In his memoirs, Doorly explains that although the tune sounds a little like the opening chorus from Gilbert and Sullivan's *The Gondoliers*, he composed the song before he knew the operetta.[20] 'Southward' was an instant success and initiated a fruitful partnership that lasted as long as the voyage. Others of the *Morning*'s crew put pen to paper, producing rollicking good-humoured verse. Some of this has survived. The work of Chief Officer England ('You May Talk About Your Engines' and 'Song of the Stores'), Lieutenant GFA Mulock (and others) seem to have been produced for recitation rather than setting to music.[21]

Doorly and Morrison pooled their talents again for a song ['Drink to] The Northland' (2) for New Years Day or Christmas (or, indeed, any occasion requiring a toast). Both of these songs (1 and 2) appear to have been written on the outward voyage.

A third song, 'Birrd, Birrdie' with its rolled Scots 'r's, was written for the birthday of the ship's Scottish doctor, GA Davidson, whose job it was to capture and preserve creatures encountered during the voyage.[22]

The song carries Gerald Doorly's name as composer as well as the intelligence that this is a parody of an 'Old Irish Air'. Doubtless sending up the Scots with an Irish tune added relish to the humour, though the supposed 'Irish Air' is almost certainly Doorly's work.

'The Ice King' (4) was written as *Morning* searched the Antarctic coast looking for *Discovery*, eventually finding Scott's ship in McMurdo Sound (Figure 8). This is the finest song of the group, aspiring to catch a sense of gravity and awe associated with the *Morning*'s departure. The ship, anchored off the edge of the ice that still trapped *Discovery*, watched the men from that ship wave them off. This song's words catch something of the inflection of the Empire ballad:

> Bearing the flag of England
> Far oe'r the frozen sea;
> Their watchword and their haven
> 'Discovery' still shall be.
> Watching the stars in their courses
> Watching the needles swing
> Doing their duty — not counting the cost,

---

20 Songs are listed here and numbered (in brackets) in their order in *The Songs of the 'Morning'* (1943).
21 See the liner notes for *The Songs of the 'Morning': a Musical Sketch* (CD, Reardon Press, ISMN: M9002068-0-0, ISBN-1-873877-52-8) 2002. England's poems are on p. 9 and p. 15 and Mulock's on p. 16.
22 No photograph of taxidermy being performed on the *Morning* seems to have survived. There is a photograph of Dr Wilson on the *Discovery* doing what is described in Doorly's song in Ann Savours (2001) *The Voyages of the Discovery*. Chatham Publishing, London.

Till the 'Morning' comes with the Spring.

Refrain:
Far away in that cold white land,
In the home of the Great Ice King!
Braving his fury, daring his wrath,
When honour and glory are showing the path;
God will keep them from harm and scathe
Till the 'Morning' comes with the Spring.

Figure 8. First page of 'The Ice King' from *The Voyages of the 'Morning'*, 1916. 'The Ice King' is, perhaps, the most dramatic and evocative of the seven songs published by the Bread and Cheese Club, Melbourne, in 1943. Doorly wrote other songs but their current whereabouts is not know, if, of course, they have survived.

As far as it is possible to tell, Markham did not hear or read these songs, but there can be no doubt that the old spirit was manifest in Doorly and Morrison's works. It seems likely that Doorly's selection of 'The Ice King' and 'Southward', both of which resulted from his collaboration with Morrison, indicates a special affection for these pieces.

As it happened the supply visit was unexpectedly short due to the weather. The exhilaration of having discovered Scott, feelings shared by supplier and supplied, was suddenly overtaken by pragmatism. Fearing that the ice would re-form, trapping the *Morning*, Scott ordered the ship back to New Zealand. A reluctant Ernest Shackleton was a passenger, having suffered the 'ravages of scurvy when returning with Scott and Dr Wilson from a 92-day's pioneering sledge journey towards the pole'.[23] So too were nine other members of *Discovery*'s crew when the *Morning* departed on 2 March 2003.[24] Shackleton and Doorly wrote the words for 'Scotland Forever' (5) jointly sending up Morrison and Dr Davidson, members of the *Morning*'s crew, both of them Scots.

It is difficult to place the last of the songs published in *The Songs of the 'Morning'*, 'Yuss!' (6) but it seems probable that it was written when the New Zealand accent was a recent, vivid memory. Essentially, Doorly saw it as a sea song 'with a fine rollicking chorus'. Once again the stalwart lyricist JD Morrison provided the words.

'The Maid's Lament' (7) followed a visit to Christchurch; Doorly suggests that this was on the outward journey to Antarctica in 1902.

While the seven published songs are not strictly a song cycle — and there are other songs in manuscript that were not included in the 1943 publication — they do document different parts of the experience of the *Morning*'s first relief voyage. In contrast, a second relief voyage in 1903 appears to have been less productive of songs. The order in which they were published is not, I think, the order in which Doorly imagined them being sung, his own notes suggesting that 'The Maid's Lament' should be sung third and 'Yuss!' sixth. In a sound recording of a musical sketch entitled *The Songs of the 'Morning'*, an eighth song by Doorly, 'Eight Bells' is also performed.[25]

The Songs of the 'Morning', published by the Bread and Cheese Club in Melbourne, is almost certainly the first music written on a voyage associated with and in Antarctica to be professionally printed and distributed as a cohesive collection. The words and music of 'Southward' and 'The Ice King' were first printed in

---

23 Doorly (1943) *The Songs of the 'Morning'*, p. 15.
24 Doorly (1943) *The Songs of the 'Morning'*, p. 15.
25 It is not clear from the liner notes booklet whose arrangement this is, though the whole is credited to Doorly. It seems likely that Doorly played 'by ear'. See *The Songs of the 'Morning': a musical sketch* (2004). Reardon Publishing, England, recorded in Wellington NZ in February 2002.

Doorly's *The Voyages of the 'Morning'* in 1916 as illustrations of activities on board that vessel in 1902.[26] They are, of course, in a tradition. James Cook, whose crew almost certainly included sailors with practical musical abilities, captained the first European ship known to have crossed the South Polar circle in 1773. It is not clear if their music included original compositions. Others followed, first in frail sailing ships and later in more robust, manoeuvrable steamers but none, as far as I can tell, generated music which was original and published. Scott's thespian troupe in the Royal Terror Theatre certainly found new words for familiar tunes and some of these can be assembled from their scattered parts; a tune from a musical, scripted material recorded in a diary or in the purpose-built periodical the *South Polar Times*, this last an amateur hand-made newspaper.

The publication of *The Songs of the 'Morning'* was the result of several pieces of good fortune. First was the philosophical position of Sir Clements Markham, as well as Markham's authority as one who had experience of polar exploration. As president and long-serving secretary of the Royal Geographical Society, he was also able to command the attention of powerful and influential allies who might support polar enterprises. Without Markham the resurgence of polar exploration in last years of the 19th century might not have happened. He was able to put into action his longstanding sense of the qualities desirable in the ideal polar explorer. He was often criticised for his dictatorial manner and his inclination to stand in the way of anybody, however successful they might have been in their polar exploits. He was not alone in this but *Morning*'s crew seem to have treated him with affection. JD Morrison's poem called 'Klementz, the President Boss of the Gheographez' might have been a song-text but the music for the piece is not known at present. It is notable for the last line in the citation below.

> Thus spake Zirklementz, Boss of Gheographers
> Boss of the people who knew about everything,
> 'Find me a man who is skilled in the depze!
> Who noz about izbergs and blizzardz and suchlike,
> And instruct him to build uz a ship at great expense
> Phitted with the meanz of taking Pickturz
> And making of music ...'

Ernest Shackleton, at one time Markham's protégé, was obliged to follow his mentor in some respects. Potential participants in a new expedition in 1909

---

26 A later edition of *The Voyages of the 'Morning'* published by Bluntingham Books, Norfolk, in 1995 includes what appear to be facsimile copies of 'Southward' and 'The Ice King' taken from *The Songs of the 'Morning'* (1943) in Edith Harrhy's arrangements. They are in the same musical hand but are not identical. See for example, the lettering of the titles of both songs.

were interviewed by Shackleton and were often asked if they were singers. Like Markham (and reworking an old proverb), Shackleton seems to have believed that those who sing together, cling together.

If Markham's primary gift of making the 1901–04 British National Antarctic Expedition happen was his major contribution, his briefing of Scott and others was equally significant. Recollections of the British Navy entertaining itself in the early 19th century probably informed his thinking.

And then there was that essential tool of polar exploration, the piano.

Doorly made the most of it and, with Morrison, gathered those around him into a close, productive relationship following Markham's directive. The songs he wrote were modest. As Morrison, his most productive and inspired lyricist, presented the would-be composer with words for 'The Northland', he exclaimed (in Doorly's transcription of Scots), with an urgency driven by his passion as well as his local success:

> Doorly, Doorly, quickly luke [look] at these words – now here's a song for ye – if ye can get a tune for that now our name's made![27]

Doorly notes, sardonically, in his 1916 memoir that Morrison was 'a bit previous'. From the beginning musically critical people might have agreed. But this is a case where context endows the products of a particular occasion with peculiar significance; a splinter of the heritage of Antarctic experience in the heroic age.

Fate, fickle as she often is, might have seen the songs consigned to even more obscurity than they suffer at present. The two pieces included in *The Voyages of the 'Morning'* would have remained accessible there as book publishing lurched into the digital age. But it was Doorly's move to Melbourne that made the difference. He became a more regular journalist, writing for the *Bulletin* and the Melbourne *Age* and, from 1938 to 1956, he was a member of the Bread and Cheese Club. The club was one of the bastions of middle-class bohemianism. Like the Melbourne Democratic Club at the end of the 19th century, under whose auspices the singer-songwriter Billy Williams got his start, Bread and Cheese encouraged and published its own. RH Croll, a now forgotten Australian literary celebrity of the 1930s and 1940s who wrote the introduction, speaks of *The Songs of the 'Morning'* standing for 'romance and high adventure'. Croll also notes that the musical arrangements in the publication were the work of the then well known Australian composer Edith Harrhy, but the central theme in all that he has to say concerns 'the comradeship and good humour' which he notes are manifestly there in Doorly's songs.

---

27   *The Songs of the 'Morning': a musical sketch* CD citing unsourced words of Doorly p. 12.

> There is no sterner test of the ability of men to live together harmoniously than would be imposed by months of confinement in such a small vessel ... They must be self-contained in all that life could mean for them; above all they must create their own entertainment — that spiritual vitamin so essential to mental health ...
>
> It seems fitting that it [*The Songs of the 'Morning'*] should be presented to the public by a Club whose motto is Mateship.[28]

Only a few physical remnants of Franklin's last, fatal voyage have ever been found. The expedition lives in imaginations fed by legend, surmise, as well as a few bones and trinkets that seem to tell a tale. In some accounts the explorer was buried in the ice not far from his beset ship. That seems strange unless his crew imagined that his remains might be recovered once his ships were free of the ice that gripped them. Others have him transported to King William Island or even the Canadian mainland to be interred in earth. A single tangible item, a relic of his knighthood, found its way back to his wife.

In Westminster Abbey a small memorial marking his achievements includes an epigraph by Tennyson who, through the voice of Ulysses, had urged his fellows to fearlessly seek the unknown, to face adversity and danger with a clear eye and a concept of the 'rightness' of the explorer/adventurer's quest.

> Not here; the white North has thy bones, and thou
> Heroic sailor soul
> Art passing thy happier voyage now
> Towards no Earthly Pole.

It was a spirit evident in the tragedy of Robert Scott at the other Pole. By comparison, Scott left much more of himself, seemingly aware of the likelihood that his name would endure. Gerald Doorly has his name forever attached to a minor peak near Mt Erebus and its smaller neighbour Mt Terror. The major peaks had been named by Captain Crozier who later commanded the *Erebus* on its final journey. As a member of the Ross party when the *Erebus* and *Terror* visited the Antarctic in 1841, Crozier had captained the *Terror*.

The Empire, in which Scott became an indelible hero, worshipped his striving until the 1950s when wide-eyed Australian schoolchildren marvelled at his leadership and the selflessness of Captain Oates. The heroic age continued, its sights upon the 'first to get there' philosophy that saw dozens die in the frozen landscape of another hostile frontier, the higher slopes of Mt Everest.

In the 1950s, Australian schoolchildren learned that such unyielding striving was desirable and important to the prestige of the Empire. It wasn't long before those children looked to the eastern sky for Sputnik as the 'space race' began.

---

28 Gerard Doorly (1943), *The Songs of the 'Morning'*, pp. 5-6.

Who would put the first man on the moon? New frontiers presented different dangers, but little changes. 'Though much is taken, much abides', Tennyson had written in 1833. There is no evidence that astronauts have been driven to eat each other. How much smaller are a few occasional songs in the scheme of things when juxtaposed with man and nature in conflict?

Doorly survived to see his modest works in print, playing a bit-part in the first heroical and then tragic expeditions of Robert Scott. Doorly's contributions were of a different order. Legends of violent death in uncontrollable circumstances seem inevitably to be more enduring than tunes and words that have grown out of fairly ordinary experience. Some remembered Franklin with a song which has endured, but the circumstances that put Captain Doorly's piano into the ward room of the *Morning* have their roots in one of the foremost tragedies of the Victorian age, which saw the very foundations of civilisation shaken. His songs remain a tangible link to the endeavours of exceptional, ordinary men whose lives intersected those judged in their time to be heroic.

Coda

One of the few upsides to the progress of global warming is that it is likely to stimulate new expeditions in search of the truth about Franklin's last expedition. Polar ice is melting and Canadian maritime archaeologists have suggested that a deep-sea search might discover the remains of the *Erebus* and the *Terror*. What clues have survived the destruction of the ships and their long immersion is a matter for conjecture, but a new post-greenhouse expedition is unlikely to carry a piano or result in the composition of songs. Another dimension of modernity is the shortage of time for the leisure to compose and perform, new technologies having made travel quicker and ready-made digitally encoded and satellite-delivered entertainment easily accessible. Deep-sea diving equipment might, following sonar mapping of the ocean floor, disclose the wrecks of *Erebus* and *Terror*. Discussion as to whether the site might be combed through archaeologically, or is seen as a place where human remains are likely to be found and left untouched, need only follow a positive identification. Just what might result from risk-taking in Arctic waters is unclear but these explorers of a new frontier will be operating in a venerable tradition.

Eating the audience

Bernadette Hince[1]

One hundred and ten years ago, a Scot in full Highland dress walked down a gangway and onto the ice of the Weddell Sea in Antarctica. It was a most improbable sight, and the expedition's leader captured it in photographs.

It was the time of the heroic era of intensive Antarctic exploration, a period which began late in the 19th century and stretched some distance into the early 20th century.[2] During this time, the man who was to lead the piper's expedition, William Speirs Bruce (Figure 1), made his first trip to Antarctica as a member of the Dundee Whaling Expedition of 1892–93. It was a relatively short voyage from Scotland, considering the distance of its destination, and Bruce found it frustrating from a natural science point of view. But it made him a polar man for life. 'I am burning to be off again anywhere, but particularly to the far south where I believe there is a vast sphere for research', he wrote.[3]

Three years later, in June 1896, he travelled north as a naturalist on the Jackson–Harmsworth Arctic expedition. Fridtjof Nansen and Hjalmar Johansen were at the expedition's Cape Flora base when he arrived. It was to be the first of many trips Bruce made to the Arctic.

With 'Scotland' emblazoned on its flag

Bruce's scientific work in both polar regions qualified him better than most to apply as a senior scientific member of Scott's British National Antarctic Expedition on the *Discovery*, which was leaving England in 1901. His request eventually led only to an offer of a junior appointment which he fairly naturally declined.

After failing to join Scott's expedition at a senior level, he organised his own expedition. Though London-born, Bruce was passionately Scottish, and the crew and scientists of his Scottish National Antarctic Expedition of 1902–04 were almost all Scottish.[4] He had met Major Andrew Coats in the Arctic during the late 1890s. Andrew and James Coats backed the expedition financially.[5]

---

1 Dr Bernadette Hince, Visiting Fellow, Australian National Dictionary Centre, The Australian National University, Canberra ACT 0200, coldwords@gmail.com.
2 Perhaps to 1913–14, perhaps into the 1920s — see Pharaoh (this volume).
3 Bruce ms, quoted in Peter Speak (2004) 'Bruce, William Speirs (1867–1921)', *Oxford Dictionary of National Biography*. Oxford University Press, www.oxforddnb.com.virtual.anu.edu.au/view/article/32137, accessed 27 July 2014.
4 Speak (2004) 'Bruce, William Speirs (1867–1921)', accessed 28 July 2014.
5 Speak (2004) 'Bruce, William Speirs (1867–1921)', accessed 28 July 2014.

Figure 1. William Speirs Bruce (1867–1921), leader of the Scottish National Antarctic Expedition.

Source: Reproduced with permission of the Glasgow Digital Library, University of Strathclyde.

Bruce's ship the *Scotia* sailed south from Scotland in November 1902. In March 1903 the ship was frozen in at what became known as Scotia Bay on Laurie Island. Here the men began eight months of ice-bound life on board. Scientifically, the expedition's legacy was significant. Ashore, they established a meteorological station, Omond House, now the oldest working observatory in Antarctica. (When the *Scotia* was freed by the ice, Bruce sailed from the Antarctic to Buenos Aires in December 1903 and persuaded the Argentinians to take over the meteorological station.[6])

---

6   William James Mills (ca 2003) Entry on William Speirs Bruce (1867–1921) in *Exploring polar frontiers A-L:* vol 1, Oxford, Santa Barbara CA, p. 104.

In their winter 'beset' in the ice, the young chief engineer of the ship, Allan Ramsay, had died of heart disease. On a crisp Antarctic day, Kerr led the coffin-bearers across the ice to shore, playing a traditional Scottish folk tune often chosen as a lament, 'The Flowers of the Forest'.[7] It is easy to imagine the emotions of the men, so far from Scotland, as they farewelled their dead companion.

Late in the southern autumn of 1903–04 the steam yacht *Scotia* was again briefly beset in the pack ice of the Weddell Sea. During the shorter besetment, one evening in March 1904 Kerr, in highland dress with his pipes, was on deck. His kilt swirled about him as he walked down the ship's gangway. Men were working on the sea ice around the frozen-in ship, and shovelling snow into a large pan for the ship's water supplies, or catching emperor penguins (numerous on the ice that day) which they skinned, dissected, and used for food.[8]

Kerr had warmed up his pipes in the comfort of shelter below decks. When he stepped onto the ice he walked briskly out away from the ship and stopped near one of penguins. When he began to play, the penguin looked up with apparent curiosity. Bruce photographed the striking sight, recording in the ship's log, 'After dinner I spent a considerable time, as it was sunny, photographing the piper, the ship and an Emperor Penguin, and a football scene'.[9]

The photographs (see Figure 2) provided what became the most recognisable scene of the expedition (one later featured on a British Antarctic Survey stamp).[10] As some of them show, Kerr was playing to a penguin which had in fact been leg-roped to a small pan full of ice.

Despite the rope, an emperor penguin could scarcely have been detained if it had wanted to leave. Expedition men and ship crews who handled them noted that the birds are fast and powerful, even on the ice.

'It was just all that one man could do to lead one up to the ship: with their beaks they bit fairly hard, and with their long flipper-like wings could hit out decidedly hard', wrote the *Scotia*'s doctor and geologist, James Harvey.[11]

---

7 RC Mossman, JH Harvey Pirie and RN Rudmose Brown (1906) *The voyage of the 'Scotia'* (originally published by William Blackwood and Sons, Edinburgh). Australian National University Press facsimile, Canberra 1978, p. 153.
8 Brian Gunning (2007) 'The Piper and the Penguin'. *Scotch Circle* [newsletter of the Canberra and District Branch, Royal Scottish Country Dance Society] 27(2) May: unpaginated.
9 Gunning (2007) 'The Piper and the Penguin'.
10 http://bit.ly/1vtjPRE, accessed 30 August 2014.
11 Mossman et al (1906) *The voyage of the 'Scotia'*, p. 241.

Figure 2. Gilbert Kerr playing his bagpipes to an emperor penguin, *Scotia* expedition, March 1904.

Source: Reproduced with the permission of the Royal Scottish Geographical Society.

Men on other expeditions had similar experiences of the unbiddability of penguins. On one Antarctic morning in January 1914 at Commonwealth Bay, 26-year-old Peter Goddard (the *Aurora*'s second steward) went out with the second engineer, chasing emperor penguins. Between them the two men caught and killed one animal. Goddard knocked down another bird three times, but it still escaped him and made the safety of the water. 'Emperor Penguins are fine big birds about 3ft 6 inches high and very broad', Goddard wrote ruefully in his diary.[12]

Standing penguins can drop onto the ice and toboggan swiftly across it, using their flippers to propel themselves. The ability to do this, combined with their considerable weight (up to 35 kg) and energetic reactions to handling, make it unlikely that penguins could have been forced to stand anywhere at all, whether near the piper or not.

But penguins are also by nature inquisitive. As visitors to Antarctica discover, penguins will approach someone who sits quietly. Sometimes, they come so close that they are too close to be photographed.

A century after Kerr played his pipes for the penguin, geographer Innes Keighren described the incident as 'a frivolous and impromptu experiment'.[13] It seems

---

12   Patrick G Quilty and Peter H Goddard (2004) 'The lower deck on *Aurora*: H.V. Goddard's diary, 1913–14'. *Polar Record* 40 (214): 193–203, p. 201.
13   Innes M Keighren (2003) 'A Scot of the Antarctic: the reception and commemoration of William Speirs Bruce'. MSc thesis, Geography Institute, University of Edinburgh, available at era.lib.ed.ac.uk/

more likely that Bruce anticipated — if not engineered — the scene of Kerr, his pipes and the penguin. Bruce had been in Antarctica before and had observed penguins before. He had scientific training. And he was the leader of a Scottish expedition, with explicitly nationalist aims for it.

He had hired Kerr to maintain morale during the voyage, as well as serving as a laboratory assistant. There were few ways in which he could better have reinforced the expedition's Scottish flavour than by taking a piper.[14]

> Science was the talisman of the Expedition [he wrote] but 'Scotland' was emblazoned on its flag. It may be that in endeavouring to serve humanity by adding another link to the golden chain of science, we have also shown that the nationality of Scotland is a power that must be reckoned with.[15]

The presence of bagpipes neatly satisfied Bruce's nationalist ambitions. No single entity is more closely tied to Antarctica (even when not leg-roped to it) than a penguin. Bruce would surely have delighted in using the typically Scottish pipes when photographing piper Kerr with that most overused of Antarctic symbols, the penguin.

James Harvey Pirie suggested another motive for the spectacle. It was, he said, an experiment designed to test the effect of music on penguins. Did the penguins like the pipes? Kerr played marches, reels and laments without apparent effect, said Pirie — there was 'only sleepy indifference'.[16]

Other penguin encounters with music

There were other orchestrated encounters between penguins and music in Antarctica during the heroic era. Two of these occurred on Shackleton's Imperial Trans-Antarctic Expedition of 1914–17. In the first incident, three Adelie penguins approached meteorologist Leonard Hussey while he was playing a banjo. Shackleton wrote that:

> The solemn-looking little birds appeared to appreciate 'It's a Long Way to Tipperary', but they fled in horror when Hussey treated them to a

---

bitstream/1842/890/1/Keighren.pdf, accessed 18 November 2013, p. 83.
14   William James Mills (ca 2003) Entry on William Speirs Bruce (1867–1921). In *Exploring polar frontiers A-L:* vol 1, Oxford, Santa Barbara CA, p. 103.
15   William Speirs Bruce (1906) in Mossman et al. *The voyage of the 'Scotia'*, p. viii.
16   Pirie in Mossman et al. (1906) *The voyage of the 'Scotia'*, p. 241.

little of the music that comes from Scotland. The shouts of laughter from the ship added to their dismay, and they made off as fast as their short legs would carry them.[17]

The second occasion reflects the polarised opinions that bagpipes can so easily produce. When Scottish biologist Robert Clark 'endeavoured to entertain our little visitors with melodies of his native highlands', expedition photographer Frank Hurley later wrote, it was unsuccessful. 'His amiable intentions failed', said Hurley, 'for when the penguins heard the bagpipes, they fled in terror and plunged back into the sea'.[18]

Much later, in the mid-1950s, a visitor to subantarctic Îles Kerguelen played an accordion to a group of penguins. The doctor at the French base on the island, Andre Migot, interpreted the penguins' reaction as positive. Though the choice of instrument was apt on a French island, the visitor was in fact an Australian, Phillip Law. Migot wrote:

> It is known that they [penguins] are very fond of music. To prove it to us Dr Law fetched his accordion and began to play 'The Dead Leaves', one of his favourite songs. There was no doubt that the penguins were interested; they stretched out their necks and turned this heads on one side as if trying to hear better.[19]

These incidents are so few and so lacking in any comparability that we can really only guess at any reaction of penguins to bagpipes and other musical instruments. Observed behaviour seems to show no consistency at all — in Kerr's there is apparent indifference, in Law's curiosity, in Hussey's and Clark's, antipathy.

The enduring image

The *Scotia* returned to Scotland in 1904 with extensive scientific collections which became the basis of the Scottish Oceanographical Laboratory Bruce founded in Edinburgh in 1907. He published seven volumes of scientific reports from the expedition between then and 1919. After his death in 1921, his ashes were scattered off South Georgia in accord with his wishes.[20]

---

17   Ernest Shackleton (1919) *South! The story of Shackleton's Last Expedition 1914–1917*. Century Publishing, London, available at www.gutenberg.org/files/5199/5199-h/5199-h.htm, accessed 27 February 2012, no pagination.
18   Frank Hurley (1948) *Shackleton's argonauts*. Angus and Robertson, Sydney, p. 38.
19   Andre Migot (1956) *The lonely South*. Rupert Hart-Davis, London, p. 177.
20   Speak (2004) 'Bruce, William Speirs (1867–1921)', accessed 27 July 2014.

More than a century after Bruce's expedition, the image of piper and penguin still has a modest but palpable life of its own in music and in literature. Scottish composer Roy Goldring used the name 'The Piper and the Penguin' for one of the dances of his *Scotia Suite*, which commemorated the centenary of the expedition. (The dance was performed in Canberra as an introduction to this paper in 2011 — see below.)

New Zealand writer Laurence Fearnley used the same title for a short story which centres around a photograph of the piper Kerr:

> Kathleen looked at the photograph once more before fixing it to the fridge door by a plastic-coated magnet. She couldn't imagine the playing of the bagpipes in such a cold climate. She imagined that the notes from the pipes would freeze in the air and then fall shattered to the ground like small shards of broken glass.[21]

Her imagery brings to mind the storytelling conceit of Rabelais, who described words which 'congeled in ayre' in intense cold, and could be heard when summer melted them.[22] On the confines of Rabelais' frozen sea,

> Words and cries of men and women froze in the air ... and now, the rigour of winter being over, by the succeeding serenity and warmth of the weather, they melt and are heard.[23]

The audience as food

In Antarctica, the presence of wildlife is emphatically seasonal, sources of fresh meat are scarce, and emperor penguin breast was once very acceptable tucker. In December 1910, on the second antarctic expedition of Robert Falcon Scott, the young Australian geologist Frank Debenham reported that Christmas dinner was a prolonged business. 'I must give you the Menu', he wrote in his diary — it was mulligatawny soup and fricassee of penguin.[24]

The men of the *Scotia* expedition who caught emperor penguins for skins and meat were continuing a practice already established on Antarctic expeditions. Bruce, like other naturalists, collected skin, skeletons and other animal

---

21 Laurence Fearnley (1998) 'The Piper and the Penguin', *Sport* 20 (Autumn): 71–80, p.75, available at www.nzetc.org/tm/scholarly/tei-Ba20Spo-t1-body-d12.html#name-140994-mention, accessed 27 June 2011.
22 Eugene S McCartney (1953) 'Antiphanes' cold-weather story and its elaboration'. *Classical Philology* 48(3): 169–72, p. 169.
23 Rabelais in du Chat and others (1807) *The works of Francis Rabelais*, 4 vols, Lackington, Allen and Co. (and others) London, vol 4 p. 36, available at http://bit.ly/1B0AoVp, accessed 27 February 2012.
24 Quoted in June Debenham, ed (1992) *The quiet land – the diaries of Frank Debenham*. Bluntisham Books, Huntingdon, p. 32.

specimens for scientific study. His officers and crew used whatever wildlife could be caught as food. Seals and penguins were sometimes the only fresh meat men had in 12 months or more.

The talk of food was constant. Aboard the *Scotia*, 'it was surprising how often conversation at meals turned towards food: each man had his especial delicacy which he associated with the return to civilisation, and which was unobtainable in our wilderness'.[25]

The men killed several emperors the day Bruce photographed Kerr with his bagpipes, and would certainly have taken the breast meat and livers of these animals into their larder. The photographs therefore represent a rare and possibly unique example of a concert in which the performer followed his musical efforts by making a meal of the audience.

After the expedition

The pipes Kerr had played came to a stirring end. In 1914 Bruce gave them to the First Edinburgh Battalion of the Royal Scots. They were lost in action during the Battle of the Somme.[26]

The ship was commemorated in the name of Scotia Bay in the South Orkney Islands, where the men had wintered, and in the Scotia Sea (and Scotia Ridge) northeast of the Antarctic Peninsula. But despite these names, the *Scotia*'s story — like some others of the time[27] — has been almost submerged in the wake of the better known voyages of Scott, Shackleton, Amundsen and Mawson. The long-lived photographs of the long-ago piper and his momentary emperor penguin audience are therefore not just an image of two almost cliched subjects, but valuable reminders of a uniquely Scottish expedition to the Far South.

Acknowledgements

At this paper's presentation at Canberra's School of Music in June 2011, the dancers of the Caledonian Society of Canberra were piped into the hall by Pipes Major Richard Harris of the City of Queanbeyan Pipe Band. Before I spoke, they performed the reel 'The Piper and the Penguin'.[28] I was able to arrange this performance through the kindness and coordination of Bill

---

25 Mossman et al. (1906) *The voyage of the 'Scotia'*, p. 100.
26 Royal Scottish Geographical Society (2012) Images for All website, caption to 'Piper Kerr and emperor penguin', rsgs.org/ifa/gems/polarpenguin.html, accessed 22 February 2012.
27 Nobu Shirase's, for example — see Summerson (this volume).
28 See youtube.com/watch?v=7Ek-_wuz_xk.

Causbrook and Caledonian Society member Brian Gunning. I thank Richard, Bill, Brian and the Caledonian Society dancers, for their generous willingness to display Scottish culture.

Grateful thanks to Arnan Wiesel of ANU School of Music for devising the conference, and to Rupert Summerson of Canberra for bringing the Hurley quotation and Laurence Fearnley's story to my attention.

Musical adventures in Antarctica

Alice Giles[1]

Music starts with Silence — it comes out of silence and goes back into it.

Silence is a very tempting concept for a musician — the equivalent of a blank canvas. It is the starting point for questions and for answers, and there are indeed many questions:

Why discuss sound and music in relation to Antarctica? Why take music there to perform? What kind of music is relevant? Who should be writing it? Even revisiting the 20th-century musical question, where does sound become music, or are they the same? Is music important? Where are the Australian compositions relating to Antarctica? Is it really silent there?

In early 2011 I travelled to Antarctica to give a concert. Every concert involves a level of exploration, a sense of journey, adventure, discovery; but this was the most extreme take on that concept in my career.

The purpose of my trip, as an Australian Antarctic Division Arts Fellow, was to present a concert at Australia's Mawson Station to commemorate the centenary of the Australasian Antarctic Expedition of 1911–14, my specific interest being to celebrate the participation in that voyage of my grandfather Cecil Thomas Madigan as meteorologist. The concert comprised words from Madigan's diaries, songs, hymns, and music he mentions in the diaries, and music by contemporary Australian composers especially written for the occasion.[2]

Madigan recorded in his diary the various hymns that kept his spirit going and the gramophone records that brought him cheer, clearly describing how live and recorded music was an essential component in maintaining equilibrium and the thread with home.

This was the thread that kept me going while preparing my trip, during my voyage and on my return. It was the concept that enabled me to relate to my voyage in a way that was natural to me professionally — something that was related to feeling, sensibility — something with a heart. I was able to accomplish this part on the continent, and develop it further in the concert presented at ANU School of Music.[3]

---

1 Ms Alice Giles, Director, Harp Centre Australia, PO Box 685, Yass, NSW 2582, alice.giles@sydney.edu.au.
2 Concert performed in the Red Shed, Mawson Station, Antarctica, 28 February 2011.
3 Live-streamed public performance of 'Alice in Antarctica' on 26 June 2011, Llewellyn Hall, School of Music, The Australian National University.

And yet surrounding this the questions remain, the philosophical ideas that I had not confronted before.

Every continent needs its own individual musical expression — this starts with observation of the natural sound world and then starts to be transformed into an expression of the inner world or emotional response to the essence, rhythms and history of the continent. Such an expression is necessary for a natural cultural understanding of a continent, and especially important for Antarctica because so few of us humans are living there for any length of time — we are distant and need translators to give us the emotional understanding, the whole picture — something best possible through the abstract medium of music.

How are we to gain this musical translation? A musical interpretation of a place will always be a complex matter, involving responses to the emotional and visual landscape, the elemental forces in place (be they magnetic, atmospheric or weather conditions), local sounds in context, or the social and historical environment. Every season in Antarctica should have its musician, and composers should be actively sought out to assist us in understanding this vast continent. Every composer has a different way of hearing and expressing things musically, depending on their personality and focus. To gain a wide view we need many composers spending time in Antarctica.

Why perform music *in* Antarctica? Most interaction with Antarctica involves bringing things back — ideas, images, scientific information. Performing there involves taking something to the continent and letting the environment accept and shape the experience. It acknowledges the fact that we have established and are continuing a human social environment there, which has moved a step beyond the exploratory Heroic Age and demands a greater subtlety of interaction. It acknowledges the fact that we are *there* as human civilisation.

Performers engage with people and facilitate action — they are the alchemists to bring an emotion alive. My Antarctic voyage will always resonate in the vibration of my sound, but I see my contribution mostly as a facilitator, as someone who can try and stimulate interest and engage imagination.

The harp is a powerful mythical symbol, and the idea of a harp in Antarctica has stimulated people's imagination in a way that indicates there is a need for this kind of narrative to be happening.

The response to the video clip of my playing the harp on Davis Beach posted on my blog[4] was very strong — beyond the actual musical content, the combination of the visual element of the harp on the beach, the sounds of the slushy ice combined with the simple composition, and the elephant seals in the background,

---

4   Improvisation on Davis Beach, February 2011 — elephant seals.

drew in many people. Perhaps this is an illustration of how performances in Antarctica can help bridge that gulf of imagination and understanding — by combining visual and sound elements *in situ* while performing composed works or improvisations in Antarctica.

One of the improvisations I made was on the West Arm at Mawson — very simple, soft, because it was starting to snow and expressing a sense of the slowness of time.[5]

On a metaphysical level: I play the harp; I do this because the harp has strings which allow me to explore within, and express to others an infinite subtlety and range of emotions and refinements of feeling. The instrument has become an extension of myself. I took my harp to Antarctica and let the natural forces take over the production of its sound. This was as though the wind, the voice of the continent, was vibrating through both harp and (by extension) me. The journey became a personal transformation, as I imagine it is for most Antarctic voyagers. Once transformed, one is forever changed and deepened. The harp, following my trip, will always have the voice of Antarctica within.[6]

In this musical context it is interesting to explore *why* time spent in Antarctica is transformative.

Firstly, our rhythm and sense of time is altered. This starts with the long sea voyage: the unpredictable rocking of the ocean rhythm, large waves and emotional wildness, the singularity of the uninterrupted horizon, the pulse of the engines drumming memories of the sounds of land from us. Then moving into the stillness of the Antarctic waters, with travel sometimes suspended in a timeless smoothness, at other times slowed by the incremental passage of icebreaking. On land the ancient ice and rock speak of a timeframe in millennia; there is a disruption of human-controlled rhythms — day and night rhythms are changed, and working patterns are unpredictably ruled by the larger weather patterns. The focus on science — the upper atmosphere with the magnetic spectrometer, the geophysical sciences — is all related to subtle subatomic and larger tectonic rhythms.

Composers could start grappling with these more abstract concepts of time/rhythm/patterns and translating them to a new expression.

Secondly, the whole world around you in Antarctica is uncluttered, which is a profoundly important lesson. There is a paring away of non-essentials, both in the natural world and in social or professional obligations, leaving one free to see the essence of things more clearly for a time. This focus has increased my

---

5   Improvisation West Arm, Mawson Station, March 2011.
6   Wind harp, Davis Station, February 2011.

ability to appreciate the beauty of nature in my everyday life; more than an appreciation, it is a refinement of love in response to the natural world. The sky over Yass will always touch me more intensely now with its colours, blue and white, tinged with sunset hues, changing but the same, as a reminder of my responses to that southern icy world.

Issues that are not much discussed today, as we don't have the language for it; maybe that is why we have music ...

Thirdly, there is an intangible intensity about the Antarctic experience that is experienced by many, but few could articulate this as well as a fellow traveller on the Australian Antarctica Division's voyage 3 for 2010–11, a scientist who had spent various periods of time there. He said he experienced greater extremes of emotions while there, and really had to gauge his behaviour differently to accommodate this change. There can be many reasons for this, to do with the different social environment, the different circadian cycles, the different magnetic forces and other natural environmental influences as yet undiscovered. The point I would like to make is that the integration of these influences is fascinating and important on a human level, and deserves translation into music by composers interested in exploring the complexities and subtleties of the emotional and natural worlds.

Once I had left the continent, back on the ship I tried to think of what I would wish to write if I could compose something for myself, and my overriding impression after my Mawson Station visit was an extremely deep vibration to reflect the all-pervasive power of the rocks — powerful bass notes in an unconventional tuning and scale, rather like the fundamentals in an overtone singing chant. This overlaid with high repeated patterns with which to reflect the sparkling brightness, the ancient patterns of the ice — again very similar to the concept of overtone chanting. I made a sketchy and unsatisfactory — for me — attempt to realise this personal response, which I will possibly develop later into a more satisfactory composition. I mention it only to illustrate that this would not have been my musical/emotional response if I had only looked at visual images of Antarctica.

A wider question now occurs to me. We have a large number of Australians who are funded to go to Antarctica (by various government, private and other organisations), but only a very few funded places selected from the humanities. I am now imagining a society which would firstly send many musicians, visual artists, and historians to the unknown continent, with funding for a few scientists each year — possibly a biologist and a LIDAR scientist[7] this year, a magnetic spectrometer researcher and geologist the next. Not necessarily more

---

7   LIDAR (*light + radar*) is a remote sensing technique for measuring distance with the use of lasers.

or less sensible — just a different perspective. (In fact scientists and performing artists are different sides of the same coin, and have more in common than other disciplines: focus, intellectual imagination, personal discipline, and practical ability.)

But this leads me to the further question: is music the cause or the result in our civilisation? You may think this a ridiculous question, but the ancient Chinese saw the keeping of particular scales as being essential for the preservation of their culture. If the pitch or modality of the scale changed, the dynasty changed as a consequence. Our musical explorations may or may not be as important as other explorations. Certainly, to be human is to feel and to express a huge range of subtle responses to the outside world — natural and social.

But then I return to the question (more questions!) — where are the Australian composers interested in writing music about Antarctica? One hundred years after Dr Madigan listened to the gramophone and sang the songs he brought with him, there remains very little music written by Australian composers that directly relates to Antarctica, even though Australians have been a consistent presence on the continent all that time. Are they waiting for commissions — is this the Australian culture of composition? Is it a reflection of the lack of cultural connection with Antarctica over the last 100 years? And why am I the one asking these questions besides Rupert Summerson?[8] Have other people noticed that there is a silence here? Why are other countries so much more ahead of us in musical expressions of Antarctica? So many more New Zealand composers are being 'tapped on the shoulder' to go and interpret the place.

I hope my arts fellowship and my voyage to Antarctica can be a starting point for many other Australians and especially composers to start asking these questions. Because if we would like an Australian public that is passionate about what happens in Antarctica, we need to know how to engage hearts and minds powerfully: music has this power.

---

8   See Rupert Summerson's paper 'On a Vast Scale' in this volume, from his presentation at the 'Antarctica and Music' conference in 2011.

Mentions of music in the Antarctic diaries of Cecil T Madigan[1]

Arnan Wiesel

Dr Cecil Thomas Madigan (Figure 1) was the meteorologist on Douglas Mawson's Australasian Antarctic Expedition. He led the eastern sledging party, and was also leader of the group of men who stayed behind in February 1913 when Mawson's party failed to return to their base at Commonwealth Bay in time to return to Australia on the relief ship. His expedition diaries were published in 2012.[2]

Figure 1. Cecil Thomas Madigan, ca 1912.

Source: Photo by Frank Hurley, courtesy National Library of Australia.

---

1 Mr Arnan Wiesel, pianist and former Head of Keyboard, ANU School of Music.
2 CT Madigan's complete diaries, held in a family archive, were published in 2012: CT Madigan (2012) *Madigan's account: the Mawson expedition — the Antarctic diaries of CT Madigan, 1911–1914*, transcribed by JW Madigan. Wellington Bridge Press, North Hobart.

The mentions of music in his diaries during Australasian Antarctic Expedition of 1911–14 show that musical activities were a vital part of daily life in the isolated and harsh environment. He mentions musical events as well as music listening sessions. These were part of an extensive creative range of social activities that included, for example, staging plays and poetry competitions.

'We have arranged Wed & Sunday as singing night', wrote Madigan on 3 April 1912. Singing activities included both secular and religious songs. It is important to differentiate between the two streams of musical styles, as each addressed very different social needs. Hymns and other religious singing gave a needed sense of security and connection with faraway home. One gets an idea of the comforting feeling, clearly articulated by Madigan:

> I am very fond of *Oh Lord & Father of mankind* to a tune called *Rest* – it has memories …
>
> The contralto *Abide with me* is beautiful — I must have that sung to me by an alto I know when I get back again to bonny S.A.
>
> The hymns always put me in a sentimental mood — I think of home and of 'Raywood'. How I long for those quiet evenings round the little organ at 'Raywood'.[3]

The hymns also had strong connotations of the British Empire. Australians are rightly very proud of the first Australian-led expedition to Antarctica, but the unmistakable colonial flavour of the music mentioned open for us a window to the real cultural heritage of the expedition. The secular music might have been more Australian in character, but the hymns represented the tradition of Empire.

Madigan mentions many, and noted that:

> We use the Congregational hymn book which I admit is better than ours. (*Hymns Ancient and Modern* — the Anglican hymn book) … Stillwell is a Congregationalist and knows their hymns very well & the good tunes.[4]

Frank Stillwell was the men's organist during services.

Even in the secular music we see the strong connection with Britain. Two of the three specific performers Madigan mentioned in his diaries during the first year give us a glimpse of popular listening of the time.

Dame Clara Butt (1872–1936) was a well-known English contralto singer whom Madigan mentions being played as part of a Sunday evening sacred music at

---

3   CT Madigan diaries, 21 July 1912. 'Raywood' was the name of the Adelaide home of Madigan's fiancée.
4   CT Madigan diaries, 19 May 1912.

the Commonwealth Bay hut, together with the British Army's Coldstream Choir. Dame Clara was a symbol of the British Empire in stature (she was more than 6 feet tall) and through her extroverted and majestic performances. During the years before the expedition she was at the height of her popularity, and was renowned for her renditions of hymns and traditional English tunes.

The second popular performer, Harry Lauder (1870–1950), was a Scottish entertainer. His contribution to the listening repertoire of the expeditioners was more with the entertainment aspect of music. As a contrast to the more traditional and secure world of hymns, the light entertainment character of Lauder's music would have perhaps fuelled the fun, creative activities of the men over the two years.

Madigan mentions of a third figure, Chapman Alexander, as part of an evening of hymns, probably reflects the influence of two evangelical trips to Australia by the American preacher Charles Alexander. Alexander (1867–1920) joined forces with John Chapman (1859–1918) and the hymns sung in these large-scale events were a vital part of the bonding process.

Figure 2. Harry Lauder popular song book, published by Francis Day in 1905.

Source: *Wikipedia, The Free Encyclopedia*, http://en.wikipedia.org/w/index.php?title=Harry_Lauder&oldid=636746009.

The Chapman Alexander Simultaneous Campaign of large-scale evangelical events started in 1908 in Philadelphia, USA, and included a visit to Australia in 1909, with a month each in Melbourne and Sydney, two weeks in Brisbane and ten days in Adelaide, as well as shorter visits to Albury, Ballarat, Bendigo, Castlemaine, Moss Vale and Townsville. It is important to note the men's services involved with these events in relation to the all-male social reality at the Mawson Hut.

Although the expedition is acknowledged as the first Australian expedition to Antarctica, interestingly, the international character of the expedition was evident in the language used in musical performances. Madigan records that songs the men sang included *Ich bin der Doctor Eisenbahn*, *Liebes Schätzeken*, *La Marseillaise* and *Treue Liebe*. Music is always an important indicator of the character and origins of people. The Swiss mountaineer Xavier Mertz contributed an international flavour to the expedition and Madigan, who had some knowledge of German, put this to use in the musical events.

Many of the expeditioners had recently finished university, so it is no wonder at Madigan's mention of various student songbooks — the *Varsity Boat Songs, Scottish Students' Song Book, The Australasian Students' Song Book,* and *The Globe Song Folio*. Madigan was to go to Oxford upon his return from the expedition and participate in the rowing program, so the 'varsity (university) boat songs would have had an important link to the future.

The more actively engaging musical activities show a great deal of creativity. As the *Adelie Blizzard,* produced in the expedition's second year at the hut (the expedition newspaper), also shows, these activities combined with plays and other events contained a great deal of humour.[5] 'Hurley as usual was the funniest — he had the gramophone horn and a length of rubber hose which he wound over his shoulder — his bass notes were a leading feature'.

The use of elements such as the Morse code in whistles gives another glimpse of the creative ideas the expeditioners came up with. A comment such as, 'We worked up in pitch at the rate of about an octave per verse & had several changes of key to get it down again' shows a healthy sense of not taking oneself too seriously.

---

5   Friends of the State Library of South Australia (2010) *The Adelie Blizzard: Mawson's forgotten newspaper, 1913,* Friends of the State Library of South Australia in association with the Friends of Mawson at the South Australian Museum, Adelaide.

Examples of musical activities from Madigan's diaries

The following passages from Madigan's diaries (transcribed by Julia W Madigan) have been selected by the author, Arnan Wiesel, and Alice Giles.

First year of expedition

26 November 1911 [Sang] all the good old songs & also our Varsity boating songs. *Mary had a William Goat* was not neglected.

2 December 1911 A farewell dinner at Mawson's[6] expense — sang *For he's a jolly good fellow* — not 'freeze'.

8 December 1911 [On the boat] we pass the time doing Morse code in whistles …We left the *Larboard Watch* to the best singers — it sounded fine in the twilight, with big seas running and the vessel heeling in big slow rolls. Wild[7] sang *Absent* and with much feeling … we also sang *Abide with me*.

9 December 1911 Chorus — *Sweethearts and Wives* / Sweethearts & wives, they are the dearest thing in our lives. / When pretty lips meet / My! What a treat / Oh who cd help loving the darlings!

18 December 1911 After tea all collected round the piano with the *Scottish Students' Song Book* and had a great old sing song. Nothing cheers one up like a few chorus songs, especially the old ones. Hoadley[8] is our pianist. Sang some good shanties on the hauling; 'A roving'. Mertz did some 'yodels' and sung German student song to the tune of 'Up-i-Dee' which made a good chorus.

31 December 1911 Just before tea we had a sing-song, some hymns and the *Australian Students' Song Book*. It was good to sing the 'Ode to Tobacco' and 'Meerschaum Pipe' and 'Waltzing Matilda' again, not forgetting 'Mary's William Goat'.

30 January 1912 First sit down meal in hut … Songs were put down [on the menu] as *Walzing Matilda* by Madigan, *Annie Laurie* by Hannam[9] & *Poor Old Jo*e by Laseron.[10] The first named has become very popular

---

6 Douglas ('Doc') Mawson (1882–1958), the expedition leader.
7 Frank Wild (1873–1939), leader, western base.
8 Charles Archibald ('Arch') Hoadley (1887–1947), geologist on the Western Party.
9 Walter Hannam (1885–1965), wireless engineer and mechanic.
10 Charles Laseron (1887–1959), taxidermist and biological collector.

with adopted Antarctic words ... The Doc got out the gramaphone [sic] — an Edison with the 'His master's voice' pictures on it. We had about a half a dozen records.

2 February 1912 We had the grama going again — some Harry Lauder, band selections, *Take a pair of sparkling eyes* etc.

11 February 1912 This is a little more like Sunday Evening. The gramophone is in splendid working order and Hurley is putting through some beautiful sacred records. All the dear old hymns — *Abide with me, Nearer my God to Thee, Adeste Fidelis* — they remind me of home ... We have now just heard Clara Butt & now comes *Christchurch Bells* played by Coldstream Guards — finished — it was beautiful.

18 February 1912 I got down the gramophone and went through a few sacred records — *Holy City, Abide with me, Nearer my God to Thee, Messiah, Holy Holy Holy, There is a green hill*. I love these old hymns. They are all good choirs. I wish we had old Wild here with his singing. He was for some years in the St Paul's Choir, London.

25 February 1912 We sang *Near my God to Thee* and *God our help in Ages past*. The little organ was unpacked and Stillwell played it.

3 March 1912 Service again today — it will be regular now. Hymns *Lead kindly Light* and *Eternal Father*.

7 March 1912 Played the grama after Caruso's [the dog's] surgical operation was over. *Soon I'll be back with the colleen I adore, Eileen Allanah, Argus Asthare*.

17 March 1912 Laseron is working the phono — the hymns by the London Mixed Choir are A.1. I love hymns.

22 March 1912 MacLean[11] on the grama — we have some bonzer pieces *Valse Espana, When the sun is sinking*, a sweet little coon song, some banjo selections, *Sparkling eyes* and others.

24 March 1912 After tea we got the little organ going. Stillwell[12] playing, and sang all the dear old hymns. Hannam has a very good tenor voice, and everyone sings a bit.

27 March 1912 [MacLean's birthday celebration:] then a musical programme to which nearly everyone contributed.

---

11 Dr Archibald MacLean (Dad) (1885–1922), medical officer.
12 Frank Stillwell (1888–1963), geologist.

28 March 1912 After dinner I started in to give a phonograph concert — I went through all records and made a selection and then arranged them. It was greatly enjoyed — nearly everyone got into bed and I expect most of them were sung to sleep. I unearthed a new song — I had always passed it over on the name *I know of two bright eyes* but this name belies its character. It is a tenor, soft and musical with beautiful words.

31 March 1912 In the evening Hunter[13] & Hurley[14] sang a parody they had made up on the subject — quite good — tune *Yip-I-Addy*.

3 April 1912 We have arranged Wed & Sunday as singing night. We went through all the old *Scottish Students' Songs* tonight & a lot of the Aust. Uni songs — a good time.

7 April 1912 Easter Sunday [For Easter service] we sang *Christ the Lord is risen today* and another hymn.

It has been the custom for the cook & messman to sing a song during dinner for some time past. Hurley & Hunter started it with their original songs. Last night Hannam & MacLean sang *Ye banks and braes*. Mertz[15] was cook today, Hannam messman & Mertz came to me as I was going to bed and asked me to help him with one. In spite of my fit of the blues I did it — we made one which was supposed to be Basilisk [the dog] singing, with a barking chorus to the tune of *Ich bin der Doctor Eisenbahn*. I put a lot of Mertz's funny sayings in, which of course he did not appreciate. I thought it very poor. Mertz taught it to Hannam & they gave it. It was most successful — cries of 'we want more' & the opinion that it was the best to date. The authorship was unknown & still is.

Sang hymns tonight after helping wash up. I wish we had old Wild here. He is a bonzer singer — once in St Paul's Choir.

8 April 1912 Murphy[16] was cook today and Close[17] messman. We gave them a fearful time at dinner for a song — neither can sing. At last old Close sang *Queen of the Earth* — it was quite pathetic. I was glad no one laughed, although it was hard not to. We gave him a good cheer.

9 April 1912 We had high jinks at dinner ... then songs & recitations all round. I fired off my beastly old timer.

---

13 John Hunter (1888–1964), biologist.
14 Frank Hurley (Hoyle) (1885–1962), photographer.
15 Xavier Mertz (1882–1913), dog-keeper.
16 Herbert Murphy (1879–1971), in charge of stores.
17 John Close (1871–1949), assistant collector.

14 April 1912   We sang hymns this evening for a long while, starting with *Lead kindly Light, Abide with me, Nearer my God* and ending with Chapman Alexander. Stillwell plays, and MacLean, Hunter, Laseron, Hannam & I & Mawson sing. Mawson is rather sacreligious — he wanted *Arise oh Christian soldier & put your burberrys on.*

18 April 1912   Had our weekly sing song tonight. *Scottish Students, Globe* and *Aust Students'* song books. MacLean sang *Afton Water* and Hannam *My Pretty Jane* as solos.

20 April 1912   Mertz sang a song at tea time — Hurley sang *Ich bin der Doctor Eisenbard* in German — or alleged German, & Mertz sang his English translation, which he gave me.

21 April 1912   Stillwell, our organist, is night watchman & having a sleep before coming on duty so we have no hymns. I put all the hymns through on the grama. We have *Abide, Holy Holy Holy, Green Hill, Christian Soldiers, Ave Maria, Nearer my God.*

26 April 1912   … and overall the absolute, almost dreadful, silence. We walked round the peninsula, sitting a while right at the point. We got a fine echo from the islands — Mertz's yodelling sounded well.

28 April 1912   Hymns this evening with Stillwell, MacLean, Hannam & myself. Stillwell is a Congregationalist and knows their hymns very well & the good tunes. We had a lot of well known ones.

2 May 1912   I picked out two records then, *La Cinquataine*, a beautiful harp solo, and *Ben The Bos'n*, a rousing song, and put them on the gramo in that order as a 'rise & shine'.

5 May 1912   [Hurley] and Hunter sang 3 songs of their own manufacture which were very funny, mostly jokes at the expense of various members …

12 May 1912   After dinner we had a great old sing of hymns.

19 May 1912   After dinner helped Bick[18] who was messman, & then we had our hymns — the usual four, Laseron, Hannam, MacLean & I with Stillwell playing. We have a good quartet, with one notable exception. We use the congregational hymn book which I admit is better than ours.

---

18   Francis Bickerton (Bick) (1889–1954), mechanic.

7 June 1912   Hymns tonight — *Dear Lord and Saviour* is becoming popular — I always suggest it.

... and started the gramo: with dreamy waltzes at 7:10, 'rise & shine' at 7:45.

The Adelie Land band got going tonight — there were Corell[19] with his piccolo, MacLean with Ninnis'[20] mouth organ, Ninnis with his concertina, Hunter with an empty carbide tin strapped in front as a kettle drum, Laseron with a comb, Hodgeman[21] with some suspended lengths of pipe and Mertz with two pot lids as cymbals. It sounded rather fine — they played *British Grenadiers, Swannee River, Yip-i-addy, Auld Lang Syne, Stop your ticklin' Jock*, etc. Hurley as usual was the funniest — he had the gramaphone horn and a length of rubber hose which he wound over his shoulder — his bass notes were a leading feature.

9 June 1912   Webb[22] played the organ, but we had no hymns tonight — Bick put our few gramo ones through.

21 June 1912   [Midwinter's Day 1912] I ran the gramo during dinner, which was a great success vide menu ... Then we sang a song Dad had made up ... Laseron sang, also Hannam ... Then the *National Anthem* and *Old Lang Syne*.

21 July 1912   After dinner we sang hymns, quite a nice little gathering of Stillwell, McLean, Laseron, Hunter and myself & Corell. Corell is probably the most musical of us all but he won't sing. He plays the piccolo beautifully, & accompanys the organ. I suppose old Alec does the same at Wild's base.

30 July 1912   We got the organ down and the *Scottish Students' Song Book*, Laseron, Hunter, Stillwell & myself. The old plantation songs always make me think of 'Yunkunger'.

3 August 1912   We have all kinds of records, many beautiful choir hymns. I put on first *Onward Christian Soldiers* which is a processional hymn starting scarcely audible, then *Abide with Me* sung in a beautiful alto & a tune I must get, *The Village Blacksmith* which is a fine old song in

---

19 Percy Corell (1892–1974), mechanic and assistant physicist.
20 Belgrave Ninnis (1887–1912), dog-keeper.
21 Alfred Hodgeman (1886–1964), cartographer and sketch artist.
22 Eric Webb (1889–1984), chief magnetician.

a manly base, a very pretty sentimental song (*I know of two white arms, waiting for me, I know of two red lips, praying for me*), *Eileen Alannah*, *Humoresque*, a violin solo, *Nearer my God Thee* etc.

16 August 1912 [Hodgeman's birthday] After dinner Hoyle got out a musical programme, consisting of *Cameron Men*, and *Ye Banks & Braes* by MacLean, Piccolo solos by Little Willeee Smith, *My Pretty Jane* by Hannam … *A Roving* by Hunter & Hurley, *Larboard Watch* by Hannam and Laseron … *Liebes Schätzeken* and *La Marsellaise* by Mertz, and *Walzing Matilda* & *The Good Rhein Wine* by myself (compulsory), also selections by the Adelie Band, concluded by *Old Folks at Home* and *Auld Lang Syne* by the company.

3 September 1912 [Hurley] has not been so lively of late, but tonight he got back his old form, & gave us some [negro] songs in his get up, pulling in and out the bellows of his wet camera like a concertina. He amuses me immensely.

8 September 1912 I gave a good selection of hymns before calling the sleepers this morning [Sunday] … After dinner I gave another gramo concert. Old Dux ipse [Mawson] quite cheered up during it, and told one or two to stop their jobs and have a holiday as it was Sunday night — a thing he has never done before.

6 October 1912 Then cigars went round, & MacLean sang a comic little French song (Anglo-French style) & Laseron sang a Pidgin-German song he invented, very good, & Hoyle did one of his dress ups, representing J.C. after the sledging, all bandages & frost-bites, & sang a song, with verses about different people, including Mertz … When this was over, a regular concert set in — Stillwell got down the organ & most of us sang something. I sang *Treue Liebe* for Mertz's special benefit. Bage[23] gave a good Kipling recitation, Laseron, MacLean, Hannam, Hunter sang, Corell gave piccolo solos (very good) & we had several choruses. It was a most enjoyable evening & bucked us up tremendously.

12 October 1912 Today was principally notable for the Grand Opera … Stillwell played the organ. There were topical songs and old songs and ordinary language — Hoyle provided most of the fun.

15 October 1912 [CTM's birthday] The Doctor made a nice speech for Hoyle & me, and we replied. I got rather sentimental in my reply, being somewhat touched. The evening closed with gramophone.

---

23 Robert Bage (1888–1915), astronomer.

17 October 1912   Mawson has divided up the MacKellar library — a few books each ... I would like to collar the hymn book, but don't like to ask for it.

18 October 1912   We invented a song between us, a copy of which is enclosed. We sang it very badly, which amused the crowd hugely. I was rather against *The Sergeant of the Line*, a gramophone tune, as I knew jolly well I was no good at the tune, but I depended on Dad, who got fearfully lost at times. We worked up in pitch at the rate of about an octave per verse & had several changes of key to get it down again.

Second year of expedition

2 March 1913   Then dinner, after which I chained all my little four-footed friends up, and came in and put all the hymns on the gramophone.

4 March 1913   And light-hearted old Xavier too; the last thing I remember him saying was the last night I ever saw him. He came into my tent on the great lone plateau, from Mawson's, and I said — 'let's sing a song'; and it was 'studio auf ein Reis'.

27 March 1913   Tonight they asked me to 'sing' — no one else would — well, I could not possibly risk it. At last I give up. The joke lies in the reflection on the talent of the oufit.

8 August 1913   I have been playing the gramophone furiously, and doing my best for the spirits of the others.

One of Uncle's[24] little diversions is to play hymns on the harmonium on Sunday afternoons, he can only manage one note, which he plays in bass and treble, we have him for the services, which are again regular. Mawson and I, vocalists of about the same calibre, usually sing a few extra ones during the afternoon.

Over the two seasons in Antarctica music gave the lives of people at the hut a diversity that complemented the somewhat dull daily routine. In recent years many of the expeditioners' diaries have been published. A close look into the music elements in these can give us important new clues to the environment they experienced — rich information for future research.

---

24   Hodge.

Body of ice: The movement of Antarctic ice through dance

Christina Evans[1]

Antarctic ice is fragile, dynamic and alive. The journey of an ice form is continually transient. Layering, compressing, flowing, cracking, floating, crumbling, dissolving, freezing and reforming occurs at a molecular level and large scale. The diverse textures, qualities and forms of Antarctic ice are extraordinary. Seasonal cycles of ice see Antarctica double in size as it expands through fierce winter and contracts through summer. Snow forms in layers on the plateau and compresses, forming ice. Glaciers flow to the coast to form ice shelves that break as icebergs. Such cycles take thousands of years, yet are always in motion. Our bodies are made up of pure water that at some point has been Antarctic ice. We are a part of the ice as well as its signs of a changing climate.[2]

Body of Ice is a contemporary dance work that explores the dynamic movement and extreme nature of Antarctic ice, as well as the human connection to and impact on it. As the first dance artist ever to be awarded an Australian Antarctic Arts Fellowship, I travelled to Antarctica for several weeks in 2010 to undertake creative research to develop this work. Many facets of Antarctic ice movement were researched, explored and integrated into choreographic processes. Collaborating with renowned sound artist Philip Samartzis, a fellow Australian Antarctic Arts Fellowship recipient, the *Body of Ice* soundscape was born from the raw, richly diverse and intricate sounds of Antarctic ice. Several art forms were utilised to create a sensory representation of the ice and one which physically connect us to it.

Creative research in Antarctica

The shapes and layers of an ice structure reveal its movement history; the many processes of action and reaction that created its current yet continually changing form. While in Antarctica I collected a vast range of movement and choreographic stimuli, ice imagery, visual and written responses and sensory

---

[1] Ms Christina Evans, 10 Birks Street, Parkside, SA 5063, christina.evans@outlook.com.
[2] From program notes for the author's contemporary dance piece *Polarity*.

impressions. The illuminated colour, textures, diversity, scale and raw beauty of the ice were phenomenal, and my physical state was altered through interacting with it. My diary entry stated:

> I am full of awe, wonder and passion. The ice lives and breathes. Beautiful, severe, natural. Delicate fluidity, rock hard strength. Staggering.[3]

I undertook research into ice types, ice cycles and ice behaviours as well as into the signs of a changing climate that are evident in the Antarctic. Although this research was somewhat basic as I do not have a scientific background, I wanted to ensure that the complexities of the ice and environmental shifts were accurately referenced within the layers of my work.

Choreographic processes

Various processes were used in translating the movement of Antarctic ice into choreographic material, including image, sensory, kinaesthetic, dynamic and structurally based explorations. Image-based responses included dancers looking at photographic images of Antarctic ice and responding to the shape, patterns, lines and layers seen within the ice forms. A physical journey of how the ice form became its current shape generated movement material, as well as moving through space in a way that an ice form tracks through the ocean or among surrounding ice. Textures, rolling, crumbling, melting and freezing were explored through intricate parts of the body and through bodies interacting with each other. Dancers could all be one piece of ice, varying types of ice, or their individual bodies could split into various types of ice with varying qualities of movement, speed and dynamics.

Water and ice itself were explored in several ways. Dancers danced with actual ice and also performed movement material on plastic sheets covered with ice in the studio. I conducted several rehearsals in swimming pools to explore the effect, sensations and qualities of being in water. The fluidity and impact water made on body movement was dramatic, and these qualities were brought into the choreographic material. Raw sounds of Antarctic ice, recorded by Samartzis, were used, with dancers reacting to the sounds of ice physically, and moving as if actually *being* the ice that was creating the sounds. The water in our physical composition was a pivotal exploration as this would have been Antarctic ice at one point in time, therefore we are literally a part of Antarctic ice and its cycles and processes.

---

3   Probably written at Davis station, Antarctica, around 7 February 2010.

Extreme qualities of ice were explored physically, such as strength, fragility, soft and hard ice, as well as the unpredictable nature of the Antarctic environment explored through kinaesthetic response. Dancers would move through a piece of choreography and I would shift the speed, direction or dynamic of the material, stating the switch and effecting sudden dramatic change in an instant. Extremely fast and extremely slow speeds were also explored, including moving at no faster than one centimetre per second for extended periods of time. Ice exploration also extended into the use of structures and fabrics, presenting the interconnected nature of the ice where one form of ice would become another. Each choreographic process had a deep link with Antarctic ice and allowed for extreme facets of choreography to develop in line with the nature of the ice.

Choreographic structure

The overall choreographic structure of *Body of Ice* follows the creation cycle and seasonal cycle of Antarctic ice. A journey from the ice plateau expands outwards through glacial flow, ice shelf formation and the breakage of icebergs, along with a range of ice interactions and qualities. A retreat of sea ice during the summer, plus the signs of excessive melting of Antarctic ice, forms the ending — a vivid image of bodies melting away. Throughout the work dancers articulate ice patterns, imagery and dynamics at a cellular level as well as through their connections with each other.

Soundscape

The soundscape by Samartzis recorded near Australia's Davis station includes sounds of Antarctic ice taken from *Antarctic Plateau, Brash Ice* at Heidemann Bay, Seal Cove and Law Cairn, *Frozen Lake* at Ellis Fjord and Trajer Ridge, *Icebergs* at Anchorage Bay, *Sea Ice* at Seal Cove and *Growler Ice* at Long Fjord.

Photographic imagery

Macro and micro photographic imagery of Antarctic ice, taken by Antarctic expeditioners Fred Olivier, Ruth Wielinga and me, is used as projection in *Body of Ice*. This visual element contextualises sections of the work with images of intricate and unique aspects of Antarctic ice.

Interaction of artistic forms

Body of Ice employs the artistic forms of dance, sound, photographic imagery and lighting. Each layer presents elements of Antarctic ice that integrate into all of the senses. The experience of Antarctic ice is one words cannot communicate, and the beauty of raw movement, real sound, vivid imagery and illumination of light and colour does present felt experiences of the Antarctic environment. The essential performance language of dance brings the Antarctic ice directly to humanity, physically connecting ourselves to Antarctic ice. The voice of the ice is brought to the performance by the extraordinary soundscape, being the true language of Antarctic ice itself. These two languages are further enhanced by photographic imagery and lighting in a stage environment.

Polarity

After June 2011, *Body of Ice* was developed into full length work *Polarity*, presented outdoors as part of the 2011 Melbourne Fringe Festival on the Federation Square carpark roof area. The scale of the area was fitting with Antarctic expanse, and the surrounding city linked the cityscape to the icescapes and presented the connection and impact each has on the other. Audience members were encouraged to walk around the large performance area to view the work from various angles, journeying to experience the ice. The presentation at Federation Square integrated the cityscape which in itself provided a language that communicated our present way of life and how it may be affecting the ice. The sheer scale of the buildings was also symbolic of the scale of icebergs in Antarctica, which seem like 'cities of ice'.

Artistic innovation

As the first dance artist ever sent by the Australian Antarctic Division to Antarctica, my proposal to create *Body of Ice* was seen as a unique, ambitious and innovative way to communicate Antarctica through the arts. *Body of Ice* translates the Antarctic ice environment through performance, highlighting scientific information about its cycles and nature, as well as its physical and emotive connection to us. *Body of Ice* is a potent reminder at this time that we are intrinsically connected to our environment and that we are a part of the cycles of Antarctic ice. The magnificent beauty and complex nature of Antarctic ice is something that is rarely experienced or acknowledged, and to see it explored through these mediums is an ambitious, yet natural, connection. The Australian

Antarctic Division seeks for Antarctica to be valued, protected and understood, and to bring Antarctic ice to the public in this way physically connects us to the ice and brings it to life.

Future evolutions

I envisage touring *Body of Ice* and *Polarity* throughout Australia as well as performing in the desert, as Antarctica is a desert. I also plan to connect my work to international audiences, presenting an experience of Antarctic ice to most who would never have the opportunity actually to experience it.

The performance of *Polarity* at Federation Square in 2011 received wide press coverage and positive responses. I was invited to the IV Antarctica Art and Culture International Conference and Festival in Buenos Aires in 2012, performing a solo version of *Body of Ice* and presenting a talk on my work and artistic vision. A film of *Polarity* was presented at the Ultimo Science Festival in Sydney 2013 as part of the Living Data exhibition. I am now working on an installation to perform live and present as a video piece for gallery and festival spaces, focusing on the impact of climate change on Antarctic ice. I plan to expand and evolve my work and continue to present it on a global platform.

The poetry of Antarctic sound and the sound of Antarctic poetry

Elizabeth Leane[1]

In 1996, the Antarctic Treaty System officially recognised the value of creative engagements with the continent, citing 'the contribution of writers, artists and musicians' as a key means of 'promotion of understanding and appreciation of the values of Antarctica'.[2] It is often hard to separate these different forms of imaginative response — textual, visual, aural — in the creative works that emerge from the continent. This is particularly the case in recent decades when various national programs have launched 'artists and writers' schemes, which send people working in diverse artistic modes to the continent. Drawn together by their similar tasks and their newness to the Antarctic community, these 'artists-in-residence' tend to form their own bonds, and learn about each other's mediums of expression. Musicians and sonic artists become inspired by written narratives of exploration; visual artists begin to write poetry on the side; poets draw on the vocabulary of art and music in their attempts to express their experiences of the continent; novelists look to musicians as the basis for characters.[3]

Thus an analysis of the relationship between sound, music and literature in an Antarctic context could fruitfully proceed by a number of different approaches. Those with expertise in both literary studies and musicology might draw on the well-developed, theoretically complex field of study concerned with the connections between music and literature — sometimes termed 'melopoetics'[4] — to shed light on this relationship. For others, like me, whose background is primarily literary, perhaps the most straightforward starting point is the representation of music — or, at least, its production and performance — in literary texts.

There is no shortage of examples. Antarctic fiction (my own speciality) furnishes plenty of relevant material: short stories and novels that deal with — that in some cases, you might say are even *about* — music and sound. An obvious

---

1 Associate Professor Elizabeth Leane, School of Humanities, University of Tasmania, Private Bag 41, Hobart, TAS 7000, Elizabeth.Leane@utas.edu.au.
2 Antarctic Treaty Consultative Meeting XX, Res. 2.
3 Music, art and writing, of course, do not exhaust the range of creative response to the continent: they are used as shorthand here for the wide range of artforms practised by those who have visited the continent, including film-making, photography, sculpture, dance and choreography.
4 Paul Steven Scher (2004) *Essays on literature and music (1967–2004)*, eds Walter Bernhart and Werner Wolf. Rodopi, Amsterdam, p. 471.

example is Graham Billing's novel *Forbush and the penguins*.⁵ A minor New Zealand classic, and often taught in schools there, it was adapted for screen, with John Hurt as the main character, in the early 1970s. The novel focuses almost entirely on a single character, Richard Forbush, a biologist who stays alone in Shackleton's hut at Cape Royds for a summer to monitor a nearby adelie penguin population. He is also an amateur musician who takes his clarinet when he journeys south (it becomes a guitar in the film). Over his months of isolation, he begins to assemble a strange and elaborate musical instrument of his own invention, which he calls the 'Penguin Major Polyphonic Music Machine'.⁶ The machine is constructed from bits and pieces guiltily pilfered from the hut itself, and its core component is a 'water-bottle xylophone made from Shackleton's sauce bottles and Professor T Edgeworth David's test tubes'.⁷ As Forbush's time in the hut continues he experiences a growing existential crisis triggered by the unrelenting cycles of birth and death among the local penguin population, and plays his instrument in a vain attempt to ward off this crisis. The eccentricity of the music machine he builds reflects his state of mind.

Music and sound have engaged another New Zealand novelist writing more recently about Antarctica, Laurence Fearnley. Her novel *Degrees of Separation* deals partly with a 'sonic artist' travelling with the New Zealand Antarctic program.⁸ She suffers from a serious case of imposter symdrome, unable to accept the legitimacy of her own work in the face of scientists and field training officers — those with 'proper jobs'.⁹ But here I want to discuss Fearnley's earlier short story called 'The Piper and the Penguin'.¹⁰ The title references the well-known image of the same name, which is reproduced in the text. The photograph comes from from the Scottish Antarctic Expedition of 1902–04, and shows a kilted bagpiper playing to a penguin surreptitiously tied to his ankle. Like her novel, Fearnley's story focuses on a fictional composer-in-residence with the New Zealand program.¹¹ This composer, Max, sends increasingly cryptic packages back from the continent to his wife Kathleen in Auckland. Kathleen, a visual artist who shares not only her name but also her occupation with history's most famous Antarctic widow, receives a series of enigmatic photographs, beginning with 'The Piper and the Penguin'. Before long, she identifies the connection between the photographs: they are all 'images of sound'. The last package, sent after Max has spent time in the field, contains a cassette tape. Having played it, Kathleen believes it to be blank. But when her husband arrives home, and

---

5   Graham Billing (1965) *Forbush and the penguins*. Holt, Rinehard and Winston, New York, 1966 edn.
6   Billing (1965) *Forbush and the penguins*, p. 86.
7   Billing (1965) *Forbush and the penguins*, p. 87.
8   Laurence Fearnley (2006) *Degrees of Separation*. Penguin New Zealand, Auckland.
9   Fearnley (2006) *Degrees of Separation*, p. 72.
10 Laurence Fearnley (1998) 'The Piper and the Penguin'. In Bill Manhire, ed. (2004) *The wide white page: writers imagine Antarctica*. Victoria University Press, Wellington, pp. 246–58.
11 Fearnley (1998) 'The Piper and the Penguin', p. 246.

listens to the tape for hours and days on end, she realises it is not blank but a recording of silence. Their relationship too is silenced, as her husband becomes increasingly non-communicative, withdrawn, and obsessed with his enigmatic encounter with the sounds of Antarctica. Max himself seems to become a silent continent.

The travails of a composer travelling on an arts fellowship are central to American writer Lucy Jane Bledsoe's recent novel *The Big Bang Symphony*.[12] Her composer, Mikala Wilbo, heads to the South Pole with the American program to write a symphony inspired by the cosmological work underway there: her rather ambitious brief to the National Science Foundation (NSF) is that she will 'musically represent the Big Bang'. Once arrived — and still dealing with a past personal trauma — she is unable to write a note. She practises scales, plays Bach and procrastinates. While she can *see* the music, she tells a fellow expeditioner, she is unable to 'create *sound*' with it. Her Antarctic experiences, however, eventually remove the obstacles to her expression, and the novel ends with the central characters listening to an orchestral performance of her piece, 'a song of aching beauty … that carrie[s] all the epic hope of that continent'.[13]

These are just a few examples of Antarctic fiction in which music and sound play a central role, but even this small sample space suggests some shared thematic preoccupations. Both Fearnley's and Bledsoe's stories highlight the anxieties of the composer sent south with an official artistic mission — but this may, of course, be a version of the novelist's own literary anxieties, disguised and distanced from the author by being projected onto a different artform. More fundamental is the sense in these literary texts that musical creativity is both an instinctive response to the continent — the way, in fact, of accessing or expressing its most essential 'voice' — and simultaneously the source of frustration, obsession and near madness.

Readers too experience a frustration, in the inability of the narrative to actually present the sonic or musical event at its heart. Readers can't, of course, hear the symphony that gives Bledsoe's novel its name and nicely resolved ending; we can't listen to the recordings that Fearnley's sonic artist makes, or even the particular kind of silence that holds the composer Max spellbound; and we don't know what noises Forbush manages to produce out of his water-bottle xylophone.

This absence is characteristic of prose fiction dealing with music and sound, which must be represented textually, through words on the page. But it doesn't characterise all literature — for sound and music bear a much more immediate relationship to the other, more aural modes of literary production: drama and

---

12 Lucy Jane Bledsoe (2010) *The Big Bang Symphony*. Terrace-University of Wisconsin Press, Madison WI.
13 Bledsoe (2010) *The Big Bang Symphony*, p. 330.

poetry. I could write here about Antarctic drama, theatre and performance — there is plenty of material. The history of theatrical uses of Antarctica is rich, if a little bizarre at times, and both sound and music are pivotal. There is, for example, the production *Australis, or the City of Zero* (1900): this was staged to celebrate Australia's Federation, and proposed, tongue-in-cheek, that the national capital be located at the South Pole.[14] Feted as an 'entirely Original, Musical and Spectacular, Pantomimic Extravaganza of the Future', it incorporated a full operatic chorus and orchestra, and featured, among other things, 'A Comic Ballet of Polar Animals'.[15] Equally peculiar but more disturbing is the opera *Das Opfer* ('The Sacrifice'),[16] with a 12-tone musical score by the composer Winfried Zillig (a student of Arnold Schoenberg), and a libretto adapted from the prizewinning play *Die Südpolexpeditions des Kapitans Scott* (1929), by Reinhard Goering. The opera, which dealt with the final days of Robert F Scott's last expedition and featured a singing, dancing chorus of penguins, closed after only a few performances, possibly due to Nazi displeasure.[17] Better known is a slightly later response to Scott's expedition, Douglas Stewart's mid-century verse play for radio *The Fire on the Snow*. In its original 1941 broadcast, the play featured only the sound of wind in addition to human voices.[18] Then there is the off-off-Broadway musical comedy *Meet the Real Ernest Shackleton* (2004),[19] in which the banjo takes a prominent part; it was this instrument, salvaged from the wreck of the *Endurance*, which helped relieve the tedium of Shackleton's stranded men. Like most theatre, Antarctic performances almost always combine literary text and sound, and often music.

But the relationship between literature and sound that I want to focus on here, after this rather long preamble, is the more inextricable one achieved in poetry — the mode of literature in which the sound of words, the rhythm of speech, the repetitions and the pauses, are most central. To put it simply: poets tend to be interested in sound. It is striking, but not suprising, how many poems about the continent deal explicitly with sound or music. Here, I have space to examine only a handful, from diverse historical, literary and geographical contexts.

---

14   Bernard Epinasse, and JC Williamson (1900) *Australis; or the City of Zero*. Libretto. J Andrew, Sydney. ML Q792.4/W 1-53, Mitchell Library, State Library of New South Wales, Sydney, p. 72.
15   Epinasse and Williamson (1900) *Australis; or the City of Zero*, pp. 1, 11.
16   Winfried Zillig (1937) *Das Opfer: Oper von Reinhard Goering*. Libretto by Reinhard Goering, piano-vocal score. Bärenreiter-Verlag, Kassel, 1960.
17   Hanne Nielsen and Elizabeth Leane (2013) '"Scott of the Antarctic" on the German stage: Reinhard Goering's *Die Südpolexpedition des Kapitans Scott*'. *New Theatre Quarterly* 29(3): 278–93, p. 290.
18   Gus Worby (1996) 'The Fire on the Snow: The Penguin's Egg'. In Douglas Stewart *The Fire on the Snow*. Currency, Paddington, NSW: ix–xviii, p. xii.
19   'Meet the Real Ernest Shackleton: a Comedy About Antarctica'. Written and dir. Michael Christian, choreographed by Ron Schwinn, music by Terry Radigan. Perf. Sande Shurin Theatre, New York City, 9–26 Sept 2004.

At the risk of being predictable, I will begin with Samuel Taylor Coleridge's 'The Rime of the Ancient Mariner,' originally published in 1798.[20] As the first example of Antarctic poetry, and arguably Antarctic literature, in English, Coleridge's gothic horror ballad has exerted an influence on the later literature of the continent that is probably second to no other text. It is also, incidentally, the earliest piece of Antarctic literature that has been put to music. Musical responses have varied considerably. They range from a cantata by John Francis Barnett, performed at the Birmingham Triennial Musical Festival in 1867 (see Figure 1), to the closing, 13-minute number of the 1984 album *Powerslave* by the heavy metal rock group Iron Maiden. It is not surprising that the poem is so readily adapted as song lyrics, because its rhyme and rhythm are so strong — a point to which I will return.

In 'The Rime of the Ancient Mariner,' the old sailor of the poem's title tells of a sea journey from Britain down to the South Polar regions and back again. In the Antarctic, the mariner for no obvious reason shoots a friendly albatross, and is thereafter subjected to all manner of hideous supernatural punishments — including the final penance of having to re-tell his tale indefinitely to people he mysteriously singles out. On this occasion he relates his story to an unwilling but enthralled wedding guest — the whole gothic tale takes place against the ironic background of the 'merry din' of the nuptial feast which the guest should be attending. In Gustave Doré's famous illustrations to an 1876 edition of Coleridge's poem, the corresponding image foregrounds the musicians (see Figure 2).

Only a relatively small section of this long poem is actually set in the Antarctic — about ten of over 140 stanzas. The following three occur at the point in the poem where the ship first enters the South Polar regions.

> And now there came both mist and snow,
> And it grew wondrous cold:
> And ice, mast-high, came floating by,
> As green as emerald.
>
> And through the drifts the snowy cliffs
> Did send a dismal sheen:
> Nor shapes of men nor beasts we ken —
> The ice was all between.
>
> The ice was here, the ice was there,
> The ice was all around:
> It cracked and growled, and roared and howled,
> Like noises in a swound. (l. 51–62).

---

20 Samuel Taylor Coleridge (1798) 'The Rime of the Ancient Mariner'. In John Leonard, ed. (2003) *Seven centuries of poetry in English*, 5th edn. Oxford University Press, Melbourne, pp. 310–24.

Figure 1. Score for John Francis Barnett's cantata 'The Ancient Mariner: a cantata' (Novello, London, n.d.).

Source: Author's copy.

Figure 2. 'Red as a Rose is the Bride', one of Gustave Doré's illustrations from Coleridge's 'The Rime of the Ancient Mariner', originally published in an 1876 edition of the poem.

Source: Wikimedia Commons.

These stanzas present the Antarctic through different senses — tactile, visual, and finally aural. They are dominated by the presence of ice, which is simultaneously beautiful and threatening. Although the ice is at first perceived as jewel-like, very soon it becomes oppressive in its unrelenting presence, relieved only by disquieting sounds. The marginal gloss (which Coleridge added in his 1817 edition of the poem) notes that these lines describe 'The land of ice, and of fearful sounds where no living thing was to be seen'. While visually the ice is disturbingly lifeless, aurally it is the opposite: the noises themselves are fearful precisely because they uncannily mimic those of a living creature — a fierce, mutable and monstrous one.

But it is the poem's own sounds as much as the sounds the mariner explicitly reports that characterise the Antarctic in the poem. The 'Rime' has an alternating tetrameter and trimeter metre, an a-b-c-b rhyme scheme (with some irregular stanzas), as well as plentiful internal rhyme, alliteration and repetition — and all are evident in these lines. These features are typical of the ballad genre, but in this poem about ice they take on particular resonances. The rhythmic repetition of the same words — 'The ice was here, the ice was there' — in these stanzas give a sense of the all-pervasiveness of the sea-ice surrounding the ship. The sense of confused, intimidating noises that the last two lines evoke is reinforced by that strange final word, 'swound' — an archaic term for 'swoon' or fainting fit — which itself confuses the rhyme. As Susan Wolfson notes in her essay 'Sounding Romantic', visually it seems to suggest not only the word 'sound' but also 'wound' and 'swoon' (par. 16), and the first-time reader might hesitate over whether it does indeed rhyme with 'around', or is merely an eye-rhyme — a visual resemblance: '*swound* is a ghost of *sound*, a rhyme-word that lurks in the aural field without precipitating … However one speaks it, the stress of *swound* hits the ear as a wounded *sound*' (par. 16).[21]

The sound of 'swound', however, is only a faint echo of what is achieved in the poem's title with the single word, 'Rime'. This is, of course, another of Coleridge's archaisms — an early spelling of the word we now write as 'rhyme' — but it is a particularly significant one. In the decades of revisions that Coleridge made to the poem, he removed many other archaisms in the text and the title, but not this one. One obvious reason for this is the significance of the pun on this word, which also can mean 'hoar-frost' — the ice deposited on surfaces by freezing fog or mist. In *Romantic weather: the climates of Coleridge and Baudelaire*, Arden Reed devotes a whole chapter just to teasing out this pun.[22] Reed argues convincingly that the Mariner himself, whose beard 'with age is hoar' (l. 620),

---

21 Susan Wolfson 'Sounding Romantic'. '"Soundings of Things Done": the poetry and poetics of sound in the Romantic ear and era'. Romantic Circle Praxis Series. Online, available at http://www.rc.umd.edu/praxis/soundings/about.html.
22 Arden Reed (1983) *Romantic weather: the climates of Coleridge and Baudelaire*. University Press of New England, Hanover.

and whose appearance startles those he encounters, is himself a 'piece of rime, or frozen mist', condemned to wander the earth continually telling the same tale, in a kind of 'suspended animation' — frozen in time.[23] Thus while only a short section of the tale takes place in the Antarctic, the Antarctic inhabits the tale-teller himself. But Reed goes on to point out a more complex relationship evoked by the pun. The Mariner's story, repeated over and over again to selected unwilling listeners, is related not in prose but in rhyme, a literary device which itself achieves its effect through constant repetition of sound; so, sound, like the Mariner, is in a sense frozen, held in suspended animation, through rhyme. The 'rime' — or hoar-frost — of the title, argues Reed, becomes a metaphor for 'frozen language'.[24]

When Coleridge wrote the 'Rime', he had never left Britain — never even crossed the English channel. He took most of his polar imagery from high-latitude travel narratives, both north and south. He had read James Cook's account of his circumnavigation of the South Polar region, and one of his school teachers, William Wales, had been a navigator on the journey.[25] Cook did not see the continent, only its surrounding waters and ice; nothing was known at this time of the interior plateau. Thus Coleridge's Antarctica is noisy, full of the cracks and groans of icebergs and sea ice.

With the exploration of the continent itself in the early 20th century, silence emerged as a key component of poetic responses. In some cases, these responses can be interpreted as attempts to ward off silence. For men sledging for days on the relatively featureless plateau, silence could be oppressive. Poetry and song, recited aloud or in one's head, formed a welcome release. Apsley Cherry-Garrard recommended the use a volume of poems in the field 'because it gave one something to learn by heart and repeat during the blank hours of the daily march'.[26] 'Sledging songs' — motivational verses composed on the march, recounting the challenges of the journey and celebrating its achievements, often put to the tune of a sea-shanty or music-hall song — were particularly important. Their rhyme and rhythm matched the repetitive onward tramp of sledging, and their personal content and well-known melodies gave a homely familiarity to the alien icescape. Morton Moyes, who spent more than two months alone in a hut on an ice shelf during the Australasian Antarctic Expedition, identified silence as one of the worst of his trials. Even music he played on the gramophone 'seemed only to emphasise the heavy burden of silence that gave no peace'. Yet, when his release from this oppression finally arrived, it was heralded by music of a different kind:

---

23 Reed (1983) *Romantic weather*, pp. 154–5, 178.
24 Reed (1983) *Romantic weather*, p. 180.
25 Bernard Smith (1992) *Imagining the Pacific: in the wake of the Cook voyages*. Melbourne University Press, Carlton, Vic., pp. 135–71.
26 Apsley Cherry-Garrard (1922) *The worst journey in the world*. Picador-Macmillan, London 1994, p. 203.

> Then came the day when I felt the solitude had at last beaten me. As I sat writing up my journal, I thought I heard a sledging song, one of those rollicking ditties we used to sing to boost our morale. I stood up, alarmed by the fancy, shaking with a sense of confusion. I'm going dippy, I thought. This is it. I stared stupidly about me. I heard the singing again, as faint and elusive as the far-off note of a bugle.[27]

The return of his companions was announced not by a visual but an aural signal, a breaking of the silence of his isolation.

For some explorers silence was not an oppressor but an active participant in the Antarctic experience, one who constantly drew or lured the expeditioner towards the south. In Edward Wilson's 'The Barrier Silence', published in the *South Polar Times* in 1902,[28] silence signifies mystery and secrecy, the enigmatic Pole he hoped to reach. In 'The Silence Calling,' often attributed to Douglas Mawson but actually the last verse of Robert Service's poem 'L'Envoi' (1909) slightly adapted by Mawson for Antarctic purposes, 'the frozen music of star-yearning heights' is likewise a lure.[29] The fatal journey of Scott, Wilson and company in 1911–12 made this metaphor less tenable, and gave polar silence other associations. In Stewart's retelling of this fateful polar journey, *The Fire on the Snow*, silence unsurprisingly signifies death: 'The living thing is the word / And the thing dead is silence. / These men of their own accord / Move away into silence / Their skis soft on the snow'.[30] At the end of the century this silence/death equation is still very evident in Antarctic poetry. Chris Wheat's 'Antarctica', which deals with a man succumbing to HIV/AIDS, begins: 'Antarctica is a continent without music, / as silent as starched sheets'.[31] The connection is particularly strong in poems written in response to the Erebus disaster, such as Michael Wilson's 'In Memory of Erebus'[32] and Mary Dilworth's 'Air Disaster, Antarctica',[33] which is why, I think, it is so effective that Bill Manhire framed his recent, more uplifting poetic commemoration of the crash as 'Erebus Voices'.[34] Another strong association is between silence and white: Alexandra Bates's poem, 'Rondeau, Ridge A, Antarctica', begins, 'Can you hear the sounds of titanium white? / Shh, we're trying to paint the quiet'.[35] Of course, silence and quiet are not exactly the same thing; the latter has more

---

27 Morton Moyes (1964), as told to George Dovers and D'Arcy Niland. Season in Solitary. *Walkabout* 30(10) October: 20–3, p. 23.
28 Edward Wilson (1902) 'The Barrier Silence'. *South Polar Times* 3: 151.
29 Douglas Mawson / Robert Service (1977) 'The Silence Calling'. *Canberra Times* 7 June, p. C5.
30 Douglas Stewart (1944) *The Fire on the Snow*. pp. 1–42 in *The Fire on the Snow and The Golden Lover: two plays for radio*. Angus and Robertson, Sydney, p. 9.
31 Chris Wheat (1996) 'Antarctica'. *Meanjin* 55(1): 132–7.
32 Michael Wilson (1989) 'In Memory of Erebus'. *Muse* (Arts Council of Australia, ACT Division) 83 Nov: 15.
33 Mary Dilworth (1993) 'Air Disaster, Antarctica'. *Riding to a Paradise*. Jacaranda, Milton, p. 76.
34 Bill Manhire (2005) 'Erebus Voices'. *Lifted*. Victoria University Press, Wellington: pp. 40–1.
35 Alexandra Bates (2010) 'Rondeau, Ridge A, Antarctica'. *Meanjn* 69(1): 226.

peaceful resonances, something that is evident in Frank Debenham's poem 'The Quiet Land' (1956).[36] But the difference between the silent continent and the quiet land is the topic for another essay.

One Antarctic poem which places a very high value on silence is Denis Glover's 'How Doth My Good Cousin Silence?', published in 1963:

> The one time silent regions of the Pole
> Are now vociferous, upon the whole.
> Where Amundsen stormed in with cold deceit
> And Scott's grim team toiled on to outface defeat
> Now Neptune navy boys, pre-heated upper lip,
> Roar in to land on Coca-Cola Strip
> And great Sir Hillary's ice-breaker jaw
> Drums in with tractors. What a bore.
>
> O Pole, thou should'st be silent as before.
>
>> But, quoth the London Committee, and the Ross
>> Sea Committee, and the chewing-gum boys, and the
>> Ob and the Grab and the IGY scientists
>> and sickeners, and Life and Time, and all the
>> quarrel-thickeners,
>>   *Nevermore.*[37]

In this playful and satirical poem, Antarctic silence signifies not death but purity, and humanity's intrusion on the continent is figured in terms of noise pollution. Perhaps ironically, from a 21st-century perspective, the speaker is disillusioned with the cushiness of mid-century Antarctic activity and the associated bureaucracy. Bookending the text are quotations from the work of two seminal poetic figures. The title is a line drawn from Shakespeare's *Henry IV, Part II*; in that play the character of Silence is mostly true to his name — the exception being the bawdy drinking songs he favours when under the influence. Like the continent, he shifts readily from near-silence to boisterousness. At the other end of the poem, of course, is the famous refrain from 'The Raven', by Edgar Allan Poe — who, as a writer of prose fiction, rivals Coleridge for his influence on Antarctic literature.

In between, Glover's poem itself uses rhythm and rhyme to reinforce its contrast of the silent, pure, pre-exploration Pole with the corporatised, tamed Antarctica of the late 1950s — the period of the International Geophysical Year (IGY). The

---

36 Frank Debenham (1956) 'The Quiet Land'. In June Debenham Backs, ed. (1992) *The Quiet Land: the Antarctic diaries of Frank Debenham*. Bluntisham Books, Bluntisham, p. 10.
37 Denis Glover (1963) 'How Doth My Good Cousin Silence?' *Denis Glover's bedside book*. Reed, Wellington, p. 122. Reproduced with kind permission from the Denis Glover estate and the copyright holder, Pia Glover.

poem takes the rough form of a sonnet, although the octave (first eight lines) is made up, unusually but appropriately enough, of heroic couplets. The turn of the sonnet pivots around that ninth line — 'O Pole, though should'st be silent as before' — which, with its faux-Shakespearean language, suggests an element of self-mockery in its expression of nostalgia. Then, when all the voices crowd in upon the continent in the last five lines — voices of committees organising the Fuchs-Hillary expedition, of Russian ice-breakers, of scientists, journalists and bureaucrats — the form turns to something like prose, signifying the mundane and banal, before Poe's raven ironically silences them all with the pessimistic pronouncement that the Pole will be silent no more.

Not all Antarctic poetry in recent years posits such a stark binary between the symbolic silence of the continent and the noise of human interest and inhabitation. I want to turn for my last example to a late 20th-century poem which foregrounds music in its attempt to evoke an Antarctic landscape. This is 'The Music Makers', by Caroline Caddy, a Western Australian poet who travelled south on a writer's residency with the Australian national program in the mid-1990s. The poem was published in her collection *Antarctica* in 1996.

> Over ice that's humped
>   like buried harps and pianos
> through wind scoops
>   melt pots of ancient
>   Chinese music
> all day we peer into the distances
>   of a bushman's song
> about a tree mistaken
> for a man.
> The sun slides on we stop
>   in the huge ocarina
>   of Antarctica.
> La da da da da I explain
>   ni naw ni naw ni he says.
> We stamp our feet and blow into
>   our cupped hands
> the colours of Neptune Jupiter and Mars
>   leaning in
>   to hear.[38]

Landscape and music seem to become one in this poem. Not only do the speaker and her companion journey through an icescape shaped like buried musical

---

[38] Caroline Caddy (1996) 'The Music Makers'. *Antarctica*. Fremantle Arts Centre, South Fremantle, p. 69. Thanks to Caroline Caddy for permission to quote from this poem, and for her comments on the poem.

instruments, the continent itself takes on the form of an ancient wind instrument — the ocarina — with wind-scoops in the ice acting as the finger holes. The actions of the expeditioners too — stamping feet, blowing into cupped hands — produce a kind of music, and their words, emptied of linguistic meaning, become nonsense lyrics.

'The Music Makers' gains a layer of complexity from its title, which references Edward Elgar's choral composition of the same name (1912), which in turn sets to music the text of British poet Arthur O'Shaughnessy's 'Ode', from his 1874 collection *Music and Moonlight*.[39] O'Shaugnessy's poem, which famously begins 'We are the music makers, / And we are the dreamers of dreams', highlights both the isolation and the significance of the poet or 'music maker'. Caddy's poem suggests a complex relationship between the poet and the environment — both 'music makers' of a kind. Commenting on her poem, Caddy notes that 'in Antarctica there is no particular rhyme in the wind and no rhythm as we know it in the cracking of the ice, and all our efffforts to describe it to ourselves can only be an echo of ourselves'.[40] With its lack of any obvious meter or rhyme scheme, absence of expected punctuation and slightly irregular spacing of words, the poem suggests a primarily visual rather than aural pattern. Its conclusion, Caddy reflects, is a 'synesthesia of colours of the late sun in Antarctica', evoking 'the colours of the planets as we seem them', Gustav Holst's orchestral suite *The Planets* and the philosophical concept of 'the music of the spheres'. This 'transposition of senses' is for the poet an effect of the vastness and unknowability of the Antarctic.[41]

I could give many other examples of recent Antarctic poems in which music and sound — or their absence — play a prominent part. But my intention is not to be exhaustive; rather, it is to establish poetry as not merely a way of textually representing the sounds of the Antarctic, but as itself a form of sonic response to the continent. It is, of course, both of these things simultaneously, and that is a key part of its power. In addition, these poems indicate the range of possible engagements with Antarctic sound. The continent is a growling beast in Coleridge's poem; the silent backdrop to the rousing tunes of expeditioners in heroic-era sledging songs; the passive auditor of a chatterbox humanity in Glover's sonnet; and an enormous natural instrument in Caddy's 'Music Makers'. Antarctica has inspired diverse poetic voices, and, as long as the continent means something to humanity, it unlikely that these will fall silent.

---

39 Arthur O'Shaugnessy (1874) 'The Music Makers'. In Caroline Blyth, ed. (2009) *Decadent verse: an anthology of Late Victorian poetry, 1872–1900*. Anthem, London, pp. 501–3.
40 Caroline Caddy 2014 letter to the author.
41 Caroline Caddy 2014 letter to the author.

Playing Antarctica: Making music with natural objects and sounds from the Antarctic Peninsula

Cheryl E Leonard[1]

The project

In 2008 I was awarded a grant from the Antarctic Artists and Writers Program of the United States National Science Foundation to develop a series of musical compositions inspired by environments and ecosystems on the Antarctic Peninsula. This grant enabled me to spend five weeks at Palmer Research Station during the austral summer of 2008–09 collecting materials for my project *Antarctica: Music From the Ice*.

The project is a set of ten musical works in which Antarctic field recordings are combined with sounds produced on natural-object instruments, primarily materials from the Antarctic Peninsula. Each piece is based on an aspect of the environment near Palmer Station and connects to scientific research underway in the region. Compositions are scored out and performed live on stage by a small ensemble. The completed works are being recorded and will be released digitally and on CD in 2015.

Antarctica: Music From the Ice grows out of my extensive previous experience creating compositions, improvisations, and instruments that investigate sounds, structures, and objects from the natural world. Over the past decade I have developed many works based on subjects such as cloud formations, estuary ecosystems, geological formations, and the properties of water. Since 2003 I have been composing with sounds from found natural materials, often building sculptural instruments from pinecones, bark, driftwood, shells, bones, feathers, and more. By amplifying such materials with contact, condenser, and underwater microphones, very quiet sounds hidden within them are revealed and voices of surprising character and intricacy emerge.

A passion for wild and remote places drives my creative process and I have a particular fondness for glaciers and alpine environments. Shrouded in ice, largely untouched, and inaccessible to most people, Antarctica was the ultimate

---

1   Ms Cheryl Leonard, 2352 Fulton St, San Francisco, CA 94118, USA, cheryleleonard@gmail.com.

subject for me, and the opportunity to make music in and about the frozen continent was endlessly exciting. I was especially curious about unique wind, wildlife, water, and ice sounds I might encounter there, and was eager to see what new voices I might coax out of Antarctic rocks, shells, bones, and ice.

At Palmer Station

Palmer Research Station is located on Anvers Island off the Antarctic Peninsula at 64°46' S, 64°03' W. It is the smallest of the three permanent research stations operated by the United States in Antarctica, with a summer population of around 40 people. There is no airstrip at Palmer, so to reach the station one must travel by boat from the tip of South America across the Drake Passage. I sailed south from Punta Arenas, Chile, on the *Lawrence M Gould*, a 76 m long US research vessel, which can carry up to 26 researchers and 15 crew members. The *Gould*'s maximum speed is around 11 knots, and the ship usually takes about four days to sail from Punta Arenas to Palmer Station.

Upon our arrival at Palmer the other visiting artist, Oona Stern, and I were schooled in station procedures, Antarctic survival, ocean rescue, and the safe operation of 'zodiacs' — the small but hardy inflatable boats used for local transport. After a few days of supervised boating we were assigned our own zodiac, dubbed the *Artboat 66*, and were free to roam within the safe boating area, which extends in a two-mile radius around the station. Although this might sound like a very limited range, we experienced no shortage of fascinating destinations. Many small islands are located within the boating limits, each with its own unique character, landforms, wildlife populations, and sounds. Several calving edges of the Marr Ice Piedmont, the massive glacier that blankets most of Anvers Island, were also within bounds, and an endless stream of icebergs and brash ice floated through the area.

Each day at Palmer, Oona and I set out from the station and explored our surroundings. If the weather was fair and winds were below 20 knots, we hopped in the *Artboat 66* and motored out to neighbouring islands or worked on the sea out of our zodiac. In stormy conditions, when boating was out of the question, I wandered around the 'backyard' behind the station, scrambling over rocky glacial moraine and up onto a little crevasse-free toe of the glacier.

One of the things that surprised me most about the Antarctic Peninsula was what a noisy and vibrant place it could be. In contrast to the usual rendering of Antarctica as a barren, white, quiet (except for the wind) land, during my visit Palmer Station's environs teemed with life, sound, and even patches of vivid colour. Krill swarmed in the sea, all the birds were nesting, seals floated by on bergy bits, and humpback whales regularly cruised through our local waters. Bright green mosses flourished in protected nooks, and splashes of brilliant yellow and orange lichen adorned rocky outcrops.

The kazooing of distant penguin colonies mixed with explosive snorts and howls from elephant seals, barking fur seals, squawking skuas, and squeaky terns. Meanwhile, the Marr Ice Piedmont punctuated the soundscape with great booms and gunshots as it calved immense towers of ice into the sea. The remains of these demolitions disintegrated into snapping, popping icebergs and great swathes of clinking brash ice that were regularly washed out into the open ocean. Beneath the glacier's dissolving walls water drips played gamelan-like melodies, and on the surface of the Marr small meltwater streams gurgled in cyclical rhythms or moaned and sang. Finally, framing all these busy sonorities were the ever present, ever changing intonations of wind and waves.

Figure 1. Small iceberg near Shortcut Island. The mountains in the distance are on the mainland peninsula about 30 kilometres away.

Source: Photo by Cheryl E Leonard.

Field recordings

During my forays through these rich environs I collected many hours of field recordings, some captured in the air, and some underwater via a pair of hydrophones.

I was immediately drawn to the melodious footsteps of the adelie penguins on Torgersen Island, and these sounds never ceased to delight me. Torgersen, on which thousands of pairs of adelies raise their young each year, is covered in shards of a dense, sonorous, igneous rock. As the penguins ambled along well-worn paths between colonies and beaches, the stone fragments clinked under their feet, producing delicate music. It was great fun to set my microphones up along the edge of a walkway and record lines of birds jingle-jangling by.

The southern elephant seals were another one of my favourite recording subjects. I first heard them during an early zodiac outing to a cove on Amsler Island. As we turned off the outboard motor and slowly drifted across the water, deep alien bellows emerged from the far end of the cove, echoing off the 30-foot tall walls of ice on either side of us. There in the water a couple of dark shapes tumbled and splashed. Several more massive creatures lay side-by-side on the shore. I quickly pulled out my pocket recorder, but after a few short minutes the seals' outlandish calls ended abruptly.

Thus began my quest to record elephant seal vocalisations. I returned to Amsler Island numerous times hoping to find them howling in the cove's sheltered waters, but instead they were always piled up on the shore, fast asleep. I made several fine recordings of snoring, snoozing seals, but still I longed to capture their haunting roars.

Finally, I decided to camp out on the island for a night. I waited for a window of fair weather and then, one balmy evening, was dropped off on Amsler a few hours before sunset. Shortly after the departing zodiac's motor faded into the distance, I heard it, the faint bawls and bellows, splashes and sputters, of southern elephant seals in the water. This time there weren't just a couple of them cavorting, there were over a dozen, sparring in pairs in the shallow cove. I don't know why it hadn't occurred to me before that the elephant seals might be nocturnal! Suddenly it was painfully obvious why they were conked out on the beach all day. In the long Antarctic dusk the seals' playful martial dances and eerie roars were mesmerizing. I watched, listened, and recorded until, in the wee hours of the night, I could no longer feel my toes.

Perhaps the most surprising animal vocalisation I heard at Palmer was the noise an Antarctic fur seal made when I happened upon it at close range. Although they look like adorable sea puppies, fur seals are creatures to be wary of. They can run faster than a human on land and have been known to bite people when they feel threatened. Thus, when I unexpectedly ran into one napping on a grassy hummock in the middle of Amsler Island it was with heightened alertness that I pulled out my microphones. The seal looked up, I got ready to run, and then it produced a kind of nervous whimpering which was not at all what I was expecting from a creature that might chase me down and chomp on me.

I also spent a lot of time recording ice: drifting brash, bergy bits and icebergs, and the disintegrating edges of the glacier. Out on the sea, I lowered my hydrophones over the sides of the zodiac to record the ice underwater at different depths, or tempted fate by leaning out over the water with a pair of expensive condenser microphones in my hand. The floating ice emitted an astonishing array of sounds. Smaller fragments clinked and thunked against each other, sometimes chaotically, sometimes in repeating rhythms. Waves thumped and boomed in hollows carved into larger pieces. Areas of pureed ice sloshed against the zodiac's rubber sides, giving the impression that we were floating in a giant slushie. Often the melting ice snapped and popped, as air that had been trapped inside the glacial ice for who-knows-how-long was released.

Figure 2. Recording brash ice from the zodiac.

Source: Photo by Oona Stern.

On land I staked out the Marr Ice Piedmont in order to capture the thunderous booms and cracks it produced as great chunks of ice calved off its waterfront edges into the sea. I also recorded small meltwater streams on the glacier's periphery and had the opportunity to descend inside two crevasses farther up on the Marr.

From the surface of the glacier the crevasses didn't look like much, just ominous cracks in the snow, but inside lay ornate azure caverns adorned with thousands of icicles. Because it was summer and temperatures were above freezing, hanging on a rope inside a crevasse was a lot like taking a shower. First, I recorded just the multitude of water drops, and then I began to play some nearby icicles, cautiously tapping them with a pair of superball mallets. Lovely clear pitches emerged. Unfortunately, often the icicles fractured just as I started to get nice resonant tones from them and they fell shattering in the icy depths beneath me. Although I knew they would grow back in a few days it was a little upsetting to be destroying the icicles. On the other hand, they produced a magnificent mad-xylophonist cacophony as they fell, bouncing and echoing for a surprisingly long time.

Collecting natural objects

In addition to making field recordings while onsite at Palmer Station, with special permission I also gathered limpet shells, penguin bones, and rocks to bring back to the United States and use as musical instruments.

On my inaugural excursion into Palmer's rubbly 'backyard' I came across a few scattered limpet shells. Delighted, and grinning like a small child on a treasure hunt, I greedily gathered up all the shells I could find — about five or six of them. They clinked pleasingly as I turned them over in my palms and wobbled them on a flat granite slab. Excitedly, I returned to the station to show off my find, but was disappointed when none of the veteran Palmerites seemed very impressed. This puzzled me, because I had walked all over the moraine behind the station and had only been able to find a few shells.

Shortly thereafter I visited DeLaca Island. As soon as I scrambled up onto the island's stony ramparts I understood — here were limpet shells heaped up by the thousands. As it turns out, Antarctic limpets (*Nacella concinna*) are very common in the Antarctic Peninsula and are an important food source for gulls and sea stars. The giant piles of limpet shells on DeLaca were the remains of many, many kelp gull meals. The gulls swallow the limpets whole and then regurgitate the shells. Interestingly, if they are not eaten sooner, *Nacella concinna* can live to be over 100 years old, so it's likely that many of the shells I collected are older than I am.

From two other islands near the station, Torgersen and Breaker, I gathered stones. Breaker Island is formed from an igneous rock that tends to break into thin plates. Tapping my way around Breaker's craggy edifices I found that many of them emitted ringing, pitched tones. I assembled a set of eight small slabs, which together form a pleasing scale, to bring home.

From Torgersen Island, home to many adelie penguin rookeries, I selected a handful of the stones these birds use to build their nests. Adelies have raised chicks on Torgersen for hundreds of years and, over that time, their nesting stones have become highly polished from use. I chose stones from an abandoned nesting site, where a now-extinct colony once thrived. The little glossy rock shards chime like pieces of glass.

Strewn among the rocks of many islands I often found small, sun-bleached bones, usually the remains of adelie penguins. In areas where adelies nest, bones are readily found on the outskirts of colonies. Skuas linger there, always on the lookout for weak chicks or injured adults to attack and eat. I amassed an assortment of adelie bones — including leg and wing bones, pelvises, breastbones, and two skulls — and was eager to see what sounds I could produce with them.

Developing compositions

After a little over a month at Palmer Station it was time to board the *Gould* once again to sail north to Chile, and then take a wearying series of airplanes home to California. Back in my studio in San Francisco I sorted through my field recordings, looking for sounds and ambiences that could form the foundation of compositions, either relatively unchanged, or edited more extensively into musical motives and structures. I also experimented with ways to play the bones, shells, and stones I brought back with me. Searching for distinctive voices, I attached contact mics to these objects or placed them under condenser microphones. I bowed, scraped, tapped, rubbed, brushed, and wobbled until I uncovered voices and textures I liked, sounds that evoked elements of Antarctica.

In order to more easily play the penguin bones and limpet shells, I found I needed to mount them somehow. So I constructed a series of one-of-a-kind instruments using driftwood to hold the bones and shells in place.

Antarctica: Music, sounds and cultural connections

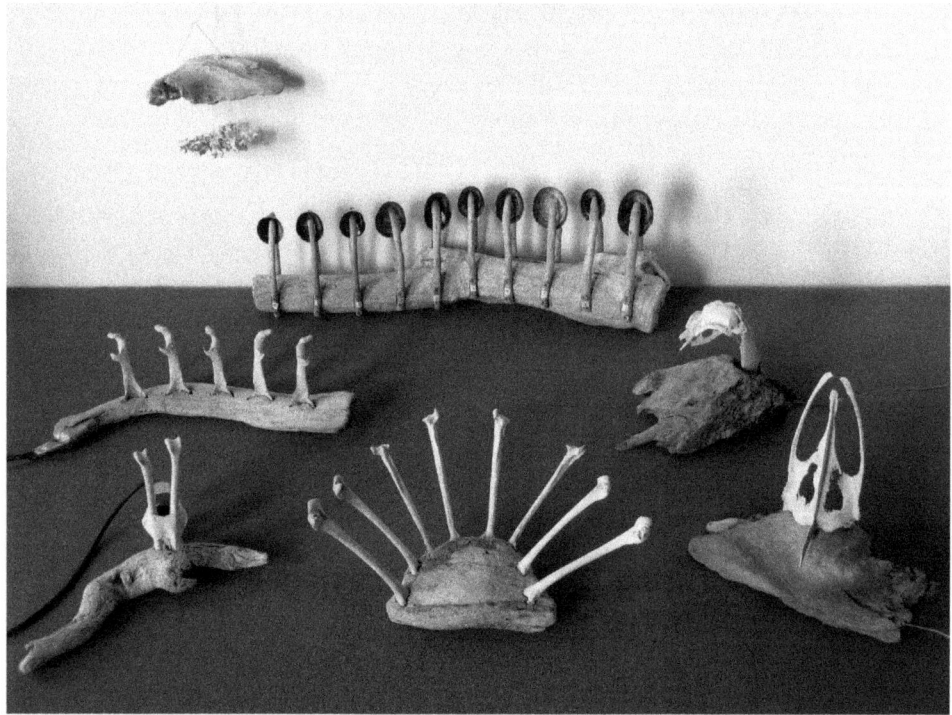

Figure 3. Musical instruments made from penguin bones, limpet shells and driftwood. Left to right: front, 'Bone Slug', 'Octobones', 'Keel'; middle, 'Coracoids', 'Skull'; back, 'Limpet Shell Spine'; hanging, 'Vertebrae Mobile'.

Source: Photo by Cheryl E Leonard.

I selected ten limpet shells that formed a satisfying scale of pitches and mounted them together. This instrument, the 'Limpet Shell Spine,' is played with child-sized violin bows, string, pine needles, and feathers. Out of a dozen or so penguin vertebrae and a piece of bone-white driftwood I built a small mobile. Swinging back and forth against each other, the vertebrae sound remarkably like tiny pieces of ice floating in water. The 'Octobones' and 'Coracoids' instruments were created by attaching penguin leg and wing bones to driftwood stands. There is also the 'Keel,' an adelie breastbone mounted upright. My favourite way to play penguin bones is to bow them. By varying bow placement and pressure, the bones produce sounds that range from soft airy breaths to loud pitched howls and warbles.

Melodies can be played on the rock slabs from Breaker Island by stroking them with wire brushes or other stones, or wobbling or dropping rounded pebbles on them. Adelie nesting stones rubbed together sound like high gusts of wind.

They can also be clinked against each other, another sound reminiscent of brash ice. Of course a wide variety of percussive sounds can also be made with the bones and shells.

After selecting my favourite field recordings and instrumental sounds, I began sculpting them into compositions. My Antarctic works develop from musical elements inherent in the original materials. Aside from amplification, the instruments are not electronically processed in any way, and field recordings are shaped only by editing and layering. Each piece has a unique theme based on an aspect of the Antarctic Peninsula's changing environments and ecosystems, and connected to areas of scientific research in the region. Many of the works relate to recent changes in the climate of the western Antarctic Peninsula: the collapse of local adelie penguin rookeries, morphing weather patterns, and the retreat of local glaciers. The theme of each piece is embodied in its instrumentation, the manner in which objects are played, melodic and rhythmic content, and organisational structures.

Scores and live performances

Because I compose for unusual sound sources, I have developed my own system of notation in order to articulate how to play each piece. I use a combination of graphics and text instructions, sometimes with sections of traditional music notation mixed in. Each piece requires a unique approach to scoring, depending on the instruments and sounds involved. Time in seconds is listed horizontally across the top of my scores, and the parts for each player, plus any field recording parts, are laid out underneath this timeline.

For 'Point Eight Ice' (see score excerpt below), I invented symbols to represent the different kinds of ice sounds in the field recording part. Vertical lines are pops, shaded-in ovals are rhythmic thunks, checkmarks are knocks, and small zigzags indicate scrapes. 'Octo' and 'Lmpts' are the instrumental parts and refer to sounds played on the 'Octobones' and 'Limpet Shell Spine.' Circled numbers specify which bone or shell to play. Playing techniques are described with text, and graphics indicate the rhythms or shapes of each musical gesture. Numbers in otherwise blank rectangles indicate seconds of rest.

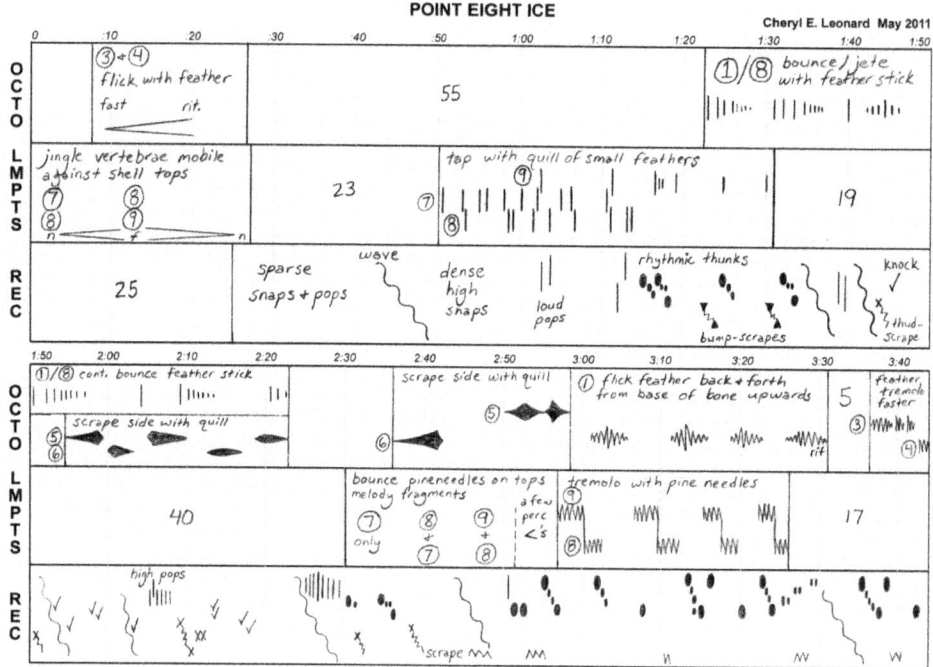

Figure 4. Page 1 of the score for 'Point Eight Ice'.

Source: Author.

I score out my Antarctic compositions so that my ensemble and I can play the pieces live in front of an audience. It is important to me that people are able to experience my Antarctic music live, that they can see the instruments set up on stage and identify how some of the unusual sounds in the music are produced. Live performances also give audiences the opportunity to ask questions, examine the instruments in person, and even try making some sounds on them.

My goal in creating these instruments, musical compositions, and performances is to share a little bit of Antarctica, especially with people who cannot visit the continent themselves. Environments, ecosystems, and the science that investigates them — these elements are important and are embedded in my works. In the end though, my principal hope is that this music helps people feel a meaningful connection to Antarctica, and conveys some of the awe and wonder I experienced during my adventures at Palmer Station.

Suggested reading and listening

Ackerman, Diane (1992) *The moon by whale light*. Vintage Books, New York.

Booth, Joan (2011) *The storied ice: exploration, discovery, and adventure in Antarctica's Peninsula region*. Regent Press, Berkeley CA.

Dunn, David (1999) *Why do whales and children sing?* Earth Ear, Santa Fe NM.

Encounters at the End of the World (2007) Dir. Werner Herzog. Discovery Films.

Gosnell, Mariana (2006) *Ice: the nature, the history, and the uses of an astonishing substance*. Alfred A Knopf, New York.

Hempton, Gordon and John Grossman (2009) *One square inch of silence*. Free Press, New York.

Hooper, Meredith (2008) *The ferocious summer: Adélie penguins and the warming of Antarctica*. Greystone Books, Vancouver.

Jarrett, Brett and Hadoram Shirihai (2008) *The complete guide to Antarctic wildlife: birds and mammals of the Antarctic Continent and the Southern Ocean*, 2nd edn. Princeton University Press, Princeton NJ.

Krause, Bernie (2002) *Wild soundscapes*. Wilderness Press, Berkeley CA.

Leonard, Cheryl (2009) *Chattermarks: Field Recordings from Palmer Station Antarctica* CD. Great Hoary Marmot Music, San Francisco CA.

Lopez, Francisco (2005) *Wind [Patagonia]* CD And/Oar, Seattle WA.

Lopez, Francisco (2007) *Lopez Island* CD. Elevator Bath, Dallas TX.

McGonigal, David and Lynn Woodworth (2003) *Antarctica: the blue continent*. Firefly, Buffalo NY.

Montaigne, Fen (2010) *Fraser's penguins: a journey to the future in Antarctica*. Henry Holt and Co., New York.

Myers, Joan(2006) *Wondrous cold: an Antarctic journey*. Smithsonian Institution, Washington DC.

Nicklen, Paul (2009) *Polar obsession*. National Geographic, Washington DC.

Post, Austin and Edward R Lachapelle (2000) *Glacier ice*. University of Washington Press, Seattle WA.

Pyne, Stephen J (1998) *The Ice: a journey to Antarctica*. University of Washington Press, Seattle WA.

Quin, Douglas (1998) *Antarctica* CD. Miramar Recordings, Seattle WA.

Rivers and Tides: Andy Goldsworthy Working with Time (2003) Dir. Thomas Riedelsheimer, Roxie Releasing.

Rogers, Susan Fox, ed. (2007) *Antarctica: life on the ice*. Solas House, Palo Alto CA.

Rothenberg, David and Marta Ulvaeus, eds (2001) *The book of nature and music*. Wesleyan University Press, Middletown CT.

Schafer, R. Murray (1977) *The soundscape*. Destiny Books, Rochester VT.

Thomas, David N (2004) *Frozen oceans*. Firefly Books, Buffalo NY.

Vear, Craig (2005) *Antarctica: Musical Images from the Frozen Continent* DVD, CD and book. Anthony Craig Vear.

Watson, Chris and BJ Nielsen (2005) *Storm* CD. Touch Music, London.

Winderen, Jana (2009) *Heated* CD. Touch Music, London.

Winderen, Jana (2008) 'Drift,' *Surface Runoff* LP. Touch Music, London.

And I may be some time…

Craig Cormick[1]

Titus Oates is alone on the ice tonight. The blizzard of the previous few days has blown itself out, and he can finally gather his thoughts again. The stars are shining down on him from the deep blackness above, sparkling on the ice. He likes the night sky when he can see it. So different from the perpetual whiteness that otherwise surrounds him and blinds him. When he holds his hands in front of his face he can't see them.

He trudges back to the tent, wondering what the others will say to him when he crawls back into the small canvas cave. He walks back to where it should be, but can't find it. That confuses him and he looks about carefully. It has to be here somewhere, he thinks, and he paces back and forward searching for any sign of it. Perhaps just the dark shape of the pyramid top jutting out of the snow.

Then he remembers, as the thoughts reassemble a little more. They are dead. The tent was collapsed on top of them by the search party. And that was years and years ago. He remembers now how he followed the slow progress of the tent as it was buried under snow and ice as the glacier slowly carried it northwards. He had even tried to estimate when it would finally reach Cape Royds on Ross Island. That would be a reason for celebration, he thinks. The Polar party finally returned.

And he wonders if Scott's hut is still there? He imagines so. People like to preserve things like that. There might be a whole row of them there now, all the huts of subsequent explorers, like terrace houses. But he also wonders if somebody hasn't packed it off back to London and reassembled it in Hyde Park or somewhere. If so, his mother and sister would have gone to visit it and walked carefully around the interior, looking perhaps at the labels on each bed and at each place at the long dining table.

One of the expeditioners might even be employed as a guide and will tell them everything he can remember about the Polar party.

He's not sure what they'll make of Scott though. Will he be considered a valiant hero or a failure?

---

1   Craig Cormick, 12 Giffen Close, Holt ACT 2615, craig_cormick@hotmail.com.

He'd like to ask somebody that. He'd like to know what happened to the Norwegians too. Did they make it back to safety? It would be an irony if they'd fallen down a crevasse or lost their bearings and failed to make it home as well. He's looked for them on the ice at times, but hasn't found any trace of them.

Sometimes, when the wind blows strongly, he can make out the voices of others calling, but can never quite tell who they are. Wailing sounds very similar in any language, he imagines.

He would like to be able to walk back to find Evans' grave though, but there are never enough calm days to allow it. The incessant winds sweep down and scatter his thoughts across the ice, and it takes so much longer to reassemble them again each time.

He imagines that sooner or later he won't be able to reassemble them at all. And that will undoubtedly be the time a party of explorers walks past, retreading Scott's path. One might pause and feel a sudden chill up his spine as Oates tries to reach out to him. But the man would just shrug and go on. What would feel unnatural about a chill in a man's bones on this continent?

They'll walk on and he'll be blown further away like tiny dancing snow particles borne before the winds and scattered forever.

And then he remembers his diary. Of course there was his diary. That was with the dead men in the tent and the expedition party that found them took all the papers away, so his words won't be lost. His written words will survive him. His mother will have received them and kept them under lock and key, guarded safely in her home to make sure no harm came to them. And researchers would be granted access to transcribe them and put them into a book. That thought gives him great satisfaction.

Then another memory comes to him. The site they had pitched their tent when he had crawled out into the blizzard had been the exact site he had recommended to Scott that they build a depot. But he had decreed it would be 30 miles further north. Bloody fool, he thinks. And he remembers the fight he'd had with him over it. Like when Scott had disagreed with his recommendation to work the horses down to exhaustion and then eat them.

It wasn't that he didn't love horses, being a cavalry man, but he knew they were knocked-up old beasts that should never have been purchased and could not be relied upon to do the job needed of them.

Scott had never known war like he had, he thinks, which was why he was unable to make the harsh decisions required. He'd not only fought in the Boer War as Lieutenant Lawrence Oates of the 6th Inniskilling Dragoons, but had been recommended for the Victoria Cross.

He wondered if the powers-that-be had now awarded him a medal for polar bravery and self-sacrifice? Or did they think him a fool as well? That worries him, that the historians will have gone through all their diaries and papers and read just how much animosity there was between them. He can now remember writing: 'I dislike Scott intensely and would chuck the whole thing if it were not that we are a British expedition.' And also that Scott was 'not straight, it is himself first, the rest nowhere…'.

Had he crawled out of that bloody tent just to get away from the others? He looks down at his hands, but still can't see them despite the air being so still. He recalls that he had severe frostbite in both his hands and feet. His war wound in his leg had been plaguing him too. It opened anew and filled with gangrene, making him limp worse than ever. Those last days were hell. Now he can recall the feeling of it. The pain in his extremities. The sickness in his stomach. The anger at knowing he was going to die through the foolishness of others. Or perhaps it was his own foolishness as well.

He'd been so determined to join the expedition and make a name for himself. There was something he had to prove, but he can't quite recall what it was. Something he was ashamed of.

Then he remembers the encounter he'd had with young Henrietta McKendrick in Scotland, as a young man. That had hardly been very heroic of him. She'd not even been quite 12 years old at the time.

He remembers his mother, and the way she had dominated his life. How he'd longed to escape her. And he remembers the men he had killed in the Boer War. He remembers so much, all flooding back at once now. And above all he remembers the loathing he had for his putrefying body, black and pus-ridden, an abomination in this beautiful harsh wilderness.

How could he have not crawled out of the tent into the blizzard?

There is something else he has to remember. But now he feels the wind picking up again. He tries to turn away from it, to maintain his thoughts. What was it he had said to Scott as he had left the tent? It was something vital to remember. Something that keeps him here. But the wind is clawing at him now and his thoughts and memories are plucked from him with its shrill song, and are sent whirling across the empty continent once more.

The nature of sound and the sound of Nature

Philip Samartzis[1]

Abstract

This paper considers ways in which audio recording can be used to offer new ways of experiencing natural environments, through a series of interviews with leading sound artists who have worked in extreme and remote locations. Its aims are to discover why sound artists are increasingly being attracted to dangerous and volatile environments, and what it is that they discover about themselves and their surroundings once they are there. It uses interviews which provide insights into each artist's motives and observations, how they have been marked by their experiences and how these experiences have subsequently influenced the work that they produce. It discusses the effects of undertaking fieldwork in remote locations including the Galapagos Islands, Antarctica, Iceland, the Amazon and the Arctic, and the strategies that each artist used to adapt to the prevailing conditions. It also examines the different concepts and methods informing location field recording and the differences between notions of authentic documentation and constructed composition. As remote locations become increasingly accessible and the popularity of field recording gains traction, it is worth asking whether the artefacts produced are in themselves unique and valuable, or whether it is the personal preoccupations, memories and perceptions of the artist articulated through their recordings that are of most value when listening to these works.

Introduction

> We think in terms of nature as being slow. But you're missing it all the time. It's very very fast.
>
> (Eastley 2006, p. 45)

---

[1] Dr Philip Samartzis, School of Art, RMIT University, GPO Box 2476, Melbourne, VIC 3001, philip.samartzis@rmit.edu.au. This chapter is adapted and enlarged from an essay titled 'Sound artists in extremis' that appeared in *Art Monthly Australia* in November 2009.

Anyone who has taken an interest in the practice of field recording has probably noticed the extremes that artists have gone to in recent years to document difficult and remote locations. Some significant works to emerge from this burgeoning trend include *Antarctica* (1998) by Douglas Quin,[2] *Baikal Ice* (2003) by Peter Cusack,[3] recorded at Lake Baikal in Siberia, *Arctic* (2007) by Max Eastley,[4] and *Wind [Patagonia]* (2007) by Francisco Lopez.[5] Works such as these provide an insight into remote and inhospitable environments that are usually inaccessible to the rest of us. The recordings are often evocative, atmospheric and strange, as faraway environments are probed for specific signifiers that mark them with a highly unusual sonic and spatial imprint.

As someone who has enjoyed the work of these and many other sound artists investigating similar concepts, I asked myself about the logistical and philosophical underpinnings of this often hazardous art practice. What is it about these types of locations that makes them so attractive, and what are the challenges that have to be overcome in order to operate there?

On one hand I am curious about the physical and psychological demands that must be met in adapting to environments that can range from oppressively hot and humid to extremely cold and dry, not to mention the technical challenges that must be overcome to produce a useful artefact. On the other hand I wonder how truly distinctive some of these remote environments are, compared with ones that are much more common and readily available. For instance, how do we differentiate common atmospheric conditions such as precipitation and wind to arrive at a specific reading of a place as being different to another? How effectively does field recording capture the spaces and resonances of a particular location to arrive at a unique experience, or does the experience hinge on a conceptual premise to remove any perceived ambiguity embedded in the recording?

While field recording provides the listener with a sense of place, theorist Rick Altman[6] suggests that the concept of 'faithful documentation' or rendition occludes the more complex relationship between techniques of sound recording and aesthetic and, relatedly, social and political concerns. As listening itself involves a highly subjective psychoacoustic process, it is arguable that any audible event can be accurately rendered, yet the relationship between technique, technology, and aesthetics provides a much more sophisticated way to engage with the environment than ideas around 'faithful documentation'

---

2 Douglas Quin (1998) *Antarctica* CD. Miramar Recordings, Seattle.
3 Peter Cusack (2003) *Baikal Ice (Spring 2003)*, CD. RER Megacorp, Surrey.
4 Max Eastley (2007) *Arctic*, CD. Cape Farewell, London.
5 Francisco Lopez (2007) *Wind [Patagonia]*, CD. And/OAR, Seattle.
6 Rick Altman (1985) The technology of the voice: Part I. *IRIS* 3(1): 3–20; (1986) The technology of the voice: Part II. *IRIS* 4(1): 107–19.

would suggest. In order to unpack these complex issues I asked some of the leading practitioners of location field recording to share their experiences, to reveal the rationale behind their practice and what they discovered about themselves when confronted with an inhospitable landscape.

Inside the circle of fire

English sound recordist Chris Watson is undoubtedly one the primary reasons that field recording has become such a popular activity among sound artists in the last 15 years. Because of the innovative amalgam of concepts and techniques informing his work, the CDs that he has published through UK label Touch provide a major reference for many working in the field (e.g. Watson 2003). Although Watson is clearly focused on the pure documentation of the natural environment, his work is often dynamic and complex, with a great sense of drama present regardless of whether it is a recording of wind, the African savannah or an Arctic iceshelf breaking.[7] I asked Watson what was the most difficult natural environment he has had to work in, and what impediments had to be overcome. He replied:

> I find this a difficult question as many environments are challenging in different ways. Deserts of varying types are some of the most difficult whether these are hot, dry and sandy or frozen glacial plains at the polar regions. However if I have to choose one particular location it would be Isla Santiago in the Galapagos Archipelago. This is a volcanic island formed entirely by swirls of black lava with no vegetation, no shade and no freshwater. I knew from experience what conditions were like on the island, so was prepared with water, sunscreen, a groundsheet to shelter under, recording equipment and food for the one day I was there. A small boat dropped me off just after sunrise and left me there until 1700h when I was collected. The island is uninhabited and I was there on my own. Midday temperatures were around 50 degrees Celsius in the middle of the island, cooler on the coast. The location was certainly unique and consequently had its own particular and special atmosphere.[8]

---

7 Watson, Chris (2003) *Weather Report*, CD. Touch, London.
8 C Watson, pers. comm., 8 May 2009.

Figure 1. Chris Watson on Isla Santiago in the Galapagos Islands.

Source: Image courtesy of the artist.

Atmosphere is an indefinable quality that marks each and every location with a particular aural presence derived from the interplay of acoustics, sound and space. Additional factors such as temperature, humidity, vegetation, and geology contribute to the way sound propagates and the attendant psychoacoustic effects that emerge to define the aural experience. In a common outdoor environment such as a park, these types of interactions produce a familiar ambience often comprised of birdsong, insects, wind and water. However, there are other types of locations whereby a unique set of aural attributes coalesce to provide a more conspicuous atmosphere. What then is it about Isla Santiago that makes it different to other islands of the Galapagos?

> The most westerly islands out in the Galapagos are the youngest, having most recently, in geological terms, emerged from the floor of the Pacific Ocean. Isla Santiago has no vegetation because it has yet to acquire any soil. Its bare volcanic rock is simply a template upon which a future island will emerge. At midday, with no wind, and away from the coastline, the sense and sound of quietness is breathtaking, and it seems difficult to break this ambience by creating any sound. Inland, and inside one of the strange lava tubes that I discovered, I managed to

record one of the quietest animal sounds I have ever heard, the faint yet determined progress of a hermit crab as it scratched its way along the floor of this natural pipeline.[9]

Faster than cold

Douglas Quin is a US-based sound recordist who has travelled widely documenting the natural soundscape — from Antarctic ice to Arctic tundra and from African savannah to Amazon rainforest. Quin's recordings of endangered and disappearing habitats represent one of the most distinctive and extensive collections anywhere. His CD *Antarctica* (1998) of emperor penguins, weddell seals and their pups, wind and glaciers, is a landmark recording that captures life on the ice with startling depth and transparency. I asked Quin about the challenges that confronted him while recording in Antarctica.

> Every opportunity that I have to work in the field presents its own unique set of difficulties and challenges, whether I am recording in a tropical, polar or temperate habitat. In the continuum of considerations that includes weather — with temperature, precipitation and humidity — terrain, accessibility, field support and other variables, I always find that there is a process of reconciling research and anticipation with actual immersion in any given environment. I never take anything for granted and am circumspect with regard to level of difficulty. I always begin my endeavours with an attitude that nothing will ever be as simple as I might, at first, expect it will be. With that said, some of the most demanding fieldwork that I have undertaken has been in polar regions — Antarctica, Greenland and Alaska.
>
> Fieldwork in Antarctica presents very particular challenges and logistical considerations. Most obviously, working outside in freezing temperatures — often well below 0 degrees Fahrenheit and compounded by significant wind, with sudden, unpredictable changes in weather, can not only make for difficult recording conditions but can be fatal if you are ill-prepared and not careful. When heading out to record, I pack not only the recording equipment but also survival gear, and make sure that I have a plan mapped out for where I am going and when I plan to return — and a back-up plan in case the weather changes and I can't make it back to camp. It is not uncommon to leave with the sun shining and a slight breeze only to have weather close in, with visibility reduced to the point where you cannot see your hand extended in front of you,

---

9   C Watson, pers. comm., 10 May 2009.

the temperature drop precipitously, and wind pick-up delivering the sting of ice and snow in your face. Hurricane blizzards, or 'Herbies' as they are called, with winds over 100 mph can come out of nowhere. Since you always travel with at least one other person, you have to make sure you are both on the same page and have talked through details and gear before you leave.[10]

Douglas Quin Recording Weddell Seals in Antarctica. Photograph © 1996 James H. Barker.

Figure 2. Douglas Quin in Antarctica.

Source: Image courtesy of the artist.

With hazards such as blizzards, hypothermia and frostbite to overcome, why would anyone want to subject themselves to this amount of hardship? It seems that there are other motives at play here than just the documentation of place. Overcoming physical and mental obstacles appears to be an important part of the creative process in which adversity heightens an artist's responsiveness to the environment.

> Challenging myself both physically and intellectually is both its own reward and a way to be more deeply engaged with the process and subject of recording — be it recording an ambience or a specific species that I am trying to understand. I am not interested in purely exploring thrill seeking or 'extreme recording' as a type of solipsistic sport. Rather,

---

10   D Quin, pers. comm., 20 May 2009.

> when I push myself in this way, I find that I gain a fuller understanding of and appreciation for what it is I am listening to. In this, listening is not simply an auditory function but something that embraces different and complementary modalities of knowing and different senses. The physicality is a reminder of where you are and what you are feeling and sensing — beyond the 'mediated' experience of your recorder and microphones. In this, there is an aspect of empathetic identification in the process of field recording which, for me, is a dimension of practice. It is not just about mastering the gear, but of doing thorough research prior to heading off and then being open to all that you may not have anticipated in the moment of listening and recording. Furthermore, each experience, whether you succeed or fail, builds a cumulative base knowledge that makes every future recording attempt richer and fuller.[11]

As Quin points out, field recording sometimes requires an element of spontaneity and improvisation in order for the recordist to successfully adapt to the conditions of a location. This can yield surprising results, in which fleeting and ephemeral sounds appear and vanish in front of the microphone. Prior knowledge of a location, however, often assists in capturing these impromptu moments, as each environment is determined by a recurring set of acoustic and spatial dynamics that modulate throughout the day or season. To achieve a worthwhile outcome the recordist must consider many questions related to microphone selection, the proximity between microphone and sound event, the type of acoustics that inform the site, what other sounds occur in the location, the best time of day to record the sound, and how the sound changes over the course of the day. Observing these dynamics over a period of time enables the recordist to apply a more rigorous recording method to reveal the nuances comprising a location that are often hidden among an omnidirectional din.

Crush grind

Like Quin, Melbourne-based sound artist Geoff Robinson also cites the cold as providing the biggest challenge in working in the field.

> I can remember several locations that I have recorded in that have all proved challenging due to one common factor, the cold. Three particular locations include recording in thigh-deep snow on the edge of a frozen lake outside of Saranac Lake in the Adirondack Mountains, New York State, and two locations in Iceland, Gullfoss and Jökulsarlon, one a waterfall and the other a lagoon at the edge of the Breiðamerkurjökull Glacier.

---

11 D Quin, pers. comm., 20 May 2009.

I am interested in the sonic potential of natural environments in flux, particularly environments that have a degree of immediate movement, through either their surrounding weather or the geomorphology of the land. Inevitably I find myself going to cold environments where dramatic shifts happen to the landscape primarily due to low temperatures, freezing water and the consequential phenomena and forms that evolve from this such as snow, ice, glaciers, etc.

All three locations involved long periods of time standing still in snow surrounded by strong cold winds. Particularly the experiences I had in the Adirondacks were challenging and also, coming from Australia, my first real experience of a cold climate. While I was prepared to some degree and dressed appropriately (thermals, waterproof snow jacket, waterproof snow boots, etc.) standing still for 10–15 minute periods recording made me realise that my body was not coping. Feeling rather numb, rigid and shaking, I remained this way for several hours even with the car heater on to full. Quite a strange sensation, considering I am so used to the temperature of the immediate environment reacclimatising your body straight away. In Iceland I learnt from these experiences and worked out ways to move while recording (toes, fingers, legs, etc.) and to set up the microphone independently so I could keep moving (sometimes this is not possible if the sound source is moving).[12]

Figure 3. Geoff Robinson in Iceland.

Source: Image courtesy of the artist.

---

12   G Robinson, pers. comm., 17 May 2009.

The burden of dreams

The physical and mental challenges that sound artists such as Quin and Robinson have had to overcome are significant, but what about the impact on the equipment used to capture these extraordinary locations? All technology is bound by a set of operational limits that determine the optimum conditions for it to function in a correct and reliable manner. What then are the effects of these punishing environments on the technology so critical to the field recordist? Melbourne sound artist Camilla Hannan describes the challenges of recording in the Amazon.

> I spent two weeks on a sound art residency program at Mamori Lake in the Amazonas region of Brazil, hosted by Mamori Art Lab and conducted by Francisco Lopez. We spent two weeks going out twice a day into the jungle to do field recordings. The heat and humidity was quite intense as were the insects. Having lived in Queensland, I was not a stranger to these conditions, but Mamori was in a league of its own. Besides the personal comfort factor, the humidity adversely affected the microphones, in particular, condenser microphones. Microphones affected by moisture generate hum. The only way to remedy this is by drying the diaphragm in a moisture-free climate-controlled environment. This wasn't an option at Mamori where there was no air conditioning, let alone facilities for a climate-controlled room. Preventative measures such as using sealed waterproof bags and desiccant crystal sachets helped somewhat. Aside from problems with humidity there were constant power outages that meant a heavy reliance on battery power.[13]

English sound artist and instrument builder Max Eastley encountered a different set of problems recording in subzero temperatures on Spitsbergen, the largest island of the Svalbard archipelago in the Arctic Ocean.

> Standard batteries will not work well in those environments so a lead acid battery is better as it can be topped up at any time, but they are heavy. Weight is crucial when you don't know how far you will have to walk over difficult terrain. Also leads can snap when the temperature is -30 Celsius, and the lubricants on a DAT recorder can freeze up, even at one or two degrees below zero. Spitsbergen has a particular problem for recording in that it is against the law to leave a settlement without being armed, as polar bears are a real danger. I had never been in an environment like that; I had to be accompanied at all times with one of the crew with a gun.[14]

---

13 C Hannan, pers. comm., 11 May 2009.
14 M Eastley, pers. comm., 14 May 2009.

Aside from technical issues I wondered how working in a volatile region such as the Arctic affected the perception and awareness of the surrounding environment.

> It changed the way I looked at the world. Human senses are dulled in urban environments, but in a remote place I found that seeing and hearing are essential to survival. Your perception is sharpened and you begin to listen and look for details in the environment. With those experiences of recording I realised how easily a series of unforeseen events could combine into a situation where you need all your resources.[15]

Oblique strategies

Can the artefacts generated by field recording *in extremis* simply function experientially to provide new knowledge of the natural world, or do they demand further questioning in order to understand an artist's intent, and therefore to measure the significance of their achievement? Of course a recording can do both, but unlike a musical composition, field recording opens itself up to interrogation, as the captured sounds and spaces are a window to the recordist's personal preoccupations, memories and subjective perceptions. Equally, field recording seems to carry with it a responsibility to educate and/or raise awareness, both individual and collective, about the importance of our often overlooked auditory environment. I certainly believe that sound artists such as Quin and Watson have provided unique insights into the natural world that reflect a sensitive engagement between artist and location. A different philosophical outlook that draws on a broader interest in sound, perception and space though guides Hannan, which I believe highlights the manner in which many sound artists are now engaging with field recording.

> Being isolated in the Amazon, away from the distractions of modern life meant I spent time thinking about how we listen and how the sonic landscape is made up. I thought a lot about the way sound is naturally spatialised, particularly in regard to depth of perception. I thought about the nature of silence, particularly within such a raucous environment. I thought about how the nature of recording changes the elements of a sound. I also considered notions of authenticity. To document an environment is not particularly important to me. What I am more interested in is how 'real' sounds can become abstractions of

---

15   M Eastley, pers. comm., 14 May 2009.

place and time. And following on from this and using ideas expounded by Francisco Lopez, how these recordings act as 'absolute sounds' devoid of reference or frameworks.[16]

Concluding remarks

The adaptation of numerous theoretical and philosophical references from acoustic ecology, soundscape composition, bioacoustics and phonography has enabled sound artists to forge new concepts and strategies to document both the natural and built environment, using increasingly portable and discreet recording equipment. Their interest and determination to access remote locations will undoubtedly continue to grow as both technology and travel become cheaper. I will be listening with great interest as new frontiers are revealed, to see how well I can spot the difference between the familiar and the strange.

---

16   C Hannan, pers. comm., 11 May 2009.

Kiwis on ice: Defining the ways in which the New Zealand identity is reflected in the Antarctic-inspired works of four New Zealand composers

Patrick Shepherd[1]

Antarctica — 'a poetical fantasy to range in'[2]

With the substantial body of work which has been produced by artists all over the world from many artistic disciplines, critics are now in a good position to examine exactly what the artist's relationship is with Antarctica, both from the artists' own words and the work they have produced. Bringing the world to the continent is certainly a literal reality for those who travel to Antarctica, but the converse is also true, as each artist brings the continent back to the world. It may also be true that Antarctica is the ultimate silence, a blank canvas upon which each artist can project their own imagination. Interpreted differently, it may be the ultimate silence because of the unique challenges it offers, what Pyne describes as 'an esthetic sink, not an inspiration. Its landscape erased those elements which provided worlds accessible, and its fantastic isolation seemingly defied any but self-referential attempts to assimilate it'.[3]

In looking at how the New Zealand artists relate to Antarctica — and in particular the four composers discussed in this paper — it is perhaps helpful to ascertain first what drivers New Zealanders exhibit. To merely describe the Kiwi relationship with Antarctica as 'unique' is unhelpful. To paraphrase *Animal Farm*, 'Everyone is unique; we're just more unique than them', says little about how one country relates to the continent. On a practical level, there are the obvious geographical, political and economic links, but they are hardly unique. The historical links such as Lyttelton and Timaru — places the heroic

---

1 Dr Patrick Shepherd, College of Education, University of Canterbury, Private Bag 4800, Christchurch, New Zealand, patrick.shepherd@canterbury.ac.nz.
2 A Kippis (1788) *The life of Captain James Cook*. Printed for G Nicol and GGJ and J Robinson, London, p. 510.
3 SJ Pyne (1986) *The Ice*. Phoenix, London, p. 150.

age expeditions of Scott departed from — have certainly helped cement a strong bond between the two places, as has a bona fide local Telecom (now Spark) dialling code for New Zealand.

New Zealand was also one of the countries to set up education, artists and writers programs. The New Zealand government was a signatory to the Antarctic Treaty. The Gateway Antarctica program continues to flourish at the University of Canterbury where, incidentally, the Council of Managers of National Antarctic Program currently resides. Of course, the Erebus disaster of 1979 where a sightseeing plane crashed into Mount Erebus killing all 257 people on board is still very raw in the Kiwi psyche.

Key indicators for the New Zealand identity

Antarctica provides the ultimate wilderness for a country whose residents exhibit a world-renowned sense of adventure and travel, as well as a love of the outdoors and nature. New Zealand is an eco-friendly country, as well it might be, for if climate change becomes a terminal reality and Antarctica reduces in size through melting, New Zealand will be one of the first places to be affected. Given all these factors the Kiwis' near-obsession with their relationship to the land is hardly surprising, particularly in the strong cultural and spiritual ties exhibited by the Maori.

The relationship with the land is argued for strongly in the album *Home, Land and Sea* (Trinity Roots 2004). *Situating music in Aotearoa New Zealand*[4] follows on from Glenda Keam's PhD thesis on the notions of national style in contemporary New Zealand music, of which landscape plays a significant part. Douglas Lilburn, the grandfather of modern New Zealand art music, believed that the land and the environment could contribute to a national musical style that he felt was missing. He also believed that there was a process whereby New Zealand composers were being subconsciously formed and creatively affected by the land and the environment, as evident in his claim that 'this environment of ours is shaping us into characteristic rhythms of living'.[5]

Of course, when all else fails, New Zealanders blame Australians, so perhaps the whole New Zealand obsession with national identity in music was in part due to Percy Grainger who spoke on New Zealand radio in 1935 giving New Zealand composers their cue to look to the landscape for musical significance,

---

4 Glenda Keam and Tony Mitchell (2011) *Home, land and sea: situating music in Aotearoa New Zealand*. Pearson New Zealand, Auckland.
5 Keam and Mitchell (2011), p. 218.

announcing that he would be awarding a prize for the best composition by a New Zealand-born composer that presented 'typical New Zealand cultural and emotional and characteristics'.[6]

Several recent studies of New Zealanders have shown that top of their list in importance is a love of, and respect for, the environment — KEA (2011), Practica (2010), Timezoneone Blog (2009), *NZ Herald* (2008). Practica's research — as reported in Jane Clifton's article 'Choice, bro'[7] — identified seven 'legends' (defining characteristics) for New Zealanders: relationship with the land, independence and freedom, masculinity of expression, importance of sport, 'mateship', being easy-going and non-confrontational, and a sense of humour. Of these, perhaps 'masculinity of expression' and 'mateship' provide some of the more subtle identifiers between Antarctica and New Zealand, a place to get away from it all with your mates in much the same way as the hunter or fisherman might trek off into the bush or high country for days on end.

On a slightly less formal note — and out of the mouths of babes, as so often the simple truths are — one need look no further than the website of Mrs Brunton's Year 8 class in room 28 at Marina View School who came up with, 'To me, being a Kiwi means that you box above your weight'; 'It means NZ has no pollution, great greenery, great oceans. Kiwis have freedom'; 'We have the chance to achieve great things'; and finally, 'To watch the All Blacks versus the Wallabies'.[8]

New Zealand's relationship with Antarctica may also be seen as part of a 'coming of age'. In much the same way as the British Empire regarded it in the heroic age, so Australia and New Zealand claiming their parts of Antarctica has been part of those countries' coming of age. Nazi Germany also saw it as strategically desirable, establishing a base there during World War II, and the Americans currently have a military presence, albeit benign. Hollywood has done much to cement Antarctica in the popular culture through movies such as *The Thing* and *Alien vs Predator* which choose the brutal isolation of Antarctica on which to project the drama.

Artist programs

The US, Australia, New Zealand, United Kingdom, Chile and Argentina are some of the countries that run — or have run — Antarctic artist schemes. From all the different countries a significant body of Antarctic-related art has been

---

6 Keam and Mitchell (2011), p. 219.
7 *New Zealand Listener* (Online), 3 Jul 2010, vol 224(3660) issn:0110-5787.
8 http://www.marinav.school.nz/Site/Archive/2007/Team_Brunton/Room_28_-_Mrs_Brunton_-_Year_8.ashx, retrieved 19 June 2011.

established. The artists who have headed to Antarctica from New Zealand have not always done so through government-assisted schemes. The practice started in 1957 with painter Peter McIntyre and, later in 1970, with Royal New Zealand Air Force official artist Maurice Conly. The New Zealand Artists to Antarctica scheme (and a parallel education scheme) ran from 1997 to 2007 in conjunction with Creative New Zealand, New Zealand's main arts funding body. Currently, two to three artists are selected annually by a panel and 'shoulder-tapped'. The 45 artists New Zealand has sent to Antarctica represent most artistic disciplines: painting, sculpture, musical composition and performance, furniture-making, choreography, play and novel writing, poetry, photography, fashion design, ceramics, printmaking, jewellery, and textile art. The Postgraduate Certificate in Antarctic Studies, part of the University of Canterbury's Gateway Antarctica program, has also seen several artists including Laura Taylor (*Antarctic Lullaby*) and Julian Evans (ice pipe installation) head south as part of their studies.

The four composers

The four composers who are the subject of this paper are Chris Cree Brown, Phil Dadson, myself and Gareth Farr. They are listed in the order in which they travelled to Antarctica, Chris Cree Brown being the first, with the musical excerpts played during the oral presentation at the conference listed at the start.

Chris Cree Brown

Under Erebus (2000) — electroacoustic

Icescape (2003) — symphony orchestra

> I had hoped to find sounds whose morphology and spectra I could digitally transform to create abstract sounds that would reflect some of the magnificence of the continent. This would create an expressive link between a real, unaltered and recognisable sound source and more abstract textures.
>
> My goal was to create an expressive work of sonic art that reflected my personal interpretation of the environment of Antarctica and my experiences while in Antarctica.
>
> Prior to going down to the Ice, I classified the Antarctic sounds into four different categories:

i) Environmental sounds: ice cracking, breaking and rumbling on the Erebus ice tongue, tapping ice crystals, ice crystals shattering, and the various types of wind (polar wind, Antarctic white out, katabatic wind).

ii) *Wildlife:* various species of penguins, skuas, petrels and underwater vocalisations of seals.

iii) Human activity: the effort in walking (panting), the squeaking of footprints on snow (the snow in New Zealand is not dry enough for this sound), ice breakers and the radio communications.

iv) Silence.

Such a significant experience as Antarctica is bound to influence one in a myriad of ways, and the Antarctic experience has allowed a new perspective on environmental issues, and the fragility of our planet.

One of the striking aspects of the Antarctic sound world is the apparent incongruity of many sounds when compared to the environment. The massive, majestic icescapes and graceful, sweeping glaciers evoke a music that embodies grand, slow moving, dense and interweaving textures. These characteristics seem to be the antithesis of the sounds that are heard on the continent.

The Antarctic Treaty acknowledges sound ecology and has set aside some few thousand square miles where mechanical and other human noise is prohibited. Ours is a world where noise (defined here as the undesirable sonic by-product of human activity) and its insidious psychological consequences on humanity has largely been ignored. In the words of Canadian sound ecologist, R Murray Schafer, 'It would seem that noise pollution has reached an apex of vulgarity in our time'.

Antarctica, by contrast, appears as a near pristine environment, not only with regard to its visual and physical environment, but also in its sonic landscape. The tranquility in Antarctica is unfamiliar and, as a consequence, marginally disturbing, especially when exacerbated by the absence of ambient sound. The sociological, psychological and cultural changes that have occurred as a direct consequence of the unrestrained increase in and excessive intensity of noise pollution must be profound. However, it is reassuring that our species has saved some small piece of the planet in terms of sound ecology, even if there is nothing there except ice.

There is little doubt that when tourism in Antarctica becomes further established, a corresponding quantity of noise will ensue and, as elsewhere on the planet, assume a low priority in the pollution stakes.

Antarctica: Music, sounds and cultural connections

Phil Dadson

Flutter (2004)

Stonemap (2005)

Chthonian Pulse (2005)

Excerpts played from *Polar Projects* (Flutter; Stonemap; Aerial Farms; Echo Logo)

> Any preconceptions I did have were made up of mental images conjured from reading explorer accounts and from photographs, all fairly typical. The actual experience far surpassed any imaginings, especially those in the Dry Valleys. Nothing prepared me for the pristine temple-like atmosphere of one stone valley floor in particular, which I nicknamed 'valley of the gods'. Wind-sculpted granite ventifacts, some strangely anthropomorphic, surreally backgrounded against giant dunes of black sand banked half way up one hundred foot high crystalline walls of ice.
>
> The Antarctic experience was one I went into with all antennae bristling, heightened somewhat by the prosthetics of a camera lens and a high-quality microphone. Above all, it reinforced for me the attitude of going into a situation with as few preconceptions as possible; keeping an ear and eye out for sounds and sonic images that might catch my attention, and welcoming the unexpected — the 'improviser' sensibility.
>
> I was making field recordings with a Uher tape recorder around the same time I first got interested in composing, and then later as a film-sound recordist, so the tape-recording medium and structuring and editing processes have always been part of my compositional thinking. I don't make any separation really, between the act of composing in one medium or another — whether it's film, video, audio, an installation, a music ensemble or combinations of — the process for me is very similar.
>
> Summertime, January 2003, and a 24/7 period of daylight. I was going out filming and recording most nights around 8 or 9 pm and returning to the tent site at 3,4 or 5 in the morning. The light at so-called 'night-time' was so much better for recording video. It was like continuous early morning or late afternoon light, devoid of the harshness of full daytime sunlight. The sun would appear to strike a medium arc across the sky during the main hours of daytime and then, at late afternoon appear to just sit at one level close to the horizon line and remain there. I was recording ice cracks for one entire night (without too much luck I have to say) and during this time sat motionless, simply watching and listening, much of the time focused on my relationship with the planet

and to the sun. Instead of watching the sun slowly creeping along the horizon line, I could literally sense the earth turning around the sun. It was a simple and profound sensation and it has stayed with me.

Polar Projects is as much a composition of elements, from my perspective, as an installation. One [memory] I regularly return[ed] to was the physical sensation of feeling an absolutely minuscule remote and insignificant dot on the surface of the planet, and at the same time, awestruck with a physical sensation of the me as a tiny dot on the earth turning around the sun.

It's a rare opportunity and one that should be available to as many artists as possible. Another time, I'd like to do a sequel that interfaced more intentionally with specific locations, and with science teams as performer/collaborators, maybe via another nation's program. It's provided a heightened sense of urgency about the politics of impermanence. It's also polished the lens through which I view landscape and geography.

Patrick Shepherd

Katabatic (2005) — chamber ensemble

Adeliesong (2005) — two clarinets

Fanfare for a Frozen Land (2005) — orchestra

Cryosphere (2005) — orchestra

I've always loved the ice and snow. Coming from the north of England some of my earliest childhood memories are associated with snow — that amazing light you sense when you first wake up and it's lighter, brighter and crisper than it usually is. I needed inspiration and thought Antarctica might be interesting. I knew Chris [Cree Brown] had gone and he reckoned it was life-changing so I decided to give it a go. I didn't expect it to become an all-consuming passion.

Conrad's *Heart of Darkness* is often used as a metaphor for Antarctic — and Arctic — exploration, and I think that anyone who goes there faces the ultimate truth that in an environment stripped bare of virtually everything there really is nowhere else to run to — it's you and nature, face-to-face. Shackleton got it right when he said that Antarctic exploration was not an outward journey but rather an inward journey of discovery.

It's really hard to try and see a stylistic change in my music, perhaps because I'm too emotionally and chronologically close to the event. Besides, people who claim they've 'changed' rarely have. I'm not concerned as much with my audience, maybe. Don't get me wrong, I want to connect but I'm less concerned with the performance playing out in my head as I write and more with the effect of the sounds. I still write at the computer but I tend to sketch first on paper; there's a freedom of expression there that you just don't get on the sequential thinking of the computer.

I'm up the top of Observation Hill, which separates Scott Base from McMurdo Station. It's snowing, I'm scared stiff because I've just climbed up a steep hill having not told anyone where I am (an absolute no-no down there) and I'm looking at the jarrah cross that bears the famous quote from Ulysses in memory of Scott and his four doomed companions. I was very proud to be British, very proud to be a Kiwi and ecstatic that I was an Antarctican. Anyone who calls Scott an idiot misses the point — there's some stuff in life bigger than life itself and dying might be the last thing that happens to you but it may not be the worst.

I expected to come away so full of inspiration that the artistic juices would flow freely. Instead, I got a kind of block which lasted for over six months. Science — that was my only way through. I had a kind of block, the subject matter was so big and there's only so much stuff you can write that sounds like Arvo Pärt, so I moved away from the purely descriptive and found inspiration in the little things, the minutiae, the scientific stuff — and the human interest aspects. I started on *Katabatic* — which was a 30 second microscore — to get me working, then I moved on to *Adeliesong*, replicating the additive rhythm call of the penguins, which I then orchestrated out into *Fanfare for a Frozen Land*. The layering of the orchestration in *Cryosphere* took its inspiration from using a Kovacs drill on field training at Scott Base and seeing the different strata of ice and debris.

Stephen Pyne's book *The Ice* was brilliant. When you're there the beakers (scientists) tend to regard the artists as a bit 'arty-farty' (which we know can be true) but we also end up putting a human and a more publicly accessible front to much of the hard science they're dealing with. If we (the artists) can bring the issues closer to people, particularly in schools, we might have a chance of getting science front and centre, too.

Gareth Farr

Terra Incognita (2007) — tenor, chorus and orchestra

There are two overwhelming things that hit you in the face when you go to Antarctica. The first is that the world is a very scary place. It's fierce, unrelenting, and non-negotiable. The second is that the world is a very fragile place. If something that appears so invincible, so powerful, and so eternal can be falling apart because of what us humans have done in the last hundred years or so, then we have really screwed up badly.

I went to Antarctica with the expectation of discovering a landscape, a physical geographical experience — but returned to New Zealand having not only experienced that, but also a foreign culture, in exactly the same way as I have in the US, in Indonesia, in Australia. There is Scott Base, which is obviously profoundly Kiwi, and there is McMurdo Station — five minutes away by road — which is just like being in the US — currency, accents, everything. But there is an overriding Antarctic culture there — an understanding of things that they all have in common that are utterly peculiar to Antarctica — such as safety/survival issues, scientific issues, general things you just have to know to exist in a space station-like environment.

I don't think my compositional style has altered because of Antarctica per se — writing a piece for bass voice and orchestra taught me a *huge* amount about balancing a singer with an orchestra, which will impact on every piece I write for singer (or any soloist for that matter) and orchestra in the future. It also was my first major dramatic piece, where I had to look at the piece as a piece of theatre, and structure/pace it accordingly.

I'm not a word person — I'd be an author otherwise — it's not my talent to put an experience into words. I've always hated the idea of expressing landscape in music — in fact I've never been that keen on expressing anything visual in music — because I don't think that music exists for that purpose. Music is music. I don't even like writing program notes — to me they seem like an apology because the music wasn't capable of communicating to the audience.

So to write a piece of music inspired by my experience in Antarctica was utterly impossible, based on my self-imposed restrictions! But there was a moment — the epiphany moment! — when I realised that it was the people who have been to Antarctica in the last hundred years; that is what I can reflect in my music.

Basically what happened is that the minute I realised the project was about people and their relationship to the continent, as opposed to a musical representation of the geographical features, I had a major epiphany. I had talked to Paul Whelan (Kiwi singer, then based in London) about a piece a few years earlier, and we had in mind a piece for bass voice and orchestra — but as always happens the idea had fallen by the wayside because neither of us had the funding to do anything. The epiphany was — 'oh my God, this is the piece — I need the epic sound of an orchestra, and I need the human communication of a singer — *this* is the piece!'

My general outlook changed in a very specific way — ecologically.

Conclusion

The experiences of the four New Zealand composers demonstrates not only how their personal horizons broadened but also how the journey south offers a unique opportunity to compare and contrast their work in a unique way. It is indeed rare to be able to make such direct comparisons between the works of people operating in a similar discipline exposed to exactly the same stimuli and as such provides an invaluable insight into not only how the creative mind operates but also how art interacts with life on the ice.

Antarctica: 'Surround Sound'

Stephen Nicol[1]

In this era of heroic Antarctic centennials we are likely to be inundated with an avalanche of sepia-bound literature reinventing the myths of the cold white continent. Chief amongst these myths is the portrayal of Antarctica as a colourless, sterile environment where the only sound is the howling of the wind and the predominant biological feature is the spectre of white men, their beards infested by icicles, struggling and dying heroically on the ice. There is, however, another side to Antarctica, rich in colour, sound and smell which derives from the ring of life that surrounds the continent and which is more attuned to the oceans to the north than to the great white hell of the interior. The Antarctica that a visitor perceives is dependent on their orientation but also depends on the mode of transport used to get there.

Antarctica is more accessible than ever these days but there are only two ways to get there — by ship or by airplane. Most people visit by ship because most tourism in Antarctica is ship-based, and even national and private expeditions use ships extensively to transport people because of their capacity for bulk transport across the ocean. Air transport is largely the preserve of the national operations — and these programs have been the source of much of what is written about Antarctica both in the sciences and humanities. Thus the views of those flown in to Antarctica tend to dominate the recent literature, yet much of what is perceived of the frozen continent comes from people approaching slowly from the north by ship. The rapid immersion into the Antarctic provided by air transport provides a wholly different perspective and imagery compared to the slow edging through the ocean and the ice that approaching by ship affords.

Travel by ship still retains an air of romance and adventure, even if the vessel is a vast, ice-strengthened luxury cruiser. To cross the Southern Ocean is still risky; it is the world's stormiest oceanic region with the highest average wave height, so there is a rite of passage involved in even the shortest crossings. Travellers who have experienced the horrors of a Force 10 in the Drake Passage can boast of their exploits for the rest of their lives, although they were probably curled, quivering and nauseous, in their first-class bunks at the time. But the storms are the province of the open ocean of the forties and fifties latitudes, and the days at sea in this region accustom the visitor to the immensity of the ocean, its movements and its deep blue emptiness. Vistas of rolling seas are

---

1   Adjunct Professor Stephen Nicol, Institute of Marine and Antarctic Studies, University of Tasmania, and formerly Program Leader Southern Ocean Ecosystems, Australian Antarctic Division, steve.nicol@bigpond.com.

punctuated by the soaring of the albatross and very little else. Consequently, approaching the continent, or the vast fractal wonderland of the pack ice, the visitor begins to appreciate the emerging landscape more keenly. The first break to the undulating two dimensionality of the ocean surface is the looming towers of icebergs. At first the bergs are sighted individually and distantly; eroded giants fast on the path to liquid oblivion. Into the sixties icebergs become more common and being younger are more varied in size, shape and colour. Vast, flat-topped bergs the size of small countries vie for attention with the crenellated ramparts of crumbling ice castles. The immense whiteness of the freshwater ice is perforated by the cobalt blue of cavities and chasms. Still more colourful are bergs shot through with vivid stripes of translucent blue and the holy grail of the ice-enthusiast, the deep green of the jade bergs. And the bergs take on the colour of the sky, changing constantly from piercing clarity at midday to subtle mauves and pinks during the timeless sunsets that merge into equally drawn out dawns. But all of this is merely the entree, a taste of the wonders that the continent and its frozen fringe have to offer.

What changes the environment so spectacularly as you approach the first barriers of ice and rock is the presence of life. Almost every living organism in or around the Antarctic continent is dependent on the ocean for its existence. Although the open ocean is not sterile, the pack ice through its melting and freezing drives an annual cycle that is astonishing in its productivity. Behind and within the receding pack ice in spring and early summer, blooms of microscopic plants explode on a planetary scale, and these prairies of the ocean are grazed upon by the vast ochre swarms of krill. Such an abundance of marine life has led to the evolution of a suite of large animals that exploit this highly seasonal cornucopia. Great whales used to gather here in their millions, travelling from their breeding grounds in the balmy tropics to gorge for a few short months which would suffice them for the long migration north and for the rest of the year. Seals breed on the ice and exploit the food supply below and around them. Flying birds come from as far as the Arctic and many breed in huge colonies that become ice free in the summertime. Penguins utilise the scattered rocky outcrops to frantically raise their young in the few short months when the snow has melted and when food is abundant. Thus, for the last hundred or two kilometres as a ship approaches Antarctica the ocean is suddenly awash with vibrant, noisy and frenetic life making the most of the narrow chance to feed, breed and hence survive another winter.

Figure 1. The colourful fringe of the Antarctic continent.

Source: Photograph by Steve Nicol.

Antarctica: Music, sounds and cultural connections

Figure 2. Life, death, colour and sound on the edge of the Antarctic continent.

Source: Photograph by Steve Nicol.

Although the pack ice, formed from frozen sea, is white on top, on the bottom it's heavily fouled by microbial communities that use the undersurface to help them stay near to the surface and hence to life-giving light. As the ice decays the green–yellow–brown of the living floes becomes exposed and life begins to tint the physical world. The seals too add daubs of colour to the floes through the startlingly blood-red piles of excrement. Seals like most of the larger animals of the pack are rather drab but their movements and the occasional flash of pink from their gaping jaws alleviate the tonal monotony. But this is not unusual — most marine mammals and birds the world over favour unexciting colour schemes; the uniforms of grey, mottled beige and contrasting black and white are common to whales, seals and seabirds from the tropics to both poles. Onshore the penguin colonies are more colourful, despite the near-monochrome nature of their inhabitants. Pink guano of digested krill seeps into every crevice to the extent that these colonies are visible from space. The nutrient-rich and pungent excrement fertilises the surrounding area, resulting in swathes of pink, yellow and green blooms of algae that colonise rocks, ice, snow and ocean. Penguin colonies are a riot of colours, smells and sounds and are a vibrant counter to the stereotypical vision of Antarctica as a colourless sterile expanse serenaded by the white noise of the wind. To be sure, the animal life of Antarctica cannot rival the primary colours visible in the tropics; there are none of the species that bring colour to more northern ecosystems — no reptiles, no amphibians, no insects and no songbirds. But the fringe of Antarctica is far from a colourless sterile environment, at least in summer.

Moving inland from the living fringe of Antarctica, the signs of life diminish and with them go the colour, the sound and the smell. Fifty kilometres inland and life retreats in scale, with drab mosses and lichens eking out a silent existence in the ice-free valleys and on exposed mountain ridges. The animals that dare to venture into the interior lose colour and blend into their environment. Snow-white snow petrels roost in crevices in the mountains and the colouration of skuas mimics that of the brown-grey rocks on which they breed. Two hundred kilometres into the continent and life is essentially extinct.

Figure 3. Riches from the sea — the brick-red guano of a penguin colony.

Source: Photograph by Steve Nicol.

Figure 4. The drab colours of life away from the coast — a skua among the rocks.

Source: Photograph by Steve Nicol.

As most visitors to the Antarctic arrive by ship in summer, the chaotic, noisy and nasally challenging spectacle of life on the fringe is what greets them. This is a marked contrast to the introduction to Antarctica experienced by those who arrive by airplane. Planes usually land near the coast, deep within the pack ice zone or on ice runways groomed on the high Antarctic plateau, far away from the ocean. Disembarking from an airplane, one is greeted by a harsh white landscape largely devoid of life except for the evidence of human activities. The sounds are those of the wind and of the mechanical appliances that permit human life in a hostile environment. The smells are largely those associated with industrialised life — kerosene, exhaust fumes and sunblock.

During the autumn, human and animal life deserts Antarctica, leaving a virtually uninhabited continent. It is during this rarely observed period that Antarctica most resembles its stereotype — cold, dark, monochrome and windy with the only sounds being those of the elements. It is paradoxical that during the long dark and largely colourless winter the sole native resident of the continent is the most colourful of the Antarctic animals, the emperor penguin.

Human activities follow the seasons. Biologists look to the ocean and the margins in summer, the region where life thrives and where the factors that encourage life and induce death can be studied in a restricted environment. The Antarctic of most biologists is a colourful, noisy, smelly and hectic environment. In contrast, the physicists and astronomers look inwards and upwards, seeing a blindingly white continent where contrast is only added though the ephemeral auroras or the artificial hues of distant stars and galaxies abstracted through complex instruments. The only life and colour that scientists at the South Pole experience is human life and introduced colour. At the Pole, the most inhospitable place on earth, only humans and microbes can survive.

Antarctica, more than most destinations, is thus defined by the perspective of the visitor. Early explorers would have found the coast a distraction as they set their sights inland to the colourless, lifeless interior. But to define this continent on the basis of its interior is as unrealistic as ignoring the diverse rainforests and reefs of Australia in favour of its remote red centre. The challenge for those who seek to describe this vast and important area of the planet is to incorporate its diversity and huge seasonality into the narratives that help to define its place in popular culture.

Frozen voices:
Women, silence and Antarctica

Jesse Blackadder[1]

This chapter explores a different kind of Antarctic silence: the silencing of certain stories and voices. It's the silence of the earliest female travellers to Antarctica.

The voices of the earliest female travellers are silent and their stories remain untold, partly because there's no place for them in the dominant Antarctic narrative of exploration and conquest. Reimagining them through fiction is one way — though with potential pitfalls — to 'unfreeze' those stories.

The history of Antarctic exploration is about the adventures of men, particularly those in the so-called 'Heroic Age' from approximately 1897 to 1922. The great names of polar exploration, like Scott, Shackleton, Amundsen and Mawson, are well known and the mythology of their exploration, successes and failures still fascinates people today. The themes of their exploration narratives concerned heroism, conquest, suffering and male bonding.

Arguably the most powerful exploration story was the race between the British Scott and the Norwegian Amundsen to the South Pole. Polar scholar Elena Glasberg says 'This celebrated competition was motivated by all the familiar elements that shaped exploration history: the cultures of nationalism, imperial science, and male adventure'.[2] Those defining moments of Antarctic history were masculine, and issues of gender were stamped on the landscape from the start.

Antarctic historian Tom Griffiths describes it thus: 'There was something spiritual about male comradeship, something pure about distant yearning and asexual love, and something incontrovertibly masculine about frontiering. The ice was their own inviolable space. In Antarctica, the presence of women could diminish a man. In their absence, one might prove oneself worthy of them'.[3]

This has led to a primary narrative of Antarctica, a tale of suffering, competition, and achieving the all-important 'first'. No one just ends up in Antarctica — there is always a journey of some sort to get there. These 'terrible journeys', such as

---

1 Dr Jesse Blackadder, Writing & Society Research Centre, University of Western Sydney, 3 Muli Court, Myocum, NSW 2481, jesse@blackadder.net.au.
2 E Glasberg (2002) 'Refusing history at the End of the Earth: Ursula Le Guin's "Sur" and the 2000–01 Women's Antarctica Crossing'. *Tulsa Studies in Women's Literature* 21(1): 99–121, p. 101.
3 T Griffiths (2007) *Slicing the silence*. UNSW Press, Sydney, p. 214.

Cherry-Garrard's 'worst journey in the world', Shackleton's epic journey to save himself and his men, the competitive journey to the South Pole between Scott and Amundsen, and Mawson's lone trek for survival, function as Antarctica's formation myths. The linear journey of exploration, the classic 'hero's journey', has become a blueprint for Antarctic stories.

Where did women fit into this masculine space?

According to polar scholar Elizabeth Leane, Antarctica itself was constructed as feminine in its literature.[4] In some Antarctic narratives from the early 20th century 'the continent resembles nothing so much as a monstrous feminine body that threatens to engulf the unwary male explorer' (2009, p. 511).[5] The heroic phase was characterised by expedition writing that characterised the continent as 'an aloof virginal woman to be won through chivalrous deeds'.[6]

This is clearly expressed in the cartoon 'Waiting to be Won', from *Punch* in 1875, which depicts the 'White Ladye of the Pole'. The verses printed with the cartoon said:

> But still the white Witch-Maiden that sits above the Pole
> In the snow-bound silver silence whose cold quells aught but soul
> Draws manly hearts with strange desire to lift her icy veil
> The bravest still have sought her, and will seek, whoever fail.[7]

Although this image relates to the North Pole, Leane points out that 'both icescapes tend to be feminised when viewed as fields of endeavour'.[8]

Women's entry into this space was obviously problematic. On a physical level women were actively — in fact, strenuously — excluded from Antarctica in the first century of its history. Access to Antarctica in that time was controlled by money, race and gender. None of the great heroic era explorers took women with them.

Although opportunities for women were severely restricted, the *desire* for adventure wasn't only a masculine one. Among Shackleton's records is this letter from three young women who asked to join his expedition:

> We are three strong healthy girls, and also gay and bright, and willing to undergo any hardships, that you yourself undergo. If our feminine garb

---

[4] E Leane (2009) 'Placing women in the Antarctic literary landscape'. *Signs: Journal of Women in Culture and Society* 34(3): 509–14, p. 510.
[5] Leane (2009) 'Placing women in the Antarctic literary landscape', p. 511.
[6] Leane (2009) 'Placing women in the Antarctic literary landscape', p. 511.
[7] Reproduced in F Spufford (1997) *I may be some time: ice and the English imagination*. Picador, New York, p. 178.
[8] Leane (2009) 'Placing women in the Antarctic literary landscape', p. 510.

is inconvenient, we should just love to don masculine attire. We have been reading all books and articles that have been written on dangerous expeditions by brave men to the Polar regions, and we do not see why men should have the glory, and women none, especially when there are women just as brave and capable as there are men.[9]

Newspaper articles report that women applied to be included in Antarctic expeditions in 1919 at the tail end of the heroic era:

THE ANTARCTIC. ANOTHER EXPEDITION.
WOMEN WANT TO GO.
LONDON October 18.
Captain Cope is inviting applications from experts in the following sciences to accompany his expedition to the Antarctic regions:- Geology, meteorology, biology, photography, surgery, cartography, and hydrography. The party will number 51, of whom 17 will be engaged on shore work. A number of the members of the expeditions which accompanied Captain Sir R. F. Scott and Captain Sir Ernest Shackleton have joined the expedition. Several women were anxious to join, but their applications were refused.[10]

Antarctic exploration moved into the mechanical era in the 1920s, using planes and motorised ships to further exploration goals. But women were still actively excluded from participating.

Twenty-five women applied to join Mawson's British, Australian and New Zealand Antarctic Research Expedition (BANZARE) in 1929[11] and in 1937 the extraordinary number of 1,300 women applied to join the proposed British Antarctic Expedition.[12] None were successful in being permitted to travel to Antarctica.

Women were known to have sailed to the Far South as companions on whaling and sealing ships plying their trade around the wild subantarctic islands in the 19th century, though their names were often not recorded.[13] In the mechanical era, it was possible for women to travel to Antarctica in greater safety and comfort as companions, providing support, care and domestic tasks. As in the history of American deep-sea whaling, generally the first women to go were the wives of the captains.

---

9   Reproduced in Spufford (1997) *I may be some time*, p. 144.
10 *The Advertiser* 10 October 1919, p. 7. 'The Antarctic: another expedition: Women want to go'. Retrieved from http://nla.gov.au/nla.news-article5633923.
11 *The Argus* (1929), p. 9.
12 *The Argus* 3 April 1937, p 17. 'Women want to go to pole: 1,300 applications: "No," says leader'. Retrieved from http://nla.gov.au/nla.news-article11053800.
13 E Chipman (1986) *Women on the ice: a history of women in the Far South*. Melbourne University Press, Melbourne, p. 11.

The first woman recorded to have set foot on Antarctica was Caroline (also spelt Karoline) Mikkelsen, who accompanied her husband south in 1935.[14] He had been working as a captain in the Norwegian whaling fleet on ships owned by Lars Christensen, with instructions to look for Antarctic lands that could be annexed for Norway. During their voyage a group including Caroline went ashore for several hours, raised the Norwegian flag, built a cairn, had afternoon tea and then returned to the ship.

Caroline neatly fitted in to the small role that could be allotted to women in the dominant Antarctic narrative: a domestic companion who was conveyed there by her husband and who set foot on the continent as an appendage to him. Although her landing wasn't publicised at the time, her 'first' was later reclaimed and now appears in Antarctic lists and timelines everywhere, as well as in books and articles by feminist scholars. If you Google 'first woman on Antarctica', hers is the name that comes up.

However, the reality's not so simple. As Chipman says, 'many of the "firsts" in the Far South are suspect and coloured by prevailing attitudes' (1986 p. 6).[15]

Four women are known to have gone to Antarctica before Caroline, but they've been largely overlooked. I'd like to tell you something of their story.

The Norwegian Ingrid Christensen first went to the Antarctic in 1931 (four years before Caroline) when she was 38 and had six children, whom she left at home. Her husband Lars was an entrepreneur who owned a large pelagic whaling fleet and personally funded much of Norway's Antarctic exploration. Ingrid went as his companion on the refuelling vessel for his factory fleet, a relatively privileged position. Ingrid and her companion Mathilde Wegger were, in 1931, the first identifiable women known to have seen Antarctica.[16] However, that year the expedition did not find a suitable landing site. Ingrid didn't achieve that all-important 'first footprint'. Mathilde faired even less well in recorded history. She was a widow and presumably went to keep Ingrid company — a role even more lowly than Ingrid's own — the companion of the companion. Chipman (1986) mentions her by name and includes a photograph of the two women together, but little other information about Mathilde survives in English-language history.

---

14   Mikkelsen is reported as the first woman to land on Antarctica in publications including the Norwegian *Main Events in the History of Antarctic Exploration* (Bogen (1957) p. 85), the Australian *A History of Antarctica* (Stephen Martin (1996) State Library of NSW Press, Sydney, p. 194); the English *Encyclopaedia of Antarctica and the Southern Oceans* (B Stonehouse (2002), John Wiley and Sons, Chichester) and the American *Encyclopedia of the Antarctic* (B Riffenburgh (2007) Routledge, New York, vol. 1) as well as on numerous websites.
15   Chipman (1986) *Women on the ice*, p. 6.
16   Chipman (1986) *Women on the ice*, p. 72.

Two years later, in 1933 Ingrid and Lars travelled to Antarctica for the second time, again leaving their children at home. This time Ingrid's companion was Lillemor (Ingebjorg) Rachlew, a woman who kept a lively diary of their trip, took photographs and from her own account, participated energetically in the voyage.

Here's one of Lillemor's descriptions:

> At one time during the morning it became a little calmer and I made my way along to the verandah — as we called the built-in deck beneath the captain's bridge — with my cine camera under my arm, to see if I could get any snaps of what could be seen of the after-deck between the waves. Suddenly the ship lurched violently and I fell and rolled in snow slush right across the verandah, coming to anchor with a crash on the port side, in the midst of some chairs and tables that were lashed securely there. Once there, I made use of the opportunity to take some snaps, and I very much hope they will be good — I'm sure I deserve it after all I went through![17]

Perhaps in the original diaries there might have been more personal reflection or some clues about what motivated Lillemor to set out on the journey. But although Lars quotes from Lillemor's diary extensively in his book, so far I've found no trace of her diaries still existing today.

An article about Lillemor and Ingrid appeared in a 1933 French journal carrying Lillemor's photographs[18] but that's one of the few contemporary media reports of their activities. Like Mathilde, Lillemor didn't have a place in the main Antarctic narrative.

Accompanied by a woman called Ingeborg Dedichen, Ingrid went to Antarctica for the third time in 1933–34 when the refuelling vessel *Thorshavn* circumnavigated the continent on a lengthy voyage.[19] Once again they didn't manage a landing anywhere. This was one of the most remote places on earth and the conditions were unpredictable and dangerous, so landing wasn't a given.

The following season, 1935, Caroline Mikkelsen was in luck. With good conditions, she made the landing.[20] She also made her own decision around

---

17 As cited in L Christensen (1935) *Such is the Antarctic* (transl. E Jayne). Hodder and Stoughton, Great Britain, p. 81.
18 C Rabot (1934) 'Voyage d'une femme dans L'Antarctique' ('Travels of a woman in the Antarctic'). *L'Illustration*, 4741 (13 January): 52–53, p. 52.
19 Chipman (1986) *Women on the ice*, p. 172.
20 H Bogen (1957). 'Main events in the history of Antarctic exploration'. *Norwegian Whaling Gazette*, Sandefjord, p. 85.

'silence'. Two years after the landing, her husband died. Caroline remarried and chose not to talk about her Antarctic experiences 'to spare his feelings'.[21] She kept silent about her story for decades.

Ingrid's fourth and final voyage was in 1936, after Caroline's landing. Lillemor went again as her companion and this time Ingrid took her youngest daughter Sofie, who was then 18. Another woman, Solveig Wideroe, whose husband was an aviator on the ship, was also with them. They carried out aerial exploration and Ingrid became the first woman to see Antarctica from the air. They attempted to go ashore where Caroline Mikkelsen had landed, but as soon as they got into the motor boat, bad weather came up. They were nearly swamped and had to turn back without landing.[22]

It seems like Ingrid's efforts to land were jinxed, and according to most recorded history, her Antarctic story ends then. Chipman, who focused on creating a complete list of women who travelled there, doesn't follow her journey any further. Lisbeth Lewander, writing about women who travelled to Antarctica between 1930 and 1990, doesn't mention any of these women.[23] Barbara Land calls Ingrid 'the whaling magnate's wife' and gives her less than two sentences in the history of female visitors to Antarctica.[24]

However, later on that voyage the four women — Ingrid, her daughter Sofie, Lillemor and Solveig — did actually go ashore at Scullin Monolith, with Lars. Because this landing wasn't a 'first', no fuss was made of it. Lars didn't mention the women at all when he set down his personal excitement at achieving this goal.[25] What Ingrid thought about it was never recorded.

To all intents and purposes, Ingrid's four trips to Antarctica were forgotten. In fact the whole unimportant matter of the first woman to land on Antarctica rested there until the 1980s when a number of books appeared about women's experiences in Antarctica, scholars started exploring issues of gender around Antarctica, and Caroline Mikkelsen's landing was brought out of obscurity and put on the record.

---

21   D Patterson (1995) 'The Vestfold Hills: the Norwegian connection'. *ANARE News* Spring/Summer: 43–44, p. 44.
22   L Christensen (1937) *My last expedition to the Antarctic*. Johan Grundt Tanum, Oslo, p. 9.
23   L Lewander (2009) 'Women and civilisation on ice'. *Cold matters: cultural perceptions of snow, ice and cold*. Umeå University and the Royal Skyttean Society Monograph no 1, 89.
24   B Land (1981) *The new explorers: women in Antarctica*. Dodd, Mead & Company, New York, p. 17.
25   L Christensen (1938) 'Charting the Antarctic'. *American Scandinavian Review* 26: 209–21, p. 217.

Then in 1998 some Australian geographic researchers (Norman, et al. 1998) took a fresh look at evidence of Klarius Mikkelsen's 1935 landing.[26] The Norwegian cairn from 1935 had been rediscovered by people working at Davis station.[27] The landing site, it transpired, was on an island.

In the world of polar exploration, landing on an island is of lesser value than landing on the mainland. Suddenly it looked like Caroline wasn't the first one to have landed on the mainland. So who was? Norman et al. say:

> The irony of the answer is manifest. Ingrid Christensen, Ingebjorg [Lillemor] Rachlew, Solveig Wideroe and Augusta Sophie Christensen, all landed at Klarius Mikkelsen Mountains (now Scullin Monolith) on 30 January 1937 [Bogen, 1957], but which of the 'ladies' touched the land first remains unknown. Ingrid Christensen was the first mentioned, but were her feet first ashore?[28]

Ingrid, Lillemor, Sofie or Solveig. Any of them might have been the first woman to land on the Antarctic continent, though at the time they wouldn't have known it, still believing Caroline had taken the honour. And so it seems that no record was made of the all-important first footstep in the ship's log or elsewhere.

This news didn't exactly set the world of polar studies on fire. No one else showed much interest in this aspect of the work of Norman and his colleagues, and once again, there the matter rested.

Within the dominant narrative of exploration and conquest of Antarctica, the journeys of all of these women have remained less than secondary. Travelling to Antarctica as companions of men, or even less importantly, as companions of women, their 'first' just doesn't make it. Having been conveyed there by men, virtually as baggage, what story could they possibly have to tell? It's likely even Caroline felt this, as she didn't speak about her Antarctic experiences until the 1990s when she was tracked down by an Australian researcher Diane Patterson — herself the first female leader of an Australian Antarctic base.[29]

According to Leane, who categorises Antarctic literature into three stages, the most recent stage is one 'in which Antarctic literature by and about women has flourished and broadened, informed by women's burgeoning opportunities to experience the continent'.[30] However, even modern women's contributions to Antarctic literature are still profoundly influenced by the masculine epic

---

26   FI Norman, JAE Gibson and JS Burgess (1998) 'Klarius Mikkelsen's 1935 landing in the Vestfold Hills, East Antarctica: some fiction and some facts'. *Polar Record* 34(191): 293–304.
27   Norman et al. (1998) 'Klarius Mikkelsen's 1935 landing in the Vestfold Hills', p. 297.
28   Norman et al. (1998) 'Klarius Mikkelsen's 1935 landing in the Vestfold Hills', p. 301.
29   Patterson (1995) 'The Vestfold Hills', p. 44.
30   Leane (2009) 'Placing women in the Antarctic literary landscape', p. 510.

journey of discovery narrative. One example in fiction is Ursula Le Guin's short story 'Sur', published in the *New Yorker* in 1982.[31] Her feminist reworking of the heroic exploration myth imagines 'an alternative history of Antarctic exploration not premised on conquest, nationalism, fame or race to finish'.[32]

Yet Glasberg argues that Le Guin's narrative, about a team of South American women beating Scott and Amundsen to the pole but leaving no trace of their expedition, functions to renarrativise masculine exploration history, and 'documents the very history it seeks to critique. Can Le Guin project a feminist fantasy of prior arrival and yet refuse the complicities of masculine teleologies of conquest?'.[33] This tendency appears in other Antarctic novels and memoirs by women, such as *Antarctic navigation*[34] and *Terra incognita: travels in Antarctica*,[35] which consciously engage with, respond to and re-enact the masculine myths of Antarctica.

My Doctor of Creative Arts (DCA) project included the novel *Chasing the Light*,[36] about Ingrid and her journey to Antarctica. The starting point for the story, the thing that fascinated me, was that Ingrid travelled to Antarctica four times, but missed out on being the first woman to land and therefore was forgotten by history. At the start of my research, and as I learned more about her, I felt a strong urge to excavate her story and tell it to a wider audience. My intent was to use fiction in developing her character and exploring her possible emotional journey, but to base the novel as closely as I could on the known historical facts about her.

Two issues arose for me in the course of the research. First was the challenge of fictionalising history. Le Guin created an entirely fictional cast, whereas I was stepping into that tricky territory of plundering history in search of a good story, the very thing for which historian Inga Clenndinnen took Kate Grenville to task.[37] I started out by using everything I could find about Ingrid and filling in the considerable blanks with my own imagination — a risky undertaking in relation to a person who died in 1976 and has living descendants. How far could I go in recreating her story if I wished to have the creative freedom and imagination to explore all aspects of it? Clendinnen's critique of novelists making free with stories from history is that empathy alone is not enough to allow novelists to understand characters who are widely separated from them by time, space and culture. She says it leads to the illusion of understanding,

---

31 Le Guin, U (1982) 'Sur'. *New Yorker* 1 February, pp. 38–46.
32 Leane (2009) 'Placing women in the Antarctic literary landscape', p. 510.
33 Glasberg (2002) 'Refusing history at the End of the Earth', p. 111.
34 Arthur, E (2005) *Antarctic Navigation*. Bloomsbury Publishing, London.
35 Wheeler, S (1996) *Terra incognita: travels in Antarctica*. Jonathan Cape, London.
36 Blackadder, J (2013) *Chasing the light: a novel of Antarctica*. HarperCollins, Sydney.
37 Clendinnen, I (2006) 'The history question: Who owns the past?' *Quarterly Essay* vol. 23. Black Inc, Melbourne.

when in fact the task of true understanding requires long observation, cool thought and the ability to resist rather than indulge intuition.[38] And of course there is the large ethical question of drawing on a known life and using it as a leaping-off point, with all the complications of that.

Second, I realised I was also deeply influenced by the pervasive Antarctic narrative of the exploratory journey of conquest. I was anything but immune to it. I found myself transposing Ingrid and Caroline into the classic Scott/Amundsen Antarctic narrative. That hero's journey with its inherent drama lent itself irresistibly to these women's stories. Caroline, as the quiet, efficient victor of the competition, stood in for Amundsen, who started later, was better prepared and ultimately won the prize of the South Pole. Ingrid became the tragic and heroic figure of Scott, the one who arrived second, who stood in her equivalent of Scott's 'awful place' knowing that she'd failed in achieving even her own modest first.

These were sobering reflections that resulted in shifts in the creative direction. I decided not to write the novel from Ingrid's point of view, but to expand it into a third-person narrative about her, Mathilde and Lillemor. I chose to create a fictional voyage that incorporated elements of all four of Ingrid's real-life voyages. These were difficult decisions, and meant to an extent letting go of the notion of rescuing Ingrid from history's cracks. My challenge was to proceed with the writing in a way that remained conscious of the influence of that great Antarctic narrative over my story, and to both reflect on it and allow other narratives to emerge.

---

38   Clendinnen (2006) 'The history question', p. 23.

Frames of silence: Some descriptions of the sounds of Antarctica

Stephen Martin[1]

People sometimes say that when watching and listening in the great silences of Antarctica, they can hear their own heartbeat. Almost paradoxically, the great silences can be the frame for a discussion of the sounds and noises of the southern continent.

Before delving into this topic it may be useful to put the listening experience into a broader context of human experience in Antarctica and its surrounding seas.

When people go south they go with an extraordinary range of feelings and expectations. They come from a culture dense with meanings, understandings, symbols and relationships that are so familiar many of them are almost unconscious or even unrecognised.

This was brought into relief as I recently travelled through Bhutan, where the human culture and geography and nature are so intertwined that it's confusing — almost overload. The contrast with a trip to Antarctica — even with 200 years of human history and such understandings as we derive from modern myth and scientific understanding — is enormous. I remember standing in a rhododendron forest with reds, yellows and creams on the trees and thinking about tales of demons and yetis and yak herders that are set in such a forest and thinking just how young are our stories of the human presence in Antarctica.

So, as you travel south you experience a moving away from the density and complexity of human culture — if by sea, you will also get physically unwell and unsettled. You move into cold — sea birds, albatross, petrels and gulls follow the ship and eventually leave. You may see whales but you will see ice — in the form of bergs and large and small pieces floating in the water, and then you'll get to the continent. The air is clearer, you can see farther. More importantly for this discussion, you can hear from greater distances — the silences are enormous and overwhelming and the sounds travels farther in the clearer, dryer air.

And perspectives change — things seem out of kilter.

---

1   Stephen Martin, 8/4 Darley St East, Mona Vale NSW 2103, stephen.martin5@bigpond.com.

For the most part you will lose the familiarity of the everyday. You won't see houses, streets, planes crossing the sky, other people as anonymous crowds. The noises we take for granted are gone.

It can be very unsettling. And into this sense of change and sensory confusion tumble the sights and smells and sounds of one of the world's most extraordinary places. You see blocks of ice that defy imagination — if at Commonwealth Bay or elsewhere, you'll see cliffs of ice hundreds of metres high. The water may be discoloured by ice or by plankton. Mountain-tops poking out of ice will be shrouded by mists, or nearly surrounded by glacier flows. The lights can at times be blinding, or subtly gloomy, a sort of light that makes the ice colours glow. In some places, the sun will set and rise again in 20 minutes — before disbelieving eyes.

It is different to everyday experiences of our northern homelands and some would now say magically so. Early visitors recorded their fear and horror, modern visitors a sense of awe and unreality.

But there are cycles and rhythms as well, seasonal cycles, cycles of light and dark, freezing and melting, a slow irregular rhythm of the glacier flow to the sea, the generation of icebergs as they calve and float slowly north.

So it is clear from this that the sounds can be quiet and ephemeral but they, like the natural noises around the planet, are also elemental and awe-inspiring.

Within this new and changing personal response, are the new sensory experiences — the sounds and noises and silences of Antarctica are experienced with fresh insights — possibly even meanings.

Composer Kyle Gann wrote about John Cage's work *4′33″*, a work of silence nearly 60 years old. Gann defines this work as:

> An act of framing, of enclosing environmental and unintended sounds in a moment of attention in order to open the mind to the fact that all sounds are music … It begged for a new approach to listening, … a blurring of the conventional boundaries between art and life.[2]

The content of the composition is meant to be perceived as the sounds of the environment that the listeners hear while it is performed. The silences highlight the range of sound in the everyday environments.

It's a bit like a form of bearing witness, a Quaker prayer meeting, a communal act of respect and listening.

---

2   Kyle Gann (2010) *No such thing as silence: John Cage's 4′33″*, Yale University Press, p. 42.

I think it has some wonderful resonances for the human experience in Antarctica. And it's a direct link to Antarctic sounds, for the silences, experienced both individually and as a group, as respectful or even awed, are a common human experience in Antarctica — a silence that accentuates the other noises, the silence in which you can hear/feel your own heartbeat.

Here's a list of some of the typical sounds of Antarctica. The sea — washing against the ice, crashing into large icebergs, yes, even gently lapping the shores; the ice (obviously a wide range), sounds of the sea-ice bumping into each other — described by one 19th-century observer as the sounds of crepitation! broken bones rubbing against each other, sea ice cracking under foot (be aware!). The strange and wonderful boom or crack of a glacier cracking — on a still day this noise reverberates through hills — sometimes it is difficult to tell where it comes from and that is a little unsettling; the wind — in the rigging, around huts, across the plateau, the gentle whistle of the wind in the bits and pieces of your clothes; the animals, whales blowing, birds calling, fur seals now repopulating the Peninsula, and penguins. We hear of one of the most unusual sound relationships — that of people, visitors and penguins.

> We have great fun with the penguins — especially making them dance by singing to them.[3]

And of course, people, including noises from talk, radio, ships, recorded music, singing, chattering and celebrations.

There is a strong, almost religious connotation to the descriptions of this silence and an accompanying sense of intrusion — of not quite belonging — which is appropriate for the levels of human occupation in Antarctic. Other sounds mark these occupations of the continent and the technologies people used in attempting to assess the meanings of the sounds or silences.

The silences are a leitmotif, a characteristic of the environment that is a reminder of people's unease and unfamiliarity in Antarctica. Sometimes it's more than this, an intimation of intrusion.

So how do these references appear in the diaries of people who go to Antarctica? They appear described directly and sometimes by implication. Interestingly, sounds and noises and music are not much described in the journals and diaries I've looked at. Obviously the recording of sounds was not a first priority for these diarists.

---

3   Apsley Cherry-Garrard in Stephen Martin (1996) *A history of Antarctica*, State Library New South Wales Press, Sydney, p. 136.

Some examples

In 1929, United States expedition leader Richard Byrd flew over the south. He soberly described the regions around the pole as a 'white desolation and solitude'; his pilot Berndt Balchen was more introspective:

> I was glad to leave. Somehow our very purpose here seemed insignificant, a symbol of man's vanity, an intrusion on this eternal white world. The sound of our engines profaned the silence as we headed back to Little America.[4]

In 1939 Byrd returned to lead another expedition at 'Little America' on the Ross Ice Shelf. This time the men had a radio setup and sent broadcasts out into the world. Byrd had misgivings, like those he expressed when he first heard morse code messages being tapped out for the first Little America broadcasts. He noted,

> When too much talk seems to be the cause of much of the grief in the world, no man could break the isolation of the Last Continent of Silence without a twinge of remorse.[5]

Byrd established a small base a few miles inland from Little America and lived there for a few months. Alone in the Antarctic winter, Byrd took the opportunity to reflect. One afternoon he 'paused to listen to the silence ... the imponderable forces of the cosmos functioning gently, harmoniously, soundlessly ... This is the way the world will look when it dies'.

In the 1930s John Rymill and his team were in the Peninsula. John Stevenson and others looked south into new territory:

> Everywhere was complete calm silence; the sound from the other tent ... we were further south than anybody else in the world, and apart from our companions at the base, there was no human being within 1,500 miles. It made one feel extremely insignificant to see and think of such vast areas untouched by man, and in which man had had no influence whatsoever.[6]

Incidentally, soon after this he listened to political radio broadcasts from Europe, so the silences and noises were then and are now tempered by contact with home.

---

4 Bernt Balchen and Richard Byrd in Stephen Martin (1996) *A history of Antarctica*, p. 179.
5 Richard Byrd in Stephen Martin (1996) *A history of Antarctica*, p. 40.
6 John Stevenson in Stephen Martin (1996) *A history of Antarctica*, p. 54.

Edward Wilson, with Robert Falcon Scott's second expedition (1910–13), wrote a report for the expedition publication. The report was of an arduous and sometimes terrifying journey undertaken to Cape Crozier in the late winter. Despite the conditions the men survived the experience. As befits such a report, it is written in a clear style but there are some engaging descriptions and references to the noises and sounds. They may appear strange, but they became a part of the common experience for Wilson and his companions.

Here are the sounds of Antarctic routines, of the surrounding environment, sometimes familiar, often as locators in the new world, sometimes frightening, threatening or dangerous.

> Tuesday June 27, '11 We camped for lunch at 2.30 pm. having made $6\frac{1}{3}$ miles from Cape Evans. The double tent was easy to pitch, and we began a routine of brushing down the inside, after removing all the contents, every time we broke camp. This routine we continued the whole way to Cape Crozier and it made a great difference to the collection of ice on the upper two-thirds of the tent.

Standing on or near the pressure ridges of ice sheets and learning to read these noises brought the men to a fuller understanding of the world around them.

> Sunday July 9, '11 These were obviously the pressure ridges, and when we stood still we could hear a creaking and groaning of the ice underneath and around us, which convinced us, and later led us to think that the tidal action of the coast here was taken up in part by the pressure ridges without forming any definite tide crack

and

> Monday July 10, '11 By noon a blizzard was blowing from the S.SW of force 6 to 8 and the air was as thick as could be with snow. This continued all day and we lay wet and warm in our bags listening to the periodic movement of the ice pressure, apparently tidal to some extent, beneath and about us.

Travelling in these lands was a new experience and one sometimes interrupted by strange new sounds.

> Wednesday July 19, '11 We had about a mile to go down snow slopes to the edge of the first pressure ridge, and our intention was to keep close in under the land ice cliffs which are very much more extensive now than they were ten years ago. Then we hoped to get in under the actual rock cliffs which had always been the best way down to the rookery in the *Discovery* days. But somehow we got down by a slope which led us into a valley between the two first pressure ridges, and we found it

> impossible to get back in under the land ice cliffs. Nor had we then seen any other way down from the land ice except by the slope we followed. The rest was apparently all ice cliff about 80 to 100 ft high. We tried again & again to work our way in to the left where the land ice cliffs joined the rock cliffs but though we made considerable headway now & then along snow slopes and drift ridges by crossing the least tumbled parts of the intervening pressure lines, we yet came time after time to impossible places & had to turn back & try another way. We tried one possible opening after another and all led to further impasses until the daylight was two-thirds gone and we found ourselves faced in a large snow hollow by a chaotic pile of ice blocks & snow drifts standing almost vertically in our path and all round us to a height of some 60 ft. and completely stopping all chance of progress forward. Here we had the mortification of hearing the cries of Emperor Penguins echoed to us by the rock cliffs on our left. We were still however out of sight of the rookery and we had still a quarter of a mile of chaotic pressure to cross, so we reluctantly gave up the attempt for the day and with great caution and much difficulty owing to the failing light retraced the steps it had taken us about three hours to make. We had been roped together the whole time and had used the sledge continually over soft and rotten looking snow bridges. It was dark by the time we reached safe ground after clambering about 5 hours to no purpose.

And they experienced severe storms. The men had set up a tent and attempted to sit out a fierce storm.

> Sunday July 23, '11 The roof went as follows. We saw, as soon as light showed through the canvas in the early morning, that the snow blocks on the top had all been blown off, and that the upward strain was now as bad as ever, with a greater tendency to flap at the lee end wall. And where the canvas was fixed in over the door it began to work on the heavy stones which held it down, jerking and shaking them so that it threatened to throw them down. Bowers was trying all he could to jam them tight with pyjama jackets & bamboos, and in this I was helping him when the canvas suddenly ripped, and in a moment I saw about six rents all along the lee wall top & in another moment we were under the open sky with the greater part of the roof flapped to shreds. The noise was terrific, and rocks began to tumble in off the walls on to Bowers & Cherry, happily without hurting them, and then the sledge fell in across our sleeping bags, and in a smother of drift Bowers & I bolted in to our own bags, and in them the three of us lay listening to the flap of the ragged ends of canvas over our heads which sounded like a volley of pistol shots going on for hour after hour.

They survived this and continued on, the weird new sounds again reminding them of a new and unfamiliar geography.

> Saturday July 29, '11 We got away before daylight and marched a good soft plod all day, making 6½ miles. Subsidences were frequent and at lunch the whole tent and contents, myself included as I was cook for the day, dropped suddenly with a perceptible bump, and with so long and loud a reverberation all round that we all stood & listened for some minutes. Cherry said it started when his foot went through some snow under the top crust, not when he was digging through this crust. The central subsidence set off innumerable others all round & these others in continually widening circles & the noise took quite some two or three minutes to die away.[7]

Here are some of the human noises and associations noted in the diaries of George Dovers of the Australasian Antarctic Expedition 1911–14. As the expedition vessel, the *Aurora*, approached the continent:

> My first impression, a cry of land on the starboard, away up we all clattered, a light snow was falling, on the port the magnificent ice barrier with the ice blink reflected over it, giant bergs lying grand and splendid between us and the as yet almost invisible land and there looming through the snow on our starboard and ahead the indistinct form of land, which gradually resolved into a sheer ice cliff a vast line with snow and ice covered slopes running back inland and some spires approx. 3 or 4,000 ft high, I will never forget the first sight, it looks very rugged and we may have some difficulty landing.[8]

Here the descriptions of human sounds in Antarctica take on a sense of community — of a small number of people in a strange land, a bit like Dover's description of people smoking in a cabin of the *Aurora*.

> They call our cabin [on *Aurora*] the smoking room after meals we all get in there and the place fairly reeks, now and then a face looms through the smoke and you can tell where a fellow is by the sound of his voice.[9]

One of those diarists who wrote evocatively about a sledging journey was Frank Hurley with the Australasian Antarctic Expedition. Often seen more as a photographer than as a writer, Hurley wrote engagingly about life in Antarctica. Hurley was with Bob Bage and Eric Webb on a sledging journey south towards the south magnetic pole in 1912–13.

---

[7] Edward Wilson (2011) *A tale for our generation: an account of the winter journey*. Australian Capital Equity, West Perth.
[8] George Dovers, Australasian Antarctic Expedition Mitchell Library, Sydney, MLMSS 3812, p. 14.
[9] George Dovers, Australasian Antarctic Expedition Mitchell Library, Sydney, MLMSS 3812, p. 16.

> 12 November [1912]. The blizzard raged throughout the night and this morning little alteration has taken place. In our tiny tent we can barely move about, while to converse with one another we have to raise our voices to a shout so terrific is the swish of drift in the blizzard din.
>
> 16 November. At 6:30 pm heavy nimbus clouds came rolling up from the south and we are wondering if it is again going to snow and blow. A halt was made and tents were erected in a dead calm! What a striking contrast to the blizzard's eternal roar. Every sound seems frozen. Our voices seem strange in this awesome silence, whilst our ears, so accustomed to continuous din, ache. What a stagnant silence! Our tent is limp, for not the gentlest Zephyr stirs. What is going to happen. Bob has just ordered our supports to throw snow on to the tent to make some noise so that we can go to sleep. What a place of excesses, and how welcome to us, wind battered toilers this cessation comes.

After leaving, the party travelled across the ice and through very strong winds which were directly into their faces. On the 16th, after the wind stopped, he wrote:

> It seems as if even sound has become frozen. The absolute calm strikes our ears making them ring. Not a buzz of insect, not even the note of the song bird but a silence awesome and spacelike. Nothing is comparable with the Antarctic Blizzard. Its awful winds and snow drifts & yet in a calmer mood its quiet would drive one mad. We are now camped on the plateau. Ice boundless as the eye can discern on all sides. Around reigns a silence stagnant that seems worse than even noise. Yet what a welcome change to us, that have been so wind battered.
>
> 25 November. About noon two snow petrels came hovering around our camp and settled on the snow a few yards away. We hailed these wild creatures with joy for they are the only signs of living things we have seen for the past fortnight. From whence they came or whither bound gave us room for discussion.

Hurley writing in the tent:

> 16 December. It was hard to imagine we were on the plateau with nearly 250 miles of ice separating us from the hut. There was not even enough wind to stir the tent and although zero, it was warm. I thought it seemed as if camped in the Australian bush and was only brought back to Antarctica by the vigorous boiling of the cooker.
>
> 19 December. An absolute hush fell over the plateau, broken only by the creak & groan of our sledge runners over the polished snow or our

occasional comment on the heat. Bob remarked that it was quite like an Australian summer's day and we could really have partaken [of] ice cream with relish.[10]

As always, it is about people, as I noted in the beginning. Here's a wonderful exchange of sounds between people and penguins as recorded by Edward Wilson during his first Antarctic trip.

> They have lost none of their attractiveness, and are most comical and interesting; as curious as ever, they will always come up at a trot when we sing to them, and you may often see a group of explorers on the poop singing 'For she's got bells on her fingers and rings on her toes, elephants to ride upon wherever she goes,' and so on at the top of their voices to an admiring group of Adélie penguins. Meares is the greatest attraction; he has a full voice which is musical but always very flat. He declares that 'God save the King' will always send them to the water, and certainly it is often successful.[11]

I finish with this lovely quote from Edgeworth David talking about watching the southern lights, the aurora australis.

> Amundsen told me that when he was at Framheim at the east of Barrier Reef just before his famous dash to the Pole, he was called out of his winter quarters one very cold night by Johansen in order to hear what Johansen described as the crackling of the aurora australis. It was a very cold and still night. Amundsen distinctly heard a very faint rhythmically repeated rustling noise in the air. After a time he discovered that this was due to the rapid freezing of the moisture from his breath, and the tiny tinkle made by the minute crystals as they slowly descended under gravity close to his face, sufficiently close for the ear just to catch the faint sound ... He said that he was now confident that this was the true explanation of what poets call the 'crackling of the Northern Lights'.[12]

You won't always have your Antarctic noises beautifully framed by silence and sometimes they will be familiar and human or just plain weird but understandable, but when you do hear a sound coming through the intense silence that a place like Antarctica can engender then you'll realise that you've been in a new and special place in the world. It is a different and remarkable sensory experience, one with strong musical undertones.

---

10 Frank Hurley in Stephen Martin (1996) *A history of Antarctica*, pp. 147–8.
11 Edward Wilson in Stephen Martin (2009) *Penguin*, Reaktion Press, London, p. 35.
12 Edgeworth David in Martin (1996) op. cit. p. 24.

Made and played in Antarctica: People's music in a far-flung place

Bruce Watson[1]

Introduction

Music plays a key role in social ritual, group bonding and broader social cohesion. It is and has been so in all societies across the world and across history. This is as true in Antarctic communities as it is elsewhere, possibly more so. The way people make and share music as part of their daily lives can provide important insights into their society and characteristics.

This chapter focuses on vernacular or community music made and played at Australia's Antarctic bases. Very little of this music has been published, and nowhere has it been systematically studied. Some is documented in station year books, newsletters and reports, and printed in the ANARE Club's journal, *Aurora*. A small number of songs have been included incidentally in books.[2] Some have come to the author through personal communication.

Despite being pervasive in daily life, community music is part of oral culture and transient by nature. It is therefore easily lost and its value easily underestimated.

History

Music has played an important social role in polar life since the first days of exploration by sea. There is a long maritime tradition recognising the effects of music on morale. Many sea voyages had musicians on board to entertain, and to lead working songs, or shanties. This tradition has been passed down to Antarctic bases.

---

1 Bruce Watson, 22 Tynan Street, Preston West, VIC 3072, jandbwatson@gmail.com, www.brucewatsonmusic.com.
2 For example, Tim Bowden (1997) *The silence calling*. Allen & Unwin, St Leonards NSW; Tim Bowden (1991) *Antarctica and back in sixty days*. ABC Enterprises, Crows Nest NSW; Archie McLean and Douglas Mawson, eds (2010) *The Adelie Blizzard: Mawson's forgotten newspaper 1913*. Friends of the State Library of South Australia, Adelaide.

Figure 1. Raising one of the foreyards by use of the capstan on the foredeck. Note chantyman sitting atop the capstan with accordion. He is providing the rhythm for the team of sailors to work to.

Source: Photograph by Frank Hurley. Australian Antarctic Division, © Commonwealth of Australia.

Francis Drake took four musicians including a trumpeter on the *Golden Hind*.[3] William Bligh took a blind fiddler on the *Bounty* for morale.[4] (It didn't work!) Being blind, he would have had no crewing function other than as a musician.

When Ernest Shackleton abandoned the ice-bound *Endurance* in 1915, he allowed everyone only two pounds of bare essentials. The one exception was Leonard Hussey's banjo. When Hussey queried whether they should take it, Shackleton said, 'It's vital mental medicine and we shall need it.'[5] And he was right. Twenty-two of Shackleton's men lived on Elephant Island in the South Atlantic for four months under an upturned boat waiting to be rescued. Frank Hurley said, 'Living in the hut we had very little to do. We used to make up songs about one another and sing them at our Saturday night concerts, where

---

3   Ian Woodfield (1995) *English musicians in the age of exploration*. Pendragon Press, Stuyvesant, NY, p. xiii; John Cummins (1997) *Francis Drake: lives of a hero*. St Martins Press, New York, pp. 49, 73.
4   Woodfield (1995) *English musicians in the age of exploration*, p. 86.
5   LDA Hussey (1949) *South with Shackleton*. Sampson Low, London, p. 65.

our only musical accompaniment was the banjo. Of course our songs were very uncomplimentary, but if someone objected, we made up a worse one about him the next week. And that way we kept ourselves alive and more or less amused.'[6]

Here is part of one of those songs, to the tune of the music hall ditty 'Solomon Levi':

> My name is Frankie Wild-o! and my hut's on Elephant Isle;
> The wall's without a single brick, and the roof's without a tile;
> Yet nevertheless you must confess, in many and many a mile,
> It's the most palatial dwelling-place you'll find on Elephant Isle.[7]

From the first presence of Australians on the Antarctic continent, 'sledgometer verse' was made up by explorers to sing or recite to themselves and others during the long blank hours of the daily march.[8] Elizabeth Leane describes this verse as motivational in both form and content. Frank Hurley's 'Southern Sledging Song' is an example, sung to the simple tune of 'Sailing, Sailing':

> Hauling, toiling, tireless on we tramp
> O'er vast plateau, sastrugi high, o'er deep crevasse and ramp
> Hauling, toiling through drift and blizzard gale
> It has to be done, so we make of it fun,
> We men of the Southern Trail![9]

This is one of many songs included in *The Adelie Blizzard*, the monthly paper of those wintering with Mawson in 1913 at Commonwealth Bay. The songs capture the hardships and pleasures of daily life in that place and time.

> 'A Song on one of the Rare Occasions on which it was Possible to Smoke Outside'
>
> (Tune: 'Eton Boating Song')
>
> Jolly smoking weather
> And a Boat-Harbour Breeze
> Walking in boots of leather
> Standing upright with ease
> And we'll smoke, smoke together
> Striking matches whenever we please
> And we'll smoke, smoke together

---

6 *Vital Mental Medicine: Shackleton's Banjo*. BBC Radio 4, broadcast 11 December 2010. www.bbc.co.uk/programmes/b00wdgr5, accessed 8 March 2011.
7 Hussey *South with Shackleton*, p. 141.
8 Elizabeth Leane (2012) *Antarctica in fiction: imaginative narratives of the Far South*. Cambridge University Press, Cambridge, p. 124.
9 McLean and Mawson *The Adelie Blizzard*. This song was included in vol. 1 no. 1, April 1913.

> Striking matches whenever we please…
> Soon we'll be back in Australia
> Where pipes don't have to be thawed
> And watches outside never fail ya
> Come into the garden, Maud!
> But we'll never forget, inter alia
> Those few calms allowed by the Lord
> No we'll never forget, inter alia
> Those few calms allowed by the Lord.[10]

Most diaries and accounts from the early days of exploration include many references to the expeditioners singing together or listening together to the gramophone.

Musical instruments were taken to Antarctica from the earliest days. Phillip Law, who oversaw the establishment of Australia's permanent presence in Antarctica, was an accomplished musician and took his accordion with him on voyages. He clearly enjoyed a good tune, and would play on many important occasions. In 1955, to celebrate the landing and establishment of Mawson base, the first on the Antarctic mainland, 'Law made hot, spiced glühwein for the occasion and played his piano accordion during the festivities'.[11]

Law recognised the bonding and the boost for morale that a singalong can provide. In the 1950s he even put together the ANARE song book.[12] There are many photos of him leading singalongs, some with the book. It was used for many decades. As recently as 2010 the station leader at Davis wrote:

> The afternoon's feasting … was consumed to the sounds of the ANARE songbook in digital form courtesy of SL (me). Funny but I haven't had many orders for the CD. My favourite number is No. 140: 'Always true to you darlin' in my fashion.'[13]

---

10 McLean and Mawson *The Adelie Blizzard* vol. 1 no. 5, October 1913.
11 Bowden (1997) *The silence calling*, p. 122.
12 *ANARE song book* (anonymous and undated) [Presumed publisher ANARE Club], Melbourne.
13 www.antarctica.gov.au/living-and-working/stations/davis/this-week-at-davis/2010/this-week-at-davis-25-june-2010, accessed 23 February 2012.

Figure 2. Phil Law playing his accordion, on ship.

Source: Photograph by Peter King. Australian Antarctic Division, © Commonwealth of Australia.

Music and community in the Antarctic

In some respects Australia's Antarctic bases are like any other community; each member brings all their personal and cultural background with them. However, they are in a very different, unique place: in a small, temporary closed society in a stunning but physically difficult environment — similar to shipboard communities.

Both these similarities and differences from mainstream society are reflected in music in Antarctica, as communities swell and contract each year. Communities are constantly changing and renewed from back home. There is some continuity of culture, and traditions develop, but there is far more rapid change than in most communities.

There is a degree of randomness in the nature of Antarctic community music at any given base in any given year, depending on who is there. It may be country, jazz, folk, pop, rock, reggae, funk, blues, singer-songwriter, and sometimes classical. Mostly it is music that people can participate in, in some way: playing (skilfully or not), tapping out percussion, singing along, or dancing. Some years a station has a 'house band'. Sometimes these bands morph from summer to winter to summer to winter, with evolving membership and repertoire.

But rituals and musical forms are passed down and have grown over the years, such as Midwinter festivities and theme-party nights.[14] These are a catalyst for making up and performing many songs.

The songs

Community music tends to be simple, catchy and repetitive. This makes it easy to share, and sharing is part of its power, as a mode of group bonding and a catalyst for it.

Cover songs are performed and are popular, as people know them and can sing along. My research focuses on the music that people have written in Antarctica. There would be hundreds of such pieces. While some have been documented, many exist only on scraps of paper tucked away in people's bottom drawers, or in the heads of those who made them up or sang along.

This paper draws on around 60 collected so far. While it is too small a corpus to enable a statistical analysis, some patterns begin to emerge:

1. Most are humorous songs, many written for special occasions. A small number are lyrical descriptions of Antarctic life. Personal songs are rare. These characteristics contrast with Antarctic poetry, where the pattern is reversed. While humorous poems do exist, Antarctic poetry is primarily lyrical and much more introspective. Community music tends to be about fun and building social cohesion through humour rather than about artistic expression.

2. Most are written to well known tunes: popular songs, folk songs, songs from musicals. This reflects the democratic nature of this music — it is not for specialist composers. Anyone can put a new set of words to an existing song, and it is often done very cleverly.

3. Of the humorous songs, almost all are about the shared experiences of Antarctic life: the weather, the living conditions, the jobs, the food, drinking, travel, equipment, animals, specific incidents — and the people.

The remainder of this section discusses some examples of these themes.

The first is about a series of incidents. It refers to weasels; amphibious snow vehicles used from the 1940s to the 1990s. Bob Dovers had a few mishaps with

---

14   Bowden (1991) *Antarctica and back in sixty days*, pp. 112 ff and passim; Bowden (1997) *The silence calling*, pp. 219–20, 228, 446 and passim.

them, breaking through the sea ice, requiring chain block winches to retrieve them. Even reading the words on the page, in one's mind's ear one can hear everybody singing along and having a light-hearted go at Dovers!

'Chain Blocks'

(Bill Harvey, Mawson 1954. Tune: 'My Bonnie')

Bob Dovers has ditched his new weasel
Bob Dovers has done it again
Three times it has been in the ocean
It's odds on he'll be there again
Chain blocks, chain blocks
Oh bring back my weasel to me, to me
Chain blocks, chain blocks
Oh bring back my weasel to me ...[15]

This next example is also about a key part of Antarctic life.

'Mawson Tractor Song'

('Frosty' McDonald, Mawson 1962. Tune: 'The Deadwood Stage')

The tractor train is rollin' over the plains
The driver's cold but he never never complains
Beautiful sky, a wonderful day
So drift stay away, drift stay away, drift stay away
The tractor train is comin' over the crest
Like a homin' pigeon a hankerin' for its nest
Twenty-three miles to cover today
So drift stay away, drift stay away, drift stay away[16]

A third example of a song describing Antarctic life is this one to the tune of 'Click Go the Shears', a popular tune to parody. This song comes from 1966, the year this tune was used for the jingle to explain decimal currency. Some of its sentiments are very dated, reflecting the culture of its time.

'Antarctic Theme Song'

(Betty Thiele for Stan Taylor, Wilkes 1966. Tune: 'Click Go the Shears')
Down in the Antarctic, no cares to bother us
No dodging Sunday drivers, all in a bloody rush
No sheilas or taxes — no decimal currency
It's a man's world down under, though it lacks luxury

---

15 Tim Bowden (1997) *The silence calling*, p. 117.
16 Pers. comm. from John 'Snow' Williams.

Chorus:

Down in the Antarctic, with the penguins and the snow
Where there are no Bondi beaches, and the flamin' blizzards blow
We're intellectual characters, so when we're feeling blue
We sing and drown our sorrows in a good old fashioned brew ...[17]

While most songs describe or recount stories about Antarctic life, many are about the people — sometimes individuals, but mostly a catalogue of the cast of characters at the base and something memorable about every one of them, often embarrassing. Again, there is a strong social and morale function: sharing stories of life and people, just like Shackleton's crew on Elephant Island.

Friendly insulting in song can strengthen social bonding by breaking down barriers of formality and role. It asserts that you belong, and those you are targeting belong, because you can do this without giving offence.

You will often read in accounts of performances that there is a bit of humorous insulting traded back from the audience. Even Mawson writes that the audience for the semi-impromptu performance of the opera *The Washerwoman's Secret* was 'crowded on a form behind the dining-table, making tactless remarks'.[18]

Much of the music at Midwinter celebrations parallels the parody structure of the *Cinderella* play which is often performed as part of Midwinter. A standard story or song is adapted to local circumstances, gently breaking rules and conventions of decency, hierarchy, customs. Colleagues are insulted and sexual innuendo and scatological humour are key ingredients!

Following are sample verses from two songs about the year's cast of characters. Variations of the first song below have been sung at different bases over many years. These songs are very long, with one or more verses per person.

'REPSTAT Song' 1966 version

(Rod MacKenzie, Wilkes 1966. Tune: 'Botany Bay')

Geoff Smith you know is our leader
A job that he does just fine
He taught us to put up the buildings
And also to sing *Clementine*
Frank Smith is our deputy leader
So you can see that we're well led

---

[17] *Aurora* [journal of the ANARE Club], March 1967, p. 33.
[18] Douglas Mawson (1915) *The home of the blizzard*, EBook #6137, ch. 11 www.gutenberg.org/files/6137/6137-h/6137-h.htm, accessed 23 February 2012.

He's a beauty at cleaning up chunder
And putting sick people to bed …[19]

'My Favourite People'

(Anon., Casey 1992, Tune: 'My Favourite Things')

Dev in a turban, chapattis and bourbon
Foods which are spicy and all things suburban
Foods with a kick, things with wheels that go quick
These are a few of his favourite things…
Pat our Pom plumber has hangovers in Summer
Works in the crap farm, the smells are a bummer
What he can do with a plunger or two
What goes in your loo he can tell you that too…[20]

Many songs are written for other special occasions, such as birthdays or Christmas.

'The Twelve Days of Christmas'

(Anon., Davis Christmas 2005)

On the 12th day at Davis the Station Leader gave to me…
Twelve-minute showers …
Eleven dodgy forecasts,
Ten tonnes of sewerage,
Nine angry tradies,
Eight all-Davis emails,
Seven types of pastas,
Six Chinese lagers,
A spaaare CASA Skiii…
Four weeks of slushy,
3-minute showers,
Two Saturday duties,
And a chopper ride to the A-mer-y.[21]

---

19   Ian Mackie (1982) 'REPSTAT summer party 1965–66'. *Aurora* 2(5) Sept: 13–14. 'REPSTAT' (rep[lacement] + stat[ion]) was the name given to the Wilkes station following its handover to Australia from the United States. It was later renamed Casey.
20   Casey station yearbook 1992, held by the Australian Antarctic Division Library, Kingston.
21   www.antarctica.gov.au/living-and-working/stations/davis/this-week-at-davis/2006/january-2006/6-january-2006, accessed 23 February 2012.

Antarctica: Music, sounds and cultural connections

Figure 3. Christmas carols on the Amery Ice Shelf, 2006.

Source: Photograph by Shavawn Donoghue. Australian Antarctic Division, © Commonwealth of Australia.

Out of context these songs may appear trite, but on the Antarctic bases they always receive a rapturous reception — without fail. There is no doubt that they fulfil that function of community bonding.

From the heroic era to the present day, the musical style may change with fashion, but there are no real differences in these characteristics of humour, parody, and the gentle insults. This suggests that they continue to fulfil an ongoing social function.

Some suggest that more recent songs are less bawdy with introduction of women and a code of conduct — but that is not necessarily the case.

One change in fashion is a trend away from traditional/folk songs and towards pop songs, mostly Australian, reflecting the same trend in Australia as a whole, as well as the strong Australian pop scene in recent decades. Here is an example.

'To the Floor'[22]

(John Innes, Davis 1999. Tune: 'To Her Door', Paul Kelly)

They got in a Hagglunds
She had to get a licence
Tomsy gave a lesson
It went a bit like this
They started up and checked it,
Then she started driving
She drove it pretty slowly
— It really was the pits
John said, 'I'm not standing by
To watch you slowly drive
Press that pedal, to the floor,
To the floor, to the floor, to the floor' …

The instruments

From the start, the piano was an essential item at every base. But it was not always used. The 1948 Heard Island party had a piano in their little rec room. It took half a day's work to get it there from the boat. Only then did someone ask, 'Who can play?' — Dead silence![23]

People have always taken their own instruments to play or to learn during the long, isolated winter: guitars, mouth organs, accordions, saxophones, trumpets, clarinets, flutes, violins, trombones, banjos, ukuleles — and more bagpipes than may be considered good taste.

There are many examples of people making their own instruments; some as basic as improvised percussion on kitchen utensils, and some very elaborate projects. The tea chest bass was common, as was the lagerphone (bottle tops nailed to a long stick which is hit with a short stick).

Some of the homemade instruments have required great ingenuity, becoming exercises in collaboration across the community. An entry from the station log at Mawson in 1960 says: 'George again spent nearly all Friday night making a bass fiddle. It looks like the genuine article, sounds good and damn me he plays it well.' Bill Singleton made a bugle at Mawson in 1984. On Macquarie Island in 1959 George Casasayas made a three-string violin from an old jam tin. The bow was made using cotton thread. The carpenter made resin for the bow by heating

---

22   Davis station yearbook 1992, held by the Australian Antarctic Division Library, Kingston.
23   Bowden (1996) *The silence calling*, p. 55.

wood from an old packing box. On Macquarie Island in 1965 John Jenkin made a drum from an old custard tin and rabbit fur. They used an encyclopedia to work out how to tan the hide and the carpenter helped with wood to stretch the skin.

Figure 4. Music room, Mawson.

Source: Photograph by Donald Styles. Australian Antarctic Division, © Commonwealth of Australia.

Music and social cohesion

Station yearbooks and reports provide recognition of how important community music is.

The 1979 Mawson station leader's report, in assessing morale that year, says: 'A limiting factor on the social scene was our lack of any really competent musicians. I realise this is the luck of the draw, but can well imagine the advantages in having a so gifted expeditioner.'[24]

---

24   Mawson station leader's report 1979, held at the Australian Antarctic Division Library, Kingston.

Keith Lodwick, describing life on Heard Island in 1954, says: 'The piano was a great asset to the camp amenities; it was always a nice relaxation for Jack Walsh who played anything from bawdy songs to Beethoven.'[25] So all that effort getting the piano there in 1948 eventually paid off!

Figure 5. A 'ding' [party], Atlas Cove, Heard Island, 1953–54.

Source: Photograph by Fred Elliott. Australian Antarctic Division, © Commonwealth of Australia.

The 2005 Davis yearbook says, 'Music played a central role in keeping people happy and sane throughout the year, whether you're one to make noise or just listen ... There's something addictive about getting together with a group of people and making music.'[26]

House bands bond and develop their skills over the winter and tend to peak in the second half of the year — just as morale often dips after Midwinter. Music provides a valuable means to counteract the annual mood cycle.

Change and continuity

Reflecting broader social change, there is less homemade music making now in Antarctica — just as there is in Australia. There are so many newer forms of

---

25 Keith Lodwick (2006) 'Notes on expedition to the Antarctic 1954–1955'. *Aurora* 5(5), Sept: 18–20.
26 Davis station yearbook 2005, held by the Australian Antarctic Division Library, Kingston.

entertainment to compete for people's attention now. In Antarctica the internet enables people to spend more time in touch with home, and for their emotional lives to be lived more at home, and less totally on the Antarctic base. There is less social bonding, and probably less need for it. The social role of music appears to be decreasing as a result.

Better station facilities have also fragmented the space in which leisure time is spent. It is no longer all in the rec room, with a negotiated timetable of shared activities, including music-making and singing. There are separate spaces for different activities and less time spent all together. The 'slushy' may still choose the music to be broadcast across the station, but it is easier for others to put on the headphones and listen to their own playlist on their iPod.

Figure 6. Singalong on ship.

Source: Photograph by Eric Philips. Courtesy Australian Antarctic Division, © Commonwealth of Australia.

For all that, there is still the occasional singalong — it is just less common. It is the same in Australia. It cannot be measured objectively, but anecdotal evidence suggests that it is more common in Antarctica than Australia because, despite the changes, there is still very strong community. Unlike most communities, Antarctic communities have a small number of people in an isolated place with a common purpose. And while public space may be more fragmented than it once was, it is nowhere near to the same extent as in suburbia or an apartment block. There is still more social need and more opportunity for making music together in Antarctica.

There are also influences that encourage community music making. These include the rise of karaoke, which is a more modern way in which way ordinary people have fun together with music, even if it doesn't involve original songs. In addition, facilities for music at Australia's Antarctic bases have developed from the piano in the rec room to organised, dedicated music rooms with keyboards, drum kits and electric guitars. This encourages the formation of bands and makes it easier to practise.

Figure 7. 'Changeover & new faces. And more beer! And a guitar player with new songs. Always a high point of the year', Mawson station.

Source: Photograph by Grahame M Budd. Australian Antarctic Division, © Commonwealth of Australia.

Conclusion

Community music plays a key role in Antarctic life and in building community: bringing joy, sharing and re-telling experiences. It continues to change, reflecting changes to infrastructure and broader cultural and technological progress in Antarctica and the world. Yet it retains its own special characteristics, reflecting the uniqueness of the place and its community life.

It is striking how these songs unconsciously, yet uncannily, distil so many facets and details of ordinary life and culture that do not otherwise get documented. The examples in this paper may lack subtlety, but if you examine the verses closely you see rich detail delivered with economy. It is all a bit of fun, but what we do for fun can tell us a lot about ourselves and our society.

'A Vast Scale: Evocations of Antarctica'

Rupert Summerson[1] and Claire Beynon[2]

Introduction

Collaboration is an exciting — and instinctual — way to work. To quote evolutionary biologist Lynn Margulis (1938–2011), 'Among the most successful — that is, most abundant — living beings on the planet are ones that have teamed up'.[3] In support of the ongoing conversation between Art and Science, we felt motivated to set up a community website that would engender discussion (initially, at least) on the relationship between music and the Antarctic environment. Our intention was to create a welcoming, easy-to-navigate site with a series of short videos featuring Antarctic landscapes overlaid with our choice of music. We would then invite members of a selected audience to interact with these short films, responding in an informal and conversational way to their content and soundtracks.

Setting up the website

After considering various web formats (including blogs — WordPress and Blogger), we concluded that a Ning community site would serve our collective needs most effectively. Ning sites are structured in such a way that they encourage members to post their own material (images, videos, blog posts, web links, etc) and to both initiate and contribute to a range of discussions. While our Ning site 'A Vast Scale — Evocations of Antarctica' was directed and managed by us both (RS and CB), responsibility for the site's success, or otherwise, largely depends on each member's participation.

Along with easy set-up, layout features and functions, Ning's advantage is that it is a secure site — something we considered necessary since it would allow members greater freedom of expression. Ning also allows for comments,

---

1 Dr Rupert Summerson, PO Box 3853, Manuka, ACT 2603, rupert.summerson@bigpond.com.
2 Claire Beynon, 22 Adderley Terrace, Ravensbourne, Dunedin 9022, NZ, clarab@earthlight.co.nz, www.clairebeynon.com.
3 Lynn Margulis and Dorion Sagan (1995) *What is Life?* University of California Press, Berkeley CA, p. 224.

discussion forums and individual members' pages (see Figure 1). Membership was by invitation and members were encouraged to invite other interested people to join the site and contribute to its life.

Our intention was to create a discussion forum rather than set up a formal survey; the logic behind this was to engender lively exchange between people from a wide range of disciplines — rather like gathering informally around a dinner table instead of in a boardroom. We deliberately avoided trying to come to any conclusions; we felt that in a field which has barely been touched, that would be far too premature. Our primary motivation was to establish a network of like-minded people and a venue within which robust and wide-ranging discussion would be welcomed. Nevertheless, we are able to report on some common themes that emerged from the discussions.

During the course of this project 38 people became members of the website 'A Vast Scale'. During the period it was active there were 877 viewings of the 13 videos and 116 coments were posted. Sadly, the site did not become the ongoing discussion site that we hoped it would and it was dismantled in 2013. All the material has been archived and is being held jointly by the authors.

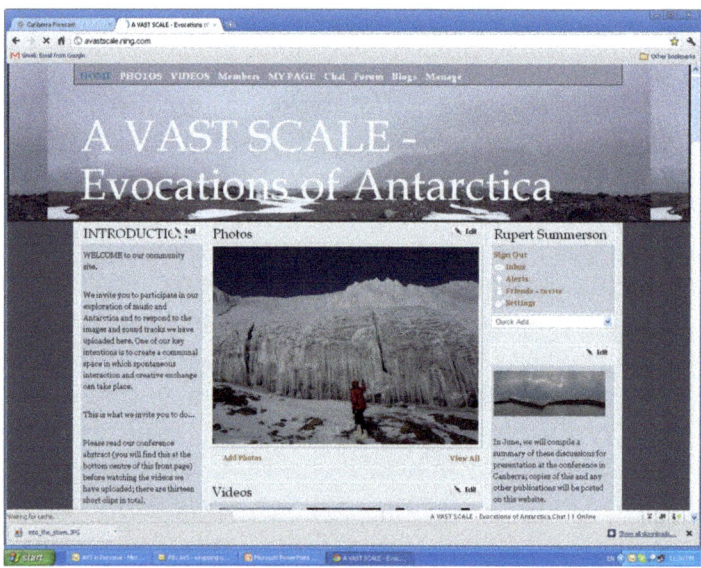

Figure 1. Screen capture of the home page 'A Vast Scale: Evocations of Antarctica'.

Source: Photograph by Rupert Summerson and Claire Beynon.

The videos

The videos are at the heart of 'A Vast Scale' and mostly comprise sets of still photos that were linked to form a movie to which a soundtrack was added. The music in the soundtracks was carefully chosen to represent music that we thought represented the landscapes. It very soon became apparent that our tastes were not universally shared! Table 1 lists the videos, the music that accompanied them and the authors of the videos.

Table 1. Videos, accompanying music and video authors, 'A Vast Scale: Evocations of Antarctica'

video name	music accompaniment	author
Antarctic Sublime	Vaughan Williams: Symphony no. 7	RS
A Voyage to Antarctica v1	Westlake: Antarctica (At the pole)	RS
A Voyage to Antarctica v2	Rachmaninov: Isle of the Dead	RS
Grimly Majestic	Bruckner: Symphony no. 8	RS
Heart of Whiteness v1	Kyorei (Traditional Japanese)	RS
Heart of Whiteness v2	Kalhor: Night Silence Desert	RS
In the Vestfold Hills	Rachmaninov: Prelude no. 9 in Eb minor	RS
In this place silence has a voice	David Raphael Katz	CB
Lacrimosa	Zbigniew Preisner: 'Lacrimosa' from Requiem for a Friend	CB
Rare sounds abound in these places where wind is dressed in white	Arvo Pärt: Fratres (Mother Night)	CB
Step out onto white not as a body bearing any weight but as a feather might	Arvo Pärt: Fratres (Fur Alina)	CB
Wandering Adélie	Zoe Keating: Optimist	CB
Weathered Systems	Andrew Bird: Weather Systems	CB

Here we each (RS and CB) describe very briefly our ideas behind the choice of imagery and music, which are followed by some comments from the other members. It is not possible to provide representative comments, as people generally did not have similar responses, so a range of comments is provided, with anonymity preserved.

Antarctic Sublime: The terror and beauty in Antarctica's landscapes (RS)

This film explores ideas of the sublime rendered into pictures and music. The pictures chosen represent landscapes that are grand, desolate and overwhelming as well as potential dangers such as bad weather. The music chosen, Vaughan Williams' Symphony no. 7, *Sinfonia Antartica*, complements the images well with the rising phrases, crashing chords, austere angelic voices and finally the wind machine.

Comments:

- 'I liked the simple statement in the title. I started out with low expectations (terror on a six-inch screen?!) but was v pleased with the effect of music (with which I was unfamiliar) and images together. Both worked with "beauty and terror" with restraint, somehow. Yes, the imagination needs to be employed but anyone who's been cold or isolated in a landscape has that to bring to the experience.'

- 'Ah, the *Sublime* again! Looks like we're on the same conceptual page. I watched the mountains piece first — couldn't help attaching the Vaughan Williams music to those pictures as well. The choral bits especially. The human voice placed against these wide, harsh, pitiless spaces is potent.'

- 'I find this painful to watch. The strident blue title screen is jarring. The quote from Bourke is displayed so briefly I there is no time to read it. The sound bursts in as if part-way into the recording. The music captures the vast scale and motion of Antarctica, but the images are static. There is also a "dead" spot at the end before the credits.'

A Voyage to Antarctica v1 (RS)

The intention of this film is to portray a voyage to Antarctica by sea, especially the final part through the sea-ice zone. The film opens with encounters with icebergs before penetrating the sea ice. A number of birds and animals are seen. The film ends with ice cliffs representing the coast of Antarctica. The music chosen for this version is *At the Pole*. *Wooden Ships* might have seemed to have been a natural choice but I preferred the excitement implicit in *At the Pole*.

Comments:

- 'Such a lot of tension and anticipated danger in the music, to me it didn't suit the images that well, even though I know it's dangerous to sail through the ice. If the climax had been a killer whale trying to take a bite out of you it might have worked better, but the music wanted a destination and I didn't feel like the slideshow had one.'

- 'There seems a general view that version 2's soundtrack is better suited; however, I like the forward rhythmic drive of the percussion and chords that characterises this one — it evokes a sense of moving forward, journeying, and a sense of anticipation and danger (even if that might be a little too exaggerated in this case). That said, I felt version 2 did fit quite well, although it didn't seem to be going forward to the same extent. You're really just talking about sound and image bites here, so a sense of journey has to be communicated a little more directly than it might otherwise be?'

- 'Music is too pounding and heavy for what are pretty calm iceberg scenes.'

A Voyage to Antarctica v2 (RS)

This film uses the same imagery as version 1 but the music is from *The Isle of the Dead* by Sergei Rachmaninov. The repetitive rhythm sounds like waves and the rather gloomy melody seems to represent the often grey skies and fogs very well.

Comments:

- 'I felt lonely watching this. The images of single creatures by themselves. Almost as if there's no way out. Stuck in a way, except the birds, but it seems like creatures would be wandering a lot, looking for something. Or at least if I were a creature there, that's what I would be doing. I'm sure they are quite content. The aerial image of the ice reminded me of farmland in the midwest (US) or farmland in the US in general. Patches. Sea and ice quilts.'
- 'Some beautiful and compelling images. I liked the simple, subtle beginning portion of the music. Toward the end it was a little too busy and dramatic for my taste as I looked at these very static, austere images. The one slide of the two ice towers reminded me of the old John Wayne westerns directed by John Ford in Monument Valley, Utah with its rock spires thrusting high above the desert landscape.'
- 'At first I wanted the images to move at a quicker pace; however, the music and images captured me and held my attention, even managed to slow me down, thank you!!! Really nice imagery and compositions. I thought the music worked really well although I would have ended the photo sequence a little earlier before the change in the music, also the music finished a little abruptly.'

Grimly Majestic (RS)

The title of this movie is a quotation from *The heart of the Antarctic* by Ernest Shackleton:

> As the days wore on, and mountain after mountain came into view, grimly majestic, the consciousness of our insignificance seemed to grow on us.

The landscapes are all stills of mountains (Figure 2). I chose part of *Symphony no. 8* by Anton Bruckner. Whilst travelling through the mountains of Alexander Island (west of the Antarctic Peninsula) many years ago I distinctly remember asking myself what sort of music best represented the landscape and thinking that the 'cathedrals of sound' that Bruckner composed seemed, to my mind, to suit it best.

This video was the most viewed and provoked the most comments. A representative selection of the comments is reproduced below.

- 'Awesome photographs. Literally. I think of the Romantic notion of the sublime, of a grandeur so vast and majestic it creates its own terror. This may be what is meant by the "grim" of the title, but to me the only thing grim is the music — by the end, I was fighting off all those 19th-century Germanic swells. I watched again without the sound — not an option — and with the level lower, but the Bruckner was still distracting. Can't help feeling this grand montage would be enhanced by some other music, perhaps something more brooding than booming.'
- 'Big, solid music matches the mountains.'
- 'I found this piece completely overwhelming. It set my ions trembling/got me panicked, so much so I wanted to switch it off and head for the closest crevasse.'
- 'Splendid music but it seemed to be proclaiming: These mountains are getting more magnificent as we go! Yes, a little overbearing.'

Figure 2. Video page for 'Grimly Majestic' (screen snapshot).

Source: Photograph by Rupert Summerson and Claire Beynon.

Heart of Whiteness v1 (RS)

This video is intended to try and represent the heart of Antarctica — the vast areas of featureless snow and icescapes that ironically very few people see or experience. The images chosen for the video are all of this inland ice, including some from the South Pole during winter darkness. The soundtrack for this first version is a traditional Japanese piece called 'Kyorei' which can be translated as 'The Spirit of Nothingness'. 'Kyorei' is part of the shakuhachi (Japanese bamboo flute) honkyoku (original music) repertoire and is characterised by almost extreme austerity and a steadily rising cadence, both of which seem appropriate for the central Antarctic ice sheet.

Comments:

- 'Yearning. The sound reminds me of a call on a Pacific conch shell — with the images it seems as if the sound is reaching out, almost pleading (for someone to hear?), across the expanse. You hold your breath waiting for a reply, but there's none, not even an echo, the sound travels towards infinity (as does the landscape). That outward travelling sound also takes your eye across the surface towards distant light or glimpsed form.'
- 'I thought the two simplicities worked well together. It was hard to tell whether the music expressed what one felt spontaneously about the landscape or was telling you how to feel about it — I suppose that's always the 'danger' of mixing media.'
- 'I think this sound track would have worked better for me with the grimly majestic mountain images. Here it is too broken along with the breaks between slides — when the imagery is all about the longest most continuous eternal wind ... whatever the sound — it needed to not change as often. I am curious about whether the change between slides would be carried better by the actual sound of wind — whether roar or whistle or ... sustained?'

Heart of Whiteness v2 (RS)

The sound track for version 2 of Heart of Whiteness is music from Khorasan in Iran — the CD is titled *Night Silence Desert* with music composed by Kayhan Kalhor. I chose this track to represent a different response to desert scenes and as with version 1 I wanted to use music that I thought would probably be unfamiliar — like the landscapes in the imagery, which are the same as version 1.

Comments:

- 'Ironically I think the stringed instrument conveys the skittering patterns created by the wind better than a wind instrument would. The very fine reverberation of the string seems to mimic the very fine etching of the surface of the ice, especially the closer views. I agree at first you associate this music with hot places, but that is perhaps our preconception — many of those places also have very cold winters and mountains. It is in the end about precision, pattern on the edge of random, fineness. I liked the fit except at the end with the darker images which seemed to ask for something more sonorous — perhaps a discord of images rather than of the match to music, which otherwise I liked best.'

- 'I really loved this piece, one of my favourites. I thought the music and images worked so well together. I found the music alluring and mysterious which made me pay close attention to what image was coming next. I find this type of sparse, slower paced music works really well, when the music is too intense it seems to overpower the image and something is lost.'

- 'Comparing versions one and two: I had a much more positive and engaged response to v2 because there was more to listen to, less of a vast emptiness as in v1. But I can see how the minimalism of v1 would be more appropriate, more evocative of actually being on the featureless plateau, where one must struggle with the lack of much to pay attention to.'

In the Vestfold Hills (RS)

The Vestfold Hills are an ice-free range of hills in the hinterland of Davis Station in eastern Antarctica. One of the largest coastal ice-free areas in Antarctica, the Vestfold Hills would be familiar to generations of Australian Antarctic expeditioners. One of Rachmaninov's piano preludes (No. 9 in E flat minor) was chosen as the soundtrack for this video in order to experiment with responses to a piece in a minor key. The rolling terrain seems to be represented very well by the music. This was the least viewed of all the videos for reasons unknown.

Comments:

- 'I make a connection between the rolling, up and down piano track and the rolling, uneven landscapes, so a good fit. Maybe the music is a bit too polished and methodical, though.'

- 'I also found the rolling tumbling music suited the rough landscape, the ending was particularly appropriate. But I felt the Rach is too romantic and lush for such barren and harsh images and didn't much like the pairing.'

In this place silence has a voice (CB)

This film incorporates porcelain bell vessels and sculptural pieces created by South African artists Katherine Glenday and Christina Bryer. Both are drawn to this medium for its translucency and fragility, for the way it holds light and sound and offers both back. When struck with a soft-headed drumstick, Katherine's vessels emit a sound like that of a Tibetan gong or cathedral angelis.

The vessels' relationship to the Antarctic landscape is reinforced by the fact that the clay body used to make these pieces (a percentage of which came from the White Cliffs of Dover) contains fossil remnants of foraminifera ('forams') and coccolithophors, clues to the scientific research that has been carried out in the vicinity of the Explorers Cove site for the past 25 years.

Christina Bryer is a mathematician as well as an artist. Periodicity is the keystone of her work. When we first sent her images of foraminifera — specifically, *Astrammina triangularis* — she delighted in the mathematical 'blueprints' employed by the forams in the design and construction of their shells and embarked on the creation of a series of exquisite sculptural tributes to the unicellular creatures.

This video features these two artists, placing them and their work purposefully and exquisitely within the Antarctic landscape they have long dreamed of.

Comments:

- 'The ring of resonance on air. The sound of the "bell" and the clarinet, as a wind instrument, seemed a great way to begin this video. There are lovely moments when the harmonics of each instrument merge, cross and linger, just as the nature of object and nature inter-react and intermingle.'
- 'I loved it. These women-made objects belong in this landscape. What an affirmation: "We belong in the landscape. Not gross egoistic intrusions into nature. Instead clear, sleek, joyous insertions into a spiritual conversation." Hurrah! Loved the music that went with the images as well.'
- 'Long notes sound, Long shadows fall. Cracks form in ice and human forms. We journey from surface to depth. Thank you, Claire!'
- 'Against the ice such small objects look like their own mountains. Everything has such delicate features. Sound and life frozen into such beautiful patterns.'

'Lacrimosa' (CB)

The choral piece accompanying this video is a track, the 'Lacrimosa' from Zbignew Preisner's album *Requiem for My Friend*. It seemed to me to embody weightiness and solemnity in a way that echoes the *gravitas* and desolation of the vast landscapes represented in the movie. There's a keening quality here that I find at once discomforting and hauntingly coherent. Several members of 'A Vast Scale' made reference to the Christchurch earthquakes; this very likely added an extra layer of breath-holding poignancy to this piece.

Comments:

- 'I really enjoy that, for many, the scale is not immediately decipherable — and yet the music is so huge. I adore the fact that the poor old eyes and head do not know on which scale the next image will resolve. And the music swells and swells as does the swing between visual scales. It was a potent compelling workout. I didn't think I would like it as a union when it started: by the end "yes". And my second-favourite collection of imagery! Stunning.'
- 'Cripes, I think I might burst if I felt an earthquake whilst listening to 'Lacrimosa' and viewing these images… how much sensory tumult can one poor hominid endure? You are of sinewy stuff.'

Rare sounds abound in these places where wind is dressed in white (CB)

For a truly exhilarating and unforgettable experience, stand at the foot of a glacier with your body braced against a mighty wind. Every cell hums, quivers, vibrates. This footage was captured during a Condition 2 storm in front of the Wilson Piedmont Glacier, on the southern rim of the Ferrar Fjord. The opening bars of Arvo Pärt's spine-chilling composition *Mother Night* expresses the tautness and tension of this environment.

Comments:

- 'I've just been watching again, over and over, and this piece just gets more fascinating. Watching that wind sweep the snow is riveting. Never gets tiring. And the music: wonderful, an altogether different mood and pace than the blowing snow. This creates an interesting relationship between the two. The Pärt does not offer commentary on the picture; indeed, to me it has little connection to what's playing before my eyes. The music creates a space to watch the wind, and the footage a space to deeply listen to that violin and shiver-making piano chord at the end. It works beautifully. Rather than being an integrated experience, the two occur side-by-side, each an experience unto itself. I am aware of myself successfully, enjoyably, doing two things at once.'
- 'What picture and music have in common: both busy, relentless, minutely detailed pattern building to a whole. Not a big fan of violins in general, but the high, scratchy sound evokes an imagined idea of the sandy blast of fine grained snow against skin, clothes or tent. The climax of the music reminds me of the deep, resonant whole that is Antarctica, made up of millenia of blowing snow packing into ice enough to sink a whole continent.'

Step out onto white not as a body bearing any weight but as a feather might (CB)

The title of this piece is the first line of 'Thin Ice', a two-line poem (Claire Beynon 2007) that reads as follows:

Step
out
onto
white
not
as
a
body
bearing
any
weight
but
as
a
feather
might

When I wanted a little more than the company of silence, Arvo Pärt's album *Fratres* — specifically 'Spiegel Im Spiegel' — was my music of choice while I was living and working at Explorers Cove, New Harbour. My camera was always poised to capture the dynamic intricacies of ice. Each day, the ice drew and re-drew itself — I found its calligraphy eloquent and surprising. When the thaw began to work its magic towards the end of the season, each step across the sea ice had to be made with extra care. Walking and listening became synonymous — almost a meditation.

Comments:

- 'Gorgeous. My only wish is that the pictures moved a bit slower. I want to savour each one. I realise this means either a longer musical selection or fewer images, but so many of the stills are so beautiful — and for their minimalism, not at all simple — I want to gaze at them from edge to edge and corner to corner.'

- 'I'm so literal! The music sounds to me just like the shapes of snow and ice, the plinking of piano and the plops of frozen water are so well matched. I agree with X, I would like more time to look at each image carefully, so I will go back and watch again.'

- 'These two seemed to work so well together I could equally imagine the music being written to the images or vice-versa. Meditative.'

Wandering Adélie (CB)

I was being a little provocative with this piece. These days, with a glut of full-length animated movies featuring penguins in leading roles, it's hard not to think *Happy Feet* when one encounters a penguin. Zoe Keating is one my favourite contemporary musicians — an avant-garde cellist whose compositions are both technologically and architecturally impressive. With our project's 'propensity for intensity', I thought it would be fun — and interesting — to see what happened when a wandering Adélie 'met' with a serious musician.

Comments:

- 'This seems like good penguin music to me. Light and quirky yet respectful of the inherent dignity of the wild animal. Not anthropomorphising, not *Happy Feet*.'
- 'Soulful and yet light. Although the title of the song, "Optimist", adds an ironic twist to the most probable fate of this little one.'
- 'Didn't like beginning as music seemed ominous — too suggestive: impending ... BUT did like rest of music ... parts very in keeping with creature. Would have most enjoyed just the part early on when you dwell on the shadow flapping — the sound track perfect here (with title KNOWN). That was the best bit and I could happily have watched and listen to the same fragment (visual) looped for minutes with the sound track!'

Weathered Systems (CB)

This piece might be considered the 'black sheep' in our 'A Vast Scale' video family; it comes to the continent from a quite different angle. I felt strongly that this aspect of Antarctica — namely, our relationship to her and with her — should be represented here, too. What wrongs we visit upon our planet. In light of these things, Andrew Bird's music seems to me to raise questions and suggest a lament. He achieves this, I think, via a sense of mournfulness, of 'active grieving'.

One of the things I wanted to say through this video was this: no matter how prettily we couch our presence in Antarctica, the impact of our being there and continuing to inhabit and explore the terrain is significant. Some might go so far as to say it is irreversible. In some way, I feel like a contradiction, having visited the continent twice. I find myself questioning my own capacity/incapacity to say 'no' should I ever be offered an opportunity to go again. How does one reconcile these conflicting pulls? When it comes to advocacy on behalf of the continent, can we assume both to go there *and* speak on her behalf? I don't know. It is all too easy to throw a soft blanket over sharp terrain.

Comments:

- 'I went into it thinking, "I am not going to like this. Human debris in the midst of pristine beauty". But the images of "stuff" are exquisite. The elements are the artists creating beauty out of things never intended to be beautiful. Reminds me of how the soul beautifies even when we pretend that we do not know it exists.'
- 'I love the last two shots — contradicting shots of human v. non human elements. I would love to see more overall shots mixed in with the detail shots earlier. It felt too closed in for me, I couldn't get a sense of the place as much. I really wanted to see the buildings; the humans hunkered down in metallic buildings. I wanted to feel small against the mountains. I think that might help the impact of the intimate detail photos if we have sort of grand photos as well.'
- 'How stunning!!! I don't see this as a piece about "waste", Claire, nor do I view it as a statement about human impacts on the environment. Indeed, it evokes just the opposite in me: the Earth system is robust and ever-changing; humanity is still subject to its force and fury, especially when the temporal scale is so gradual that it's barely perceptible (revealed as years of weathering seen in your images).'
- 'There's not much romance or beauty in what contemporary human habitation brings to Antarctica, is there? My ambivalence about going there as an artist or tourist is predicated on this: Antarctica doesn't need another human waste contributor. What is beautiful there is entirely what people haven't touched (though Jane Ussher's photos suggest at least the old huts have a venerable glow). The mournful tone of the song seems a sadness that utility is usually so ugly there.'

Two members of 'A Vast Scale' added their own videos to the site but discussion of them is beyond the scope of this paper.

The discussion forums

In addition to the videos we instigated four discussion forums. A selection from the discussion follows.

Music and silence: Without resorting to four minutes and 33 seconds of silence (ref. John Cage[4]), how might one represent silence in music?

- 'Having watched/listened to most of the videos here, I can say my preference to accompany Antarctic images is very much for minimalist music. The more different instruments, the more insistent the melody or rhythm, the less I appreciated what the different soundtracks have added. At times I longed for the "silence" of wind, or imagined the sounds of my own body on the ice. Crunching footsteps, whispering waterproof clothing, my own breath condensing, my heart beating hard ... There are some lovely passages in Kim Stanley Robinson's novel *Antarctica* where he describes the ambient sounds of walking across the ice in "silence".'

- 'I think X hits the nail on head for me: my experience of profoundly silent places (cold places — stilled places — whether polar, northern winter or desert night) and the sublimeness of them is they are not so silent: I hear myself. Exactly what X says, my breath, my heart, the blood flow near my ears, the shift of clothing, crunch of ice or sand with slight change in body weight-position... an involuntary sniff becomes horrendously loud and intrusive. On occasion I have let the nose run on down just to avoid such obscene disruptions. So let silence be sound of us, our body, slowly resolving into distinguishable then identifiable sound, or similarly the sound of wind or ice creak–snap–groan–report, but not necessarily constant — let it come and go unexpected. Or something human but atonal — something along the lines of the sustained throat singing of the Sami?'

Is it the music, the landscape or your own experience?: When you view the videos what does the music evoke; feelings for the landscape or memories of your own experiences or both or neither?

- 'I'm afraid I have found the music distracting and have mostly turned it off to enjoy the imagery in silence.'

The ethics of music-making in Antarctica: Given that silence is a key characteristic of Antarctica, is it ethical to make music in the world's last great wilderness?

- 'I think this question presupposes a narrow definition of music. In general, there is no such thing as silence, apart from that space created by an anechoic chamber. Even our own bodies make music, even if we don't necessarily hear it. Every sound is comprised of the harmonics and disharmonics of music, as discovered by Helmholtz. It is not as if bringing music into the landscape is a breach of ethics. Perhaps it is making something heard? Perhaps it is

---

4   John Cage (first performed 1952) *4′ 33″* [*Four minutes, thirty-three seconds*], http://johncage.org/4_33.html.

like bringing in another layer of language. Perhaps it is more a question of respect, or intent?'
- 'What I aim to do with an improvisation is to give the silence a voice, in a way. When people stop their ordinary activities to listen I think it is sometimes helpful if the silence has a few frames around it, especially if they are not used to it.'

Music, the environment and higher understanding: Does the combination of the music and environment together evoke a 'higher' understanding? Would you consider the whole to be greater than the sum of the parts?

- 'If you have sat on the Ross Ice Shelf on your own, miles from the nearest human, held you breath and listened to silence (bugger the heartbeat) and enjoyed the sensation, then music would be pollution. But if you wish to augment a themed set of slides or a movie with music (minor or major key) then choose carefully — getting it right should "evoke a higher understanding".'

And a member of 'A Vast Scale' contributed a fifth forum:

Absolute dance. For me, Antarctica is pure line and movement, with no need to add music.

- 'These ideas really resonate; thank you. I am inclined to agree with you ... If we think in terms of Antarctica as pure line and movement, then it surely follows that line and movement = music? This then begs the question "what = music in the context of a place like Antarctica?" Does the addition of anything to that landscape become extraneous, intrusive, a form of moral disregard or disrespect? We are so wired towards thinking our response needs to be something tangible, whether this be in an auditory, visual, sensual, textural way, when in reality any attempt to add to that which is already pure, complete — sublime — could be interpreted as a violation of sorts, a subtraction?'
- 'For me, Antarctica is more about surface than line. There is plenty of movement, to be sure, the imperceptible creep of the glaciers and the flexing of the ice shelves with the tides at one end of the movement spectrum to the howling katabatic at the other where the air is travelling so fast it will sweep you off your feet. But it is the surfaces that catch your eye, whether they be the sensual shapes of wind-blown snow or the insidious bow in the surface that hints at a 100-metre drop hidden just below the surface. And beneath the surface is that entrancing and mysterious blue. And anyway, lines are unreliable — is that the horizon, a cloud or a mirage?'

- 'I agree with William Fox (2000)[5] when he refers to Antarctica as a mirror. Our responses to Antarctica reflect more about our different ways of knowing than about the place. Lines in my mind's eye, drawings and animations, describe flows of energy that I understand from looking at scientific visualisations and that I can reconcile with physical experience.'

Wrap-up survey

In mid-2011 we decided that we should draw the discussion together by asking our members to contribute to a brief survey.

Question 1. Which was your favourite video (i.e., the one where you thought the music best matched the imagery) and which did you like the least?

- '"Weathered Systems" and "Silence Has A Voice" (porcelain vessels) were my favourites. Wonderful meld between images and music.'
- '"A Heart of Whiteness" Version 2, liked best for the match — the fine music with the fine etching of skittering wind patterns over the ice.'

Question 2. Early in this conversation, one of our group members suggested, 'Comments so far indicate a preference for Antarctica simply speaking for herself.' Two months down the track, it seems the continent might not be entirely averse to our attempts to harmonise with her. Do you agree or disagree?

- 'I think Antarctica is just hanging out for a good conversation and I think you are having one of them.'
- 'Agree that it's an interesting project to link them up — we find different ways into understanding and appreciating places, and wherever we find resonances (musical or otherwise) that's no bad thing.'

Question 3. If you were in the heart of Antarctica what instrument do you think would harmonise with your surroundings best?

- 'Wind instruments.'
- 'Possibly a clarinet.'
- 'If I were in the heart of Antarctica, both my bare lips or fingers would freeze before I had a chance to harmonise with anything. If I were a singer, likely I would sing a song to harmonise with my surroundings, assuming I'm not in a whiteout. Since I have a harmonica and it would be more practical to

---

5   William L Fox (2005) *Terra Antarctica: looking into the emptiest continent.* Trinity University Press, San Antonio, Texas.

carry it, I think a lonesome harmonica ode, such as "Home on the Range" or an "Icecap Blues" would do nicely, much as it would on a hot, dry "lone prairie", where "seldom is heard a discouraging word".'

Concluding discussion

The introduction on the home page of the website 'A Vast Scale' reads:

'We invite you to participate in our exploration of music and Antarctica and to respond to the images and sound tracks we have uploaded here.'

This has been exactly that — an exploration of music and Antarctica. The scope has been limited in some ways, indeed we have only scratched the surface of both Antarctica and the infinite number of ways to respond musically to it. Indeed, the project begs the question 'what is music?' A number of themes have, nevertheless, emerged. The first is the very great interest in music and Antarctica and the number of ways those two ideas can be configured: how to respond musically to Antarctica, can one represent Antarctica in music, is it okay to play music in Antarctica, does one instrument capture the spirit of Antarctica better than another, etc. There is, of course, no one answer to any of these questions but the discussion brings out ideas, prompts the expression of opinions and brings vitality to the community. A second theme is that there was a general preference for less rather than more, in other words fewer instruments or possibly only one, and a minimalist (reduced to the minimum), though not necessarily Minimalist (as with composers Philip Glass and Steve Reich) score. The human voice also seemed to be preferred, though again in a minimalist setting. Finally, although never actually expressed, there did seem to be a yearning for something distinctly Antarctic; music that expresses the seventh continent, setting it apart from the other six.

Index

Adams, John (US President), 24
Adams, John Luther, ix
Admiralty Range, 38
Agate, Alfred, 28
Alexander, Chapman, 91, 97
Alexander, Charles, 91
Alexandra Mountains, 39
Altman, Rick, 140–141
Amsler Island, 124–125
Amundsen, Roald, 6, 59, 169, 170, 176, 177, 187
Anchorage Bay, 103
Antarctic bases, 189–204
    Bolling Advance Weather Base, 11
    Cape Flora Base, 73
    Commonwealth Bay Hut, 91–100
    Davis Station, 103, 175, 192, 201, 212
    Framheim (base), 187
    Mawson Station, 83, 86, 192, 199, 200
    Mawson's Hut ('Main Base'), Cape Denison, 15–17, 18–19, 21
    McMurdo Station, 12, 158, 159
    Omond House, 74
    Palmer Research Station, 121, 122–123, 126, 127, 130
    Scott Base, 158, 159
    Shackleton's Hut, 108
    West Arm (Mawson Station), 85
Antarctic Circle, 23, 38
Antarctic Expeditions
    Amundsen's South Pole Expedition (1910–12), 37, 80. *see also* South Pole
    Astrolabe/Zélée Expedition (1837–40), 24
    Aurora Expedition. *see* Antarctic Expeditions, Australasian Antarctica Expedition (1911–14)
    Australasian Antarctica Expedition (1911–14), ix–x, 2, 15, 18, 89–90, 115, 185
        centenary of, xi, 1, 83
    Australian National Antarctic Research Expeditions (ANARE), 189, 192
    Belgian Antarctic Expedition (1897–98), 12
    British National Antarctic Expedition (1901–04), 59, 60–61, 63, 65, 67, 69, 73
    British, Australian and New Zealand Antarctic Research Expedition (BANZARE) (1929–31), 2, 8, 171
    Deep Sea Drilling Project (1968–83), 23–24
    Discovery Expedition (1901–04). *see* Antarctic Expeditions, British National Antarctic Expedition
    Discovery Expedition (1929–30; 1930–31), 15
    Dundee Whaling Expedition (1892–93), 73
    Endurance/Aurora Expedition (1914–17). *see* Antarctic Expeditions, Imperial Trans–Antarctic Expedition (1914–17)
    Erebus/Terror Expedition (1839–43), 24, 70
    Imperial Trans–Antarctic Expedition (1914–17), 77
        as *Endurance/Aurora* Expedition (1914–17), 19
    Japanese Antarctic Expedition (1910–12), 37–50, **43**
        music of, 39–47
        poetry of, 47–49
        songs of, 45–47
    Nimrod Expedition (1907–09), 15, 18
    Penola Expedition (1934–37), 19
    Scottish National Antarctic Expedition (1902–04), 73–81, 108
    Shirase Antarctic Expedition. *see* Antarctic Expeditions, Japanese Antarctic Expedition (1910–12)
    Terra Nova Expedition (1910–13), 19, 110, 116, 183
        Oates, Lawrence, 70, 133–135
    United States Exploring Expedition (1838–42), 23–26, 27, 32, 34, 35
        ships of, 24–26
    Wilkes Expedition. *see* Antarctic Expeditions, United States Exploring Expedition (1838–42)
    Wyatt Earp Expedition (1935–37), 19
Antarctic Peninsula, 25, 80, 121, 122, 126, 129, 182
Antarctic Plateau, 103
Antarctic Treaty, 1, 2, 3–4, 50, 107, 152, 155
Antarctica
    Australian exploration of, 1–12. *see also* Antarctic Expeditions
    composing and, 51–71, 79, 86, 87, 121–132, 151–152, 154–160
    dance and, 101–105
        Body of Ice (composition, 2010), 101, 103–105
        as *Polarity* (composition, 2011), 101, 104, 105
    fiction and, 107–109

Antarctic Navigation (2005 novel), 176
The Big Bang Symphony (2010 novel), 109
Chasing the Light (2013 novel), 176
Degrees of Separation (2006 novel), 108
Forbush and the Penguins (1965 novel), 108
film and
  Alien vs Predator (2004 film), 153
  Encounters at the End of the World (2007 film), 13
  The Thing (1982 film), 153
memoir and, 176
  Terra Incognita: Travels in Antarctica (1996), 176
multimedia productions and
  A Vast Scale: Evocations of Antarctica (collection of short films, website and discussion forum), 205–221, **206**, **210**
music and, 32, 34–36, 83–87, 189–204, 205–221. see also Antarctica, composing and
  Adeliesong (2005), 157, 158
  Antarctica (1998 recording), 140, 143
  Antarctica: Music from the Ice (2015 recording), 121–132
  Arctic (2007 recording), 140
  Baikal Ice (2003 recording), 140
  Chthonian Pulse (2005), 156
  Cryosphere (2005), 157, 158
  Under Erebus (2000), 154
  Fanfare for a Frozen Land (2005), 157, 158
  Flutter (2004), 156
  Icescape (2003), 154
  Katabatic (2005), 157, 158
  Stonemap (2005), 156
  Terra Incognita (2007), 159
  Wind [Patagonia] (2007 recording), 140
musical instruments and, 39–45, 60, 190–191, 192, 199, 201, 202–203
  accordion, 78, **190**, 192, **193**, 199
  bagpipes, 73, 75, 76–77, 79, 80, 199
  banjo, 40, 77–78, 190–191, 199
  hand organ, 60
  harp, 84–85
  improvised, 108, 199–200
  natural objects, built from, 121–122, 126–130, **128**
  piano, 40, 61–62, 201, **201**
  pianola, 40, 60
  reed organ, 60
  shakuhachi, 42–44
natural sounds of, 84, 122–126, 139, 143–145, 155, 156, 181–187
  contrasted with silence, 8–13, 180–181
  ice sounds, 102, 103, 161–167, 181
New Zealand and, 151–160
poetry and, 17–18, 23–36, 107–119
  'Air Disaster, Antarctica' (1993 poem), 116
  'Antarctica' (1996 poem), 116
  'Erebus Voices' (2005 poem), 116
  'How Doth My Good Cousin Silence?' (1963 poem), 117–118
  'In Memory of Erebus' (1989 poem), 116
  'Rondeau, Ridge A, Antarctica' (2010 poem), 116
  'The Music Makers' (1996 poem), 118–119
  'The Quiet Land' (1956 poem), 117
  'The Silence Calling' (1909 poem), 116
  'Thin Ice' (2007 poem), 215
  Antarctica (1996 collection), 118
  The Rime of the Ancient Mariner (1798 poem), 23, 28, 111–115
  Thulia: a Tale of the Antarctic (1843 poem), 23–36
    republished as *The Antarctic Mariner's Song*, 29–31, 34, 35, **35**, 36
silence of, ix, x, 8–12, 15, 169–177, 179–187
  as inspiration, 83, 108–109, 115–119, 151, 155
singing and, 60–61, 90–100, 191–199, **198**, **202**, 202–204. see also Antarctic Expeditions, Japanese Antarctic Expedition (1910–12)
songwriting and, 64–71. see also Doorly, James Gerald, as composer of *The Songs of the 'Morning'* (1943)
theatre and
  Australis, or the City of Zero (1900 musical), 110
  Das Opfer [The Sacrifice] (1937 opera), 110
  Die Südpolexpeditions des Kapitans Scott (1929 play), 110
  The Fire on the Snow (1941 radio play), 7, 110, 116

Meet the Real Ernest Shackleton (2004 musical), 110
   wildlife of, 73–80, 122–123, 124, 143, 155, 162–167, 181. *see also* penguins
      birds, 32, 122, 162–166, **164**, **166**, 179, 186
      krill, 33, 122, 162, 164
      limpets, 1226–127
      purple sea snail, 32
      seals, 80, 84, 122–123, 124–125, 143, 164, 181
      whales, 123, 162, 164, 179, 181
   women and, 169–177
Antarctica Music Festival and Conference, ix, x, 1, 5
Anvers Island, 122
Australian Antarctic Division, xi, 83, 104–105

Bage, Robert (Bob), 99, 185
Balchen, Berndt, 182
Barnett, John Francis, 111, **112**
Barrier, the. *see* Ross Ice Shelf
bases. *see* Antarctic bases
Bashō, Matsuo, 47
Bates, Alexandra, 116
Bay of Whales, 39
Beattie, Owen, 56
Bernacchi, Louis, 11–12
Beynon, Claire, 215
Bicherton, Francis, 97
Billing, Graham, 108
Bird, Andrew, 207, 216
Bledsoe, Lucy Jane, 109
Bligh, William, 190
Bolling Advance Weather Base, 11
Borchgrevink, Carsten, 10, 11
Bowden, Tim, 17
Bread and Cheese Club (Melbourne), **64**, **66**, 67, 69
Breaker Island, 127, 128
Brown, Chris Cree, xi
Bruce, William Speirs, 73–74, **74**, 77, 78, 79–80
Bruckner, Anton, 207, 209–210
Bryer, Christina, 212, 213
Butt, Clara, 90–91, 95
Byrd, Richard, 6, 10, 11, 182

Caddy, Caroline, 118, 119
Cage, John, 180, 218
Campbell, David, 8–9

Campbell, Peter, 6–7
Cape Adare, 11, 38
Cape Crozier, 183
Cape Evans, 183
Cape Flora Base, 73
Cape Royds, 108, 133
   Shackleton's Hut, 108
Casasayas, George, 199
Casey, Richard, 3
Chapman, John, 91
Chaturvedi, Sanjay, 6
Cherry-Garrard, Apsley, 115, 169
Chipman, Elizabeth, 172, 174
Christensen, Ingrid, 172–173, 174, 175, 176, 177
Christensen, Lars, 172, 173, 174
Christensen, Sofie, 174, 175
Clark, Robert, 78
Clarke, Reverend WB, 34
Clenndinnen, Inga, 176–177
Clifton, Jane, 153
climate change, 1, 4, 105, 152. *see also* global warming
Close, John, 96
Coats, Andrew, 73
Coats, James, 73
Coleridge, Samuel, 23, 28, 111, 114, 115, 118, 119. see also Antarctica, poetry and, *The Rime of the Ancient Mariner* (1798 poem)
Collis, Christy, 6, 7
Commonwealth Bay, x, 9–10, 76, 180, 191
Commonwealth Bay Hut, 91–100
composing. *see* Antarctica, composing and
Conly, Maurice, 154
Cook, Frederick, 12
Cook, James, 23, 25, 68, 115
Cooper, Alan, 36
Corell, Percy, 98, 99
Coulman Island, 38, 39
Cree Brown, Chris, 154–155, 157
Croll, RH, 69–70
Crozier, Francis, 70
Cusack, Peter, xi, 140

Dadson, Phil, xi, 154, 156–157
Dana, James Dwight, 25, 32–35, **33**
dance. *see* Antarctica, dance and
Darwin, Charles, 32, 33–34
David, Edgeworth, 6, 17, 187
Davidson, GA, 65, 67
Davis Beach, 84

Davis Station, 103, 175, 192, 201, 212
Dawson, Peter, 53
Debenham, Frank, 79, 117
Dedichen, Ingeborg, 173
DeLaca Island, 126
Dickens, Charles, 55–56
Dilworth, Mary, 116
Dodds, Klaus, 6
Doorly, James Gerald, x, 61, 62–68, 69, 70, 71
   as composer of *The Songs of the 'Morning'* (1943), 64–70
Doré, Gustave, 111, **113**
Dovers, Bob, 194–195
Dovers, George, 185
Drake Passage, 122, 161
Drake, Francis, 190
Dry Valleys, 156
Dumont d'Urville, Jules, 24

East Antarctica, 25
Eastley, Max, 140, 147–148
Edward VII Land, 39
Eisert, Regina, 13
Elgar, Edward, 53, 119
Ellis Fjord, 103
Ellsworth, Lincoln, 19
England, Rupert, 65
Evans, Edward, 61
Evans, Julian, 154
exploration. *see* specific expeditions under Antarctic Expeditions
Explorers Cove, 215

Farr, Gareth, xi, 154, 159–160
Fearnley, Laurence, 79, 108, 109
Ferrar Fjord, 214
film. *see* Antarctica, film and
Fisher, James and Fisher, Margery, 20
Fitzroy, Robert, 31
Flynn, John, 7
Ford, John, 209
Fox, William, 220
Framheim (base), 187
Franklin, Jane, 54
Franklin, John, 51, 53–54, 58, 71
   Franklin expedition to the Arctic (1948), 51, 53–57, **55**, 70, 71
Fusen, Kamiya, 45

Galapagos Archipelago, 141–143
Gann, Kyle, 180

Gaudian, Gudrun, 12
Géricault, Théodore, 56
Giles, Alice, ix, 94
Glasberg, Elena, 169, 176
Glass, Phillip, 221
Glenday, Katherine, 212
global warming, 1, 5, 71. *see also* climate change
Glover, Denis, 117–118, 119
Goddard, Peter, 76
Goering, Reinhard, 110
Goldring, Roy, 79
Gorton, John, 3
Gould, Laurence McKinley, 10
Grainger, Percy, 152–153
Great Ice Barrier. *see* Ross Ice Shelf
Greenpeace, 12
Gregory, JW, 6
Grenville, Kate, 176
Griffiths, Tom, 169

Hains, Brigid, 7–8
Hamre, Ivor, 37
Hannam, Walter, 94, 95, 96, 97, 99
Hannan, Camilla, 147, 148
Harrhy, Edith, 69
Harvey, Bill, 195
Harvey, James, 75
Haward, Marcus, 4
Heard Island, 199, 201
Heidemann Bay, 103
heroic age. *see* heroic era
heroic era, 4, 37, 70, 73, 151–152, 169, 170
   end of, 15, 19–21, 84, 171
   music in, 39, 77, 198
Herzog, Werner, 13
Hoadley, Charles, 94
Hodgeman, Alfred, 98, 99, 100
Holst, Gustav, 119
Horiuchi, 43
Hunter, John, 96, 97, 98, 99
Hurley, Frank
   diaries of, 185–187
   in Madigan's diaries, 95, 96, 97, 98, 99
   music and, 78, 93, 190–191
Hurt, John, 108
Hussey, Leonard, 40, 77, 78, 190–191

ice, 1, 12–13, 101–105, 155, 180, 208. *see also* Antarctica, natural sounds of, ice sounds
   ice sheets, 5–6, 183

icebergs and glaciers, 122–123, **123**, 126, 181
   pack ice, 162, 164
   sea ice, **125**, 125–126
Îles Kerguelen, 78
Innes, John, 199
Iron Maiden (band), 111
   Powerslave (1984 album), 111
Isungset, Terje, ix

Jenkin, John, 200
Johansen, Fredrik, 187
Johansen, Hjalmer, 73

Kalhor, Kayhan, 207, 211
Katz, David Raphael, 207
Kawaja, Marie, 2
Keam, Glenda, 152
Keating, Zoe, 207
Keighren, Innes, 76
Keneally, Thomas, 7
Kerr, Gilbert, x, 75, **76**, 76–77, 78, 80
Kirkby, Syd, 6
Knox Coast, 24
Knox, Samuel, 24, 28

Lambert, Andrew, 54, 57, 58
Land, Barbara, 174
Laseron, Charles, 6, 11, 20–21
in Madigan's diaries, 97, 98, 99
Lauder, Harry, 90, **92**, 95
Laurie Island, 74
Law Cairn, 103
Law, Phillip, 20, 78, 192, **193**
Le Guin, Ursula, 176
Leane, Elizabeth, 170, 175, 191
Lenz, William, 28, 31, 32, 36
Lewander, Lisbeth, 174
Lilburn, Douglas, 152
literature. *see* Antarctica, fiction and; Antarctica, memoir and; Antarctica, poetry and
Little America Base, 182
Lloyd, Marie, 60
Lodwick, Keith, 201
Long Fjord, 103
Lopez, Barry, 10
Lopez, Francisco, 140, 147, 149

MacAyeal, Douglas, 13
MacKenzie, Rod, 196
MacLean, Archibald, 95, 96, 97, 98, 99, 100
Macquarie Island, 199, 200

Madigan, Cecil, x, 6, 9–10
   diaries of, xi, 83, 87, **89**, 89–100
Madigan, Julia, 94
Main Base (*Aurora* Expedition). *see* Mawson's Hut ('Main Base')
Manhire, Bill, 116
Margulis, Lynn, 205
Markham, Clements, 52, **52**, 58–61, **59**, 67, 68–69
   donation of piano by, 61–62, 69
Marr Ice Piedmont, 122, 123, 126
Mawson Base. *see* Mawson Station
Mawson Station, 83, 86, 192, 199, 200. *see also* West Arm (Mawson Station)
Mawson, Douglas, 6, 7–8, 25, 80, 169, 171, 196
   expeditioners with, 11, 171, 191
   expeditions of, 2–4, 37, 170
   in Madigan's diaries, 80, 89, 94, 95, 97, 99, 100
   poetry and, 116
   silence and, 9, 15–21, **16**
Mawson, Francisca, 3
Mawson's Hut ('Main Base'), Cape Denison, 15–17, 18–19, 21
McDonald, 'Frosty,' 195
McInnes, Brendan, 38, 42, 45
McIntyre, Peter, 154
McMurdo Sound, 63, 65
McMurdo Station, 12, 158, 159
Meares, Cecil, 40
mechanised era, 20
Menzies, Robert, 3
Mertz, Xavier, 40
   in Madigan's diaries, 93, 94, 96, 97, 98, 99, 100
Migot, Andre, 78
Mikkelsen, Caroline, 172, 173–174, 175, 177
Mikkelsen, Karoline. *see* Mikkelsen, Caroline
Mikkelsen, Klarius, 175
Morrison, JD, 65, 67, 68, 69
Morse code, 15, 16–17, **21**, 93, 94
Mount Erebus, 70, 152
Mount Terror, 70
Moyes, Morton, 11, 115
Mulock, GFA, 65
Murakami, 43–44
Murphy, Herbert, 96
Murray–Smith, Stephen, 5
Musashi, Miyamoto, 47
music. *see* Antarctica, music and

musical instruments. *see* Antarctica, musical instruments and

Nansen, Fridtjof, 73
Ninnis, Belgrave, 98
Nolan, Sidney, 7
Nomura, Naokichi, 38, 42, 50
Norman, F.I., 275

O'Shaughnessy, Arthur, 119
'Ode' (1874 poem), 119
Observation Hill, 158
Olivier, Fred, 103
Omond House, 74
Ōwada, Kenju, 46

Palmer Research Station, 121, 122–123, 126, 127, 130
Palmer, James Croxall, 23–24, 25, 26–32, **27**, 34, 35, 36
Pärt, Arvo, 207, 214, 215
Patterson, Diane, 175
penguins, 4, 127, 162, **164**, 166
  music and, 40, 73–80, **76**, 181, 187, 216
  sounds of, 11, 123, 124, 184
Preisner, Zbigniew, 207, 213
Pyne, Stephen, 151, 158

Queen Mary Land, 11
Quin, Douglas, xi, 140, 143–145, **144**, 147, 148

Rabelais, François, 79
Rachlew, Lillemor (Ingebjorg), 173, 174, 175, 177
Rachmaninov, Sergei, 207, 209, 212
Rae, John, 55, 57
Ramsay, Allan, 75
Reed, Arden, 114–115
Reich, Steve, 221
Rexroth, Kenneth, 48
Roberts, Lisa, ix
Robinson, Geoff, 145–147, **146**,
Ross Ice Shelf, 11, 38–39, 182, 219
Ross Island, 12, 133
Ross Sea, 38, 63
Ross, Chet, 37–38, 41, 44
Ross, James Clark, 24, 26
Rymill, John, 19, 182

Samartzis, Philip, 101
Schafer, R Murray, 155
Scotia Bay, 74, 80
Scotia Ridge, 80
Scotia Sea, 80
Scott Base, 158, 159
Scott Island, 38
Scott, Robert, 52, **59**, 67, 79, 80, 169. *see also* Antarctic Expeditions, British National Antarctic Expedition (1901–04); Antarctic Expeditions, Terra Nova Expedition (1910–13)
  Amundsen and, 59, 169, 170
  death of, 21, 37, 70–71, 133–135, 158
  music and, 40, 68
  women and, 171, 176, 177
Scott, Walter, 57
Scullin Monolith, 174
Seal Cove, 103
Service, Robert, 18, 116
Shackleton Ice Shelf, 26
Shackleton, Ernest, 80, 157, 169, 170–171, 209. *see also* Antarctic Expeditions, Imperial Trans–Antarctic Expedition (1914–17)
  music and, 67, 68–69, 77–78, 190–191
Shackleton's Hut, 108
Shepherd, Patrick, 157–158
Shirase, Nobu, 37, 39, 43–44, 47, 48, 50
silence. *see* Antarctica, silence of
singing. *see* Antarctica, singing and
Singleton, Bill, 199
Skelton, Reginald, 60–61
songwriting. *see* Antarctica, songwriting and
sound recording, 139–149
South Orkney Islands, 80
South Pole, 23, 57, 109, 110, 167, 185, 211
  first reached, 1, 37
  race to, 52, 59, 169, 170, 177
South Victoria Land, 38
Spencer, Baldwin, 6
stations. *see* Antarctic bases
Stern, Oona, 122
Stevenson, John, 182
Stevenson, William, 38, 42
Stewart, Douglas, 7, 110, 116
Stillwell, Frank, 90, 95, 97, 98, 99
Summerson, Rupert, 87
Suzuki, Daisetzu, 48
Swan, RA, 37

Tada, Keiichi, 38, 42–44, 47, 48–49
Takeda, 39, 42

Taylor, Griffith, 6
Taylor, Laura, 154
Taylor, Stan, 195
Tennyson, Alfred Lord, 57–58, 70, 71
theatre. *see* Antarctica, theatre and
Torgensen Island, 124, 127
Toshitaka, Sekiya, 41, **41**
Trajer Ridge, 103
Tsunabuchi, Kenjo, 42, 43–44, 46, 47, 48

United States National Science Foundation, 109, 121
Ussher, Jane, 217

Vestfold Hills, 212
von Helmholtz, Hermann, 218
von Humboldt, Alexander, 34

Walker, William M., 28
Walsh, Jack, 201
Watson, Chris, 141–143, **142**, 148
Wayne, John, 208
Webb, Eric, 98, 185
Weddell Sea, 73, 75
Weddell, James, 25
Wegger, Mathilde, 172, 177
West Arm (Mawson Station), 85
Westlake, Nigel, 207
Wheat, Chris, 116
Whelan, Paul, 160
Wideroe, Solveig, 174, 175
Wielinga, Ruth, 103
Wiesel, Arnan, 94
Wild, Frank, 12, 94, 95, 96, 98
wildlife. *see* Antarctica, wildlife of; penguins
Wilkes, Charles, 24–25, 25–26, 34, 36. *see also* Antarctic Expeditions, United States Exploring Expedition (1838–42)
    court–martial against, 25
Wilkins, Hubert, 19
Williams, Billy, 69
Williams, Vaughan, 207, 208
Wilson Piedmont Glacier, 214
Wilson, Edward, 67, 116, 183–185
Wilson, Michael, 116
wireless communication, 18–21. *see also* Morse code
Wolfson, Susan, 114

Zillig, Winifred, 110

www.ingramcontent.com/pod-product-compliance
Lightning Source LLC
Chambersburg PA
CBHW040313240426
43666CB00030B/2926